KW-438-608

PUBLIC POLICY DISASTERS IN WESTERN EUROPE

In recent years Europe has witnessed some spectacular failures in government policy, which have, in some cases, contributed to the downfall of governments. *Public Policy Disasters in Western Europe* considers these failures in policy-making, asking what is meant by policy 'disaster', the different forms that they can take, and why they have occurred.

The study opens with an overview of the trends in the explanation of 'disastrous' policy and examines the problems that arise when policies are evaluated. These issues are then explored in nine contrasting cases drawn from both the European Union and its member states. These include: the devastating crisis in the Belgian political system following the exposure of a paedophile ring; the crisis in the Dutch fight against drugs; 'mad cows' and the 'Arms to Iraq' affair in the UK; monetary union between West and East Germany; the Swedish monetary crisis of 1992; Italian policy towards the South and the EU's Common Fisheries Policy and policies towards civil war in Yugoslavia.

Drawing common strands from these cases, the contributors argue that broader trends towards increasing social and technological complexity render policy failures more likely. They show how some 'successful' government policies can become 'failures' when exposed to the mass media and a less deferential public opinion. This book is an excellent study of how and why policies can go wrong, and it highlights the limits of what governments can achieve in Western Europe.

Pat Gray is Senior Lecturer in Public Policy at the University of Luton. **Paul 't Hart** is Associate Professor in the Department of Public Administration, University of Leiden.

ROUTLEDGE RESEARCH IN EUROPEAN PUBLIC POLICY

Edited by Jeremy Richardson, *University of Essex*

Other titles in the European Public Policy series:

PUBLIC POLICY DISASTERS IN WESTERN EUROPE

Edited by Pat Gray and Paul 't Hart

London and New York

First published 1998
by Routledge
11 New Fetter Lane, London EC4P 4EE

Simultaneously published in the USA and Canada
by Routledge
29 West 35th Street, New York, NY 10001

© 1998 Edited by Pat Gray and Paul 't Hart

Typeset in Baskerville by Routledge
Printed and bound in Great Britain by Biddles Ltd, Guildford and King's Lynn

All rights reserved. No part of this book may be reprinted or
reproduced or utilized in any form or by any electronic,
mechanical, or other means, now known or hereafter
invented, including photocopying and recording, or in any
information storage or retrieval system, without permission in
writing from the publishers.

British Library Cataloguing in Publication Data
A catalogue record for this book is available from the British Library

Library of Congress Cataloguing in Publication Data
A catalogue record for this title has been requested

ISBN 0–415–17070–2

UNIVERSITY OF PLYMOUTH

Item No.	900 3623142
Date	3 0 JUN 1998
Class No.	320·6 PUB
Contl. No.	0415170702

LIBRARY SERVICES

CONTENTS

CONTENTS

CONTENTS

ILLUSTRATIONS

Tables

Figures

LIST OF CONTRIBUTORS

Rob Baggott is Reader in Public Policy at De Montfort University, Leicester, UK

Mark Bovens is Professor of Legal Theory and Philosophy, University of Utrecht, the Netherlands

Sander Dekker is a research student in the Department of Public Administration, University of Leiden, the Netherlands

Pat Gray is a senior lecturer in the Department of Politics and Public Policy, University of Luton, UK

Paul 't Hart is Associate Professor in the Department of Public Administration, University of Leiden, the Netherlands

Lode Van Outrive is Professor of Criminology at the Catholic University of Leuven, Belgium

B. Guy Peters is Howard Falk Professor of American government at the University of Pittsburgh, USA

Ella Ritchie is a senior lecturer in the Department of Politics, University of Newcastle on Tyne, UK

Wolfgang Seibel is Professor of Political and Administrative Sciences at the University of Konstanz, Germany

Joanne van Selm-Thorburn is a lecturer in the Department of Political Science and Public Administration, Free University of Amsterdam, the Netherlands

Eric Stern is a research associate in the Department of Political Science, Stockholm University, Sweden

Bengt Sundelius is *Docent* (senior lecturer) in the Department of Government, University of Uppsala, Sweden

Robert Sykes is a senior lecturer in the School of Health and Community studies, Sheffield Hallam University, UK

LIST OF CONTRIBUTORS

Bertjan Verbeek is a lecturer in the Department of Political Science and Public Administration, Free University of Amsterdam, the Netherlands

Gerdien Verheuvel is a research student in the Department of Public Administration, University of Leiden, the Netherlands

Eline de Vries is a research student in the Department of Public Administration, University of Leiden, the Netherlands

Anthony Zito is a lecturer in the Department of Politics, University of Newcastle on Tyne, UK

SERIES EDITOR'S PREFACE

We live in an age of disillusionment with governments following three decades of optimism in the aftermath of the Second World War. During this earlier period, the state was seen as 'good' in the sense that state intervention was generally seen as benign, even by Conservative administrations. The welfare state was created in Western Europe and state intervention in industry was often seen as a means of reducing the pain caused by the operation of crude market forces. When problems arose, it was common to see groups, of all political colours and persuasions, calling for the state to 'do something'. The current wave of disillusionment takes three main forms. First, there has been an increase in public cynicism towards politicians and conventional politics more generally since the mid-1960s. This has manifested itself in a number of ways, such as increased voter volatility, decline in party membership, and increased resort to new social movements as a means of securing policy change. Second, we saw the emergence of a new school of thought in the 1970s, which emphasized the fact that governments might be *overloaded* and had over-reached their capacities to act effectively. Third, we have seen the emergence, from the early to mid-1980s, of an almost hegemonic policy fashion for less government, deregulation and privatization. The emphasis has been on the *limited* capacity of governments to solve societal problems.

Taking note of these cross-national trends, casual observers could be forgiven for thinking that the 1980s and 1990s have been the decades of the retreat of the state. Less government, so the argument ran, would lead to better government in those areas remaining the concern of the state. In practice, the reverse has often been the case. In an effort to reduce the role of government in society, governments have often been more dirigiste, not less, and have embarked on very ambitious public policy reform programmes. In practice governments have tried to do less by doing more in terms of policy innovation. Some very radical policy change has been introduced in the past two decades, presenting the prospect of even bigger policy failures. Thus, it would be nonsense to see modern governments as increasingly sitting on the sidelines of society and to assume, therefore, that the old 'overload' questions are no longer relevant. It is more a case of 'business as usual' than of a completely new style of governing in which the state plays a less important role. Even the concept of the 'new governance' is rather misleading in that the post-war western European state has always been characterized by power sharing, dependency relationships, and the need to mobilize complex networks of actors (both public and private) in attempts to solve societal problems. As Sammy Finer pointed out some forty years ago, the whole system of public administration is founded on the assumption that private actors will co-operate in the implementation of public policy.

One central feature of 'business as usual' is, of course, policy failure and even policy disasters. The knowledge base of public policy-making has improved over time (both quantitatively and qualitatively), the range of participants in public policy-making has been greatly extended, and the technology of policy monitoring and evaluation has improved dramatically. Yet governments seem just as prone to run into disasters, often of their own making. Despite the arrival of 'new' public management and all sorts of new decision-making techniques, governments seem as disaster prone as ever. As the Editors of this innovative volume point out, however, this is not to suggest that *all* government action leads to failure or even disaster. There is much routine policy-making which is successful, governments often seem to muddle through somehow, and some big problems are addressed reasonably successfully. This volume is concerned with one end of the spectrum of governmental action – focusing on when things go spectacularly wrong and where public policies (such as the Common Agricultural Policy, one of the case studies here) seem to create far more problems than solutions.

The intellectually exciting aspect of studying this end of the spectrum of policy-making is that it focuses on the central function of modern government – namely *societal problem solving*. The downside is that it leaves one depressed as a citizen! As Mark Bovens, Paul 't Hart and Guy Peters suggest in the concluding chapter, 'major mishaps continue to emerge at all levels of governance, including the European Union, and span the entire range of governance domains'. Indeed, they lean towards a view that policy failure might be on the increase, not simply because there is better monitoring of policy outcomes and greater media interest in failure, but also because of the trend towards increasing social and technological complexity and the closer coupling of social, political and technological systems in the modern world. As they suggest, the study of policy failures has a bright future! This volume brings together the study of a wide range of policy failures in Europe and is a stimulating contribution to what is likely to become a new academic 'industry', as political science again tries to come to grips with the difficult question of why policies fail and why all governments, sooner or later, seem to get into a terrible mess.

Jeremy Richardson
University of Essex

ACKNOWLEDGEMENTS

The authors wish to acknowledge the assistance of the University of Luton, the Netherlands Science Foundation (NWO) and the University of Leiden in providing the financial and other support to the workshops which made this volume possible.

Part I

INTRODUCTION

1

POLICY DISASTERS IN EUROPE

An introduction

Pat Gray

A study of major failures

We appear to be living in a new age in which our older fears – of totalitarianism, global war and economic collapse – have been replaced by more diverse, less predictable anxieties, which neither markets nor governments seem able to resolve (Beck 1992, 1995). Indeed recent years have offered some unusual spectacles: the great monetary crisis of 1992, which stripped many European governments of their reserves as they struggled to protect their currency from the speculative attacks of the world's money markets; the impotence of established and emerging institutions of the European Union to prevent civil war in the former Yugoslavia, or handle its consequences; the extraordinary 'mad cow' scare, which started in the UK with a handful of cases of BSE, but spread across Europe, disrupting diplomatic relations and the integration process. A nation such as Belgium, previously seen as a model of consociational democracy, entered a prolonged and agonizing institutional crisis prompted by unprecedented allegations against the police and criminal justice system following the uncovering of a murderous ring of paedophiles. In the former GDR the momentum of German reunification stalled on the dislocation caused by currency union and large-scale privatization, while in Italy massive political renewal failed to halt the deepening divisions between North and South, or the relentless advance of 'corruption politics'. In Britain, the 'Arms to Iraq' affair generated a public inquiry into the inner workings of the British state which contributed to the collapse of the conservative regime after eighteen years in power. These events might be excused on the grounds that they are exceptions within a wider picture of competent governance; yet even successful and stable nations such as Holland experienced a similar crisis of confidence in essential components of their administrative systems from apparently small beginnings.

This book is about these contemporary policy disasters in Europe. It seeks to describe how they happened, and provides different ways of analysing their backgrounds and causes. By discussing examples from different European countries

3

and policy sectors, as well as including two chapters that involve policies of the EU and its institutions, this study provides a stepping stone for comparative analysis.

Although it is focused on cases where policy-making has been found to have gone seriously wrong, this study does not rest on the assertion that modern governance is 'disaster prone'. Of course there is more policy to go wrong, but there are also better opportunities for communication, new technologies and new approaches to organizational learning. The above instances of high-profile failures represent merely the extreme end of a continuum that also contains the bulk of 'ordinary' policies – where governments seek to make small gains by muddling through whilst minimizing risks – and even a number of conspicuously successful interventions. The aims of this study are therefore limited. We seek to provide a record of some of the most chronic dilemmas which have recently faced western European governments, and of those government actions and inaction that have solicited the greatest criticism, controversy and disappointment. In so doing we seek to stimulate debate, to open a door to further study and reflection about the nature of 'disastrous policy', and particularly the circumstances under which public governance may fail, through an exploration of the links between human agency, institutions and wider cultural and historical factors in determining the fate of policies.

The complexity of modern policy-making

Pessimism about modern government is not a recent phenomenon. In the United States, for example, the experiences of the Vietnam war and the gap between the rhetoric and reality of the Kennedy/Johnson years were a serious shock to the optimism of postwar social reformers. Studies such as Derthick's (1972) *New Towns in Town* and Pressman and Wildavsky's (1973) famous account of the Oakland urban regeneration project cast doubt on the capacity of even well-funded and well-supported state intervention to contribute to the creation of any 'Great Society'.

By the mid-1970s a number of analysts, particularly in Europe, began to argue that governments were not merely suffering from an implementation gap caused by weaknesses in their systems of programme delivery, but had taken on too many responsibilities overall. Moreover, the problems government sought to tackle had become more complex too – with high levels of interdependence and rapid change contributing to low understanding, and to interventions which triggered unexpected and unwanted side-effects. Attempts to increase the scope of government to enable it to tackle more problems more effectively seemed to founder, not through a lack of resources or of relevant technologies, but because ultimately such efforts increased complexity and hence proved self-defeating (King 1975: 286).

At much the same time, critics on the left were advancing arguments which seemed similarly to question the competence of the state. For Habermas (1976), as for Offe (1984), the state under capitalism worked to ensure the continued private use of capital for profit, whilst simultaneously engineering the loyalty of all its citizens. The role of the state was therefore inherently contradictory and crisis prone. Habermas, however, suggested that the crisis was more diverse than one of simple overload: at the economic level, the system might fail to provide the requisite economic resources; at the political level, the system could suffer a 'rationality' crisis and be unable to decide key questions or suffer an inability to legitimate itself; and, finally, at the 'socio-cultural' level, there could be a crisis of 'motivation', in which the meaning of action for citizens would be lost. Habermas saw the prevalence of the two latter, less tangible types of crisis as a feature of modern capitalism and as a symptom of the increasing dominance of 'technical rationality' in society.

Whilst the experience of the Vietnam War had seemed to reinforce arguments against intervention by the American state overseas, the Watergate scandal suggested a deeper malaise might be lurking at the heart of democratic systems, which had previously been seen as a bulwark against bad government. Given the predominance of American writers in the field of public policy, it was not surprising that the 1980s became a decade in which big government faced intense criticism and the previously unfashionable ideas of the New Right achieved new prominence, against a background of increasing recession and fiscal crisis. New Right ideas had served to render the 'overload' thesis more sophisticated. Utilizing the insights of classical economics, William Niskanen (1971, 1973) sought to demonstrate the inevitability of bureaucratically inspired budget growth, a growth unconnected with any rise in demand for services and unmitigated by any necessary connection with service improvements (cf. Dunleavy 1991). Mancur Olson (1965, 1982) cast doubt on the efficacy and legitimacy of interest group behaviour and the capacity of democratic politics to produce policy which reflected anything other than the short-term interests of the most powerful groups in society. Such arguments proved controversial, but were ultimately successful in persuading many governments to reduce the range of problems they felt obliged to tackle and to re-examine the means they used to tackle those which remained (Self 1993: 69). The 1980s were pre-eminently an age of attempts to 'roll back the state' and to 're-engineer' the processes of government, often through the development of new systems of control or 'governance', and through large-scale privatization and retrenchment (Hood 1991; Pollitt 1990). This was accompanied by – in some nations – a more sceptical approach to interest groups and vigorous attempts to control, harness or bypass their power (Gamble 1988).

The 1980s also saw the first major attempts to draw comprehensive theoretical conclusions from multiple case studies of failure; Ingram and Mann (1980) drew together many of the ideas from the previous decade, producing a list of eighteen separate factors tending to produce policy failures (see also Peirce 1981). Peter Hall (1982) examined a number of prestige capital projects and found uncertainty to be a common feature in their failure: uncertainty in their environment, uncertainty about related decisions elsewhere and uncertainty over how they would be valued by citizens (see also Feldman and Milch 1982; Collingridge 1992). Barbara

Tuchman (1985) studied major acts of political, diplomatic and military 'folly' from history, attributing failure to the 'wooden-headedness' of the powerful and to the influence of group thinking (see also Janis 1998; Shiels 1991; Cohen and Gooch 1991). Hogwood and Peters (1985) and Yehezkel Dror (1986) offered conceptual frameworks to facilitate the understanding of policy predicaments and failures. Hogwood and Peters, in particular, used analogies with medical sickness to suggest distinctions between congenital failures (in which the original policy contained the seeds of its own destruction), organizational pathologies (linked to internal bureaucratic factors), informational pathologies (affecting the supply of information), delusions (which affected the way in which information was used), and various forms of obesity and budgetary disorder. At the same time, Markovits and Silverstein (1988) and Heidenheimer, Johnston and Levine (1989) turned their attention to the roots, dynamics and implications of political scandals and political corruption, respectively, both growing areas of concern in Western democracies (see also Doig 1984).

As the 1980s proceeded, theorists of 'globalization' began to conceive of national governments as working within complex webs of dependency relationships and presiding over problems whose boundaries exceeded their jurisdiction, while new media technologies brought events on the far side of the world unwanted on to the domestic political agenda (Rosenau 1980, 1990; McGrew and Lewis 1992; Sklair 1991; Waters 1995). The logic of these trends was that national governments could act on many problems only through complex, and hence risk-prone, international networks. To some, this seemed to suggest that the world was developing in precisely the opposite way from that which would render government once again effective, and hence respected (Beck 1995).

Moreover, the end of the 1980s saw a more fundamental challenge to the assumptions on which much government action rested, in the sense of a new scepticism about the very notion of risk itself. Hitherto, the management of risk had largely been seen as a purely technical matter, and failures in government as easily attributable to errors in the calculation of risk, weaknesses in implementation or the intrusion of unpredictable external factors. Now the very notion that risk could be rationally calculated was increasingly challenged (Adams 1995; Clarke and Short 1993), along with any easy assumptions about the value of scientific experts in the policy process (Fischer 1990). The belief that governmental regulation of hazards always increased public safety was also shown to be questionable (Perrow 1984; Wildavsky 1988). Indeed, it became possible to argue that regulation and the careful assessment of risks were no longer possible in a world of accelerated change.

For Beck, for example, advances in technology had created new forms of risk which could not be limited, either through social controls or through the passage of time; nor could they be processed within 'the prevailing rules of causality, guilt and liability' (Beck 1992: 2). These new risks, Beck argued, had changed the business of government from one of distributing the benefits of technological growth to one of distributing its hazards, and had given rise to new forms of political resistance which the old orders were unable to tackle.

Ubiquitous pessimism about governance?

Although pessimism about modern government therefore has a long history, the rationale for pessimism changes over time and according to the viewpoint of the observer. As the brief overview above shows, we have continuously moved the focal point of our concern about governance. We began by worrying about the capacities of organizations to deliver programmes, then signalled an imbalance between the demand for government and its supply, deepening into structural tendencies towards crisis, to end up concerned about unprecedented new predicaments, the competence and integrity of the people in charge, and the institutional arrangements of modern parliamentary democracy, bureaucracy and the nation-state.

However, although pessimism about government appears to be pervasive, much of it may be apparent rather than real. The early studies of implementation failure, for example, were motivated by a belief that government intervention could be improved. If we could obtain a clearer definition of the features of those endeavours which were likely to fail we could begin to identify the checks and balances that would enable weaknesses to be acted upon. Even the theorists of the New Right retain a faith in the capacity of institutional design (and redesign) to produce better outcomes for all, despite the inevitable limitations of self-interested actors and inherent problems in the supply of public goods. Some writers, for example Barbara Tuchman, see failure as by its nature extraordinary. She depicts it as comprised of occasional acts of small, powerful groups in society who from time to time misunderstand situations or wilfully ignore warning signs. Such an approach locates disasters at the level of human error and is profoundly *optimistic* in comparison with the structural determinism of Claus Offe or the technologically determined radical environmentalism of Ulrich Beck. Each of these theorists sees disaster as endemic and located in deep features of political systems as a whole.

This book is not intended to add to the long list of 'pessimisms'. In writing it we make no attempt to claim a single cause for all failures. Rather we will treat existing theories as potential sources of explanations which may or may not be fruitful in the cases we examine. Indeed, as we shall see, one fundamental feature of disasters is precisely the existence of multiple causes: an 'overdetermination', in which any number of potential causes could singly – or in combination – lie behind debacle. This analytical complexity in the explanation of policy disasters is compounded by the existence of multiple conflicting theoretical frameworks. It is these qualities which make policy disasters so difficult to research and yet so interesting.

7

Identifying policy disasters: towards a definition

Peter Hall (1982) defines a disastrous project as one which has caused great financial loss and which is 'perceived by many people to have gone wrong'. Definitions
of disaster, however, are not quite so easy, as disasters are diverse, multifaceted
phenomena. Hall, for example, distinguishes between negative disasters which are
abandoned after considerable efforts and expense, and positive disasters which
were 'implemented despite much criticism and even more opposition', thus
alerting us to the possibility that disasters may be handled in different ways by
political systems. Tuchman (1985: 3) defines folly (as distinct from other kinds of
failure) as 'the pursuit of policy contrary to the self-interest of the constituency or
state involved'. Folly has four characteristics: it must be perceived as folly in its own
time; a feasible alternative to the disastrous policy must exist; it is a product of
groups and, most particularly, ways of thinking which affect entire groups and
milieux; and it involves a 'perverse persistence in a policy demonstrably unwork-
able or counter-productive' (Tuchman 1985: 140). Dunleavy builds on these
definitions to suggest that disasters are 'significant and substantially costly failures
of omission or commission by government' (Dunleavy 1995: 52), adding
Tuchman's proviso that such disasters are 'eminently foreseeable – but decision
makers systematically choose to ignore an abundance of critical or warning voices'
(Tuchman 1985). Gray suggests a narrower definition, arguing that policy disasters
may involve policies which have failed against nearly every possible criteria of
evaluation, caused considerable disruption which was foreseeable and/or avoidable, and triggered complex trails of unintended consequences. Even the passage
of time fails to soften judgements of truly disastrous policies. Typically such events
involve a considerable loss of control by political authority (Gray 1996b: 74–83).
Each of these writers would thus seem to agree that 'folly' and 'disaster' not only
are unusual in their scale, but may share a common *process* or be marked by the
existence of particular patterns of beliefs about events.

Bovens and 't Hart (1996) have recently made the first comprehensive attempt
to explore these complex issues. In the process they have developed a conceptual
framework which is instructive for understanding how events come to be viewed as
disastrous in a policy community or political system. They define a policy fiasco as
'A negative event, that is perceived by a socially and politically significant group of
people in the community to be at least partially caused by avoidable and blameworthy failures of public policymakers' (Bovens and 't Hart 1996: 15). They thus
add an additional element to previous definitions, suggesting that blaming and the
search for responsible agents are crucial elements in the process of identifying
disasters. Their work then establishes four key elements in this process:

1 *Assessing events*: a certain set of events has come to be viewed as highly undesirable.
2 *Identifying agents*: the negative events are viewed as a consequence of well-
  defined acts of omission or commission by responsible public officials.

8

3   *Explaining behaviour:* the key acts or omissions producing the negative events are seen as the product of avoidable failures.
4   *Evaluating behaviour:* there is a widespread feeling that blame has to be apportioned to those responsible for the course of events.

(Bovens and 't Hart 1996: 11–14)

These elements are not separate stages, with one step following another as disasters unfold. Rather they are analytical categories which enable us to understand the different claims that underlie the labelling of events as 'disastrous'. In the playing out of policy disasters, arguments about who is to blame, how much damage has been done and who is responsible become entangled with each other in what is often a highly politicized, adversarial, discursive process. Key pieces of these arguments are often missing or intensely contested by various protagonists. Most importantly, careful investigations and systematic policy evaluations of what happened can help only so much, since assertions about blame, damage and responsibility can never be established authoritatively by dispassionate, objective analysis. Disastrous events are thus socially and politically constructed, rather than 'discovered' by scientific evaluation.

Evaluation of policy is a political act carried out in a political context. Perceptions of policies as disastrous are also conditioned by media involvement, and by the conscious efforts of powerful political actors and their opponents to structure and even dominate the language of evaluation. Such processes can sometimes account for the conundrum of policies which are broadly successful in achieving their objectives yet come to be seen as disastrous – and vice versa (Bovens and 't Hart 1996: 29–39). This distinction between the legitimacy of a programme or the belief in its effectiveness and the outcomes of a programme is one of the issues explored further in this book. When claims are made that the outcomes of policy are a 'disaster', significant unavoidable biases and the exercise of political and media power serve to render all such judgements subject to dispute.

The use of short *time frames* to analyse policy outcomes may well lead actors to exclude the inevitable complexity of long-term interactions and knock-on effects in policy areas with high levels of interdependence. Short time frames may also render judgements more critical, particularly regarding the kind of policy which requires gradual, long-term adjustments of the attitudes and behaviour of large numbers of people or the assembling of complex implementation processes. Sudden intensive shifts in public opinion or 'moral panics' can render short-term judgements faulty, as can the existence of hidden weaknesses in policy which are only revealed by some later changes in circumstances. By contrast, evaluations which use long time frames may be harder to undertake, as many policies are iterative and constantly adjust their objectives to changing circumstances. For such policies there is no long-term objective against which achievement can be assessed, and their wider impact must be examined instead. Long time frames may also fundamentally change the grounds upon which evaluation is undertaken, with

9

major shifts in values rendering before and after comparisons incommensurable or not worth undertaking (Bovens and 't Hart 1996: 21–48).

A second major bias in identifying disasters is *spatial* rather than temporal. Taking the Common Fisheries Policy (more fully discussed in Chapter 9) as an example, an evaluation centred on the fishing centre of Cornwall, in the UK, would suggest significant losses as a result of the policy. By contrast, an examination concentrating on the overall impact of the policy on the UK economy as a whole would show a negligible impact. Taking a Europe-wide view, the policy would clearly have very different impacts on different fleets. Moreover, the wider the boundary is drawn, the harder it would become to assess impacts, as other factors intervene. Such 'boundary' problems form a core method problem in attempts to form rational judgements about the impact of major policy initiatives, and have created great controversy in the implementation and evaluation of large capital projects with major environmental consequences (Bovens and 't Hart 1996: 27–29).

A third bias is that of *culture* (see Douglas and Wildavsky 1982; Douglas 1992; Schwarz and Thompson 1990). Viewed from a rationalistic, technocratic perspective, the Italian government's attempts to develop the economy of the *Mezzogiorno* may appear wholly ineffective, resulting (as is shown in Chapter 5) in the spending of gigantic sums for little long-term gain. The policy may also have assisted the growth of Mafia organizations and reinforced corrupt systems of patronage in the South, and hence hastened pressures for the disintegration of Italy as a nation-state. From the perspective of a familial culture accustomed to high degrees of clientilism and patronage, the policy might, however, be seen as highly beneficial and successful.

A fourth bias in identifying disasters is what Bovens and 't Hart classify as the '*goal-based*' bias, in which the explicit objectives of a policy or programme are used as the basis of its evaluation. In some cases, however, policy has no clear goals and is more a vehicle for garnering support from divergent political constituencies, a fudge between political interests. Much policy is itself the process of adjusting between inherently incompatible objectives, in which achievement of one goal inevitably undermines another. Much policy constantly adjusts to changed circumstances and hence does not stay still long enough for achievement to be measured. Most importantly of all, perhaps, goal-based evaluation prevents the evaluation of government inaction, which may lie at the heart of many conspicuous failures. Criticisms of inaction, however, themselves contain a bias, one which assumes that governments can and should be involved with everything (Bovens and 't Hart 1996: 44).

Highly ambitious goals may produce a self-evident, yet in many ways irrelevant, image of disastrous failure when government fails to achieve them. In political terms the very business of building and maintaining support for particular programmes sometimes requires that optimistic bright new futures are promised which can never be realized and that underachievement is dressed up as significant progress. Moreover, even when the goals of policies are fully achieved they – or the methods used – may be utterly unacceptable in terms of the values of populations subject to them. Many policies also have wider unintended impacts far outside the immediate goals set for them by policy-makers. Above all, evaluation of what happened precludes the equally important question of what might have happened had a different policy been pursued.

Errors or circumstances?

This overview of potential biases shows that there are good reasons why any negative evaluation of policy outcome is always open to dispute.[1] Moreover, according to Bovens and 't Hart (1996), the mere existence of negative outcome assessments is not enough to make an event a full-blown policy disaster. In the political arena it must also be shown that the negative outcome arose because of some avoidable acts of commission or omission by policy-makers. This is rarely an easy task. It is hard to identify not only who did what in a particular disastrous sequence of events, but also which part of a particular sequence of decisions and actions was crucial to the resulting outcome.

The inquiry into the 'Arms to Iraq' affair in the UK (discussed in Chapter 7), for example, spent considerable time trying to find out who had approved a decision to allow machinery to be exported to Iraqi munitions plants, a decision which subsequently triggered a massive public outcry. Many observers were frustrated and disappointed that the inquiry report did not clearly point the finger at any one person. Ministers had agreed to allow the exports, but the advice they had received from civil servants was not clear about the risks involved; the civil servants, in turn, had not seen many important warnings; and the firm doing the exporting had not told the whole truth in its applications to export. The decision itself had evolved through a series of meetings involving different personnel. In such a complex environment, the identification of agents is always inherently contestable, even more so when the time span of analysis is long, different groups of policy-makers and advisers have come and gone, and relationships and systems have changed.

Indeed, before one can even begin to trace 'who did what' in contributing to disaster one must have some prior view of how things are decided. The identification of causal chains in disastrous events is itself dependent on the particular view held of the policy process one is examining and which individuals, institutions, classes or groups one is predisposed to consider powerful. This is a problem not merely for social scientists, but also for political actors. A particular case which illustrates this point is a spate of escapes from UK prisons in 1994–95, which provoked intense controversy and demands that the minister involved should resign (Gray 1996a). Inquiries into the escapes were conducted primarily in a 'bottom-up' manner, by visits to the prisons concerned, and by detailed questioning of those staff most directly involved and their immediate superiors. The opening assumption of the investigators, therefore, was that some kind of breakdown had occurred at the front line of service delivery which could be mapped backwards from the escape itself. The inquiries therefore made little attempt to investigate wider relationships to political authority or to go back in time to understand the context in which prisons operated (Lewis 1997: 175). The inquiry reports were thus able to dwell on the many obstacles staff faced in carrying out their duties, and were inevitably highly critical of Prisons Head Office and the overall management of the service (Home Office 1994, 1995). Ultimately, the head of the Prison Service was dismissed as a result of these findings. Opposition parties traced the origins of the escapes back even further, to a spate of ill-considered policy initiatives, a defective management style used by the home secretary and a legacy of underfunding in the prisons. This tended to produce an equally convincing account that it was the minister who was responsible and who ought to have been removed. The minister, by contrast, used a 'top-down', or 'forward-mapping', approach, which started with the government's policy intentions and pursued whether they had been carried out. Inevitably, it found widespread evidence of weaknesses in implementation and thus thrust responsibility on middle- and lower-ranking officials. The conflict over responsibility therefore lay not at the level of fact (in organizational complexity), but in the prior image the participants had of how the Prison Service operated and in the methods they used to uncover the truth.

All such debates about 'who was responsible?' relate to the extent to which events may be seen as bad luck or sheer misfortune. Bovens and 't Hart have suggested a typology of 'misfortunes in governance' to aid classification of such arguments about who (if anyone) is responsible for particular episodes. These misfortunes range from the totally unexpected act of God, which no government might have been expected to prepare for, to clear cases in which widespread warnings of events which were clearly avoidable or controllable may have been given (see Table 1.1).

Again, however, it often proves impossible to label events in ways which will command universal acceptance. Political oppositions will aim, as far as possible, to place negative events into category 1, where allegations of negligence and incompetence can be made, whilst governments will produce extensive arguments which seek to shift the image of events in the other direction, towards category 4, where claims can be made that neither foresight nor control was feasible. Attributions of responsibility may also be influenced by our cultural and ideological leanings – fatalists, for example, are less likely to assume that events are foreseeable or avoidable than are managerial rationalists, who have an entirely different conception of the world, believing its tendencies to be both knowable and controllable. Identifying responsibility for disastrous events is thus intricately tied up with how we see social and political systems operating, and with how we see misfortune mitigating that responsibility. However, it is also linked to how we think political systems *should* operate and what we believe to be the 'feasible limits of institutional efforts to control social life' (Bovens and 't Hart 1996: 90). In analysing disasters we do not merely construct a description of 'what happened?' and 'who did what?'; we also operate with an explicit or implicit view of what ought to have happened.

Table 1.1 Bovens and 't Hart's typology of misfortunes in governance

	Foreseeable events	*Unforeseeable events*
Controllable	1	3
Uncontrollable	2	4

Source: Bovens and 't Hart (1996: 76)

Notes:

Misfortunes of type 1 generally occur in stable policy areas, where there is good knowledge of risk and high levels of government control. Here it is easy to construct arguments that disasters are both foreseeable and avoidable, and to claim that government is 'responsible'. This category is therefore the logical opposite of 'misfortune'.

Misfortunes of type 2 may be of various kinds: inherently risky situations (e.g. hazardous expeditions, new processes, complex implementation) or different kinds of 'tragic choices' in which all available options have negative outcomes. Here it is possible to construct arguments that despite the facts that risks were well known, little could have been done to avoid them.

Misfortunes of type 3 involve completely unexpected developments that may knock even the best laid plans awry – complex interaction effects or sudden and unpredictable shifts in external circumstances. Here it is possible to claim that, although plans were reasonable and rational, events or circumstances beyond foresight intervened to undermine them.

Misfortunes of type 4 may involve policy predicaments well beyond either foresight or control (e.g. acts of God). These include major natural disasters and surprise invasions by major foreign powers.

This tension lies at the heart of approaches to explaining disasters. It is to this third layer of analysis that we now turn.

Explaining policy disasters

At the start of this introduction, some vividly contrasting examples of explanations for policy failures were offered, which ranged from those with broadly optimistic implications through to the deeply pessimistic. Each of these explanations operated at different levels of analysis, with different objects and methods of study, and very different normative implications. However, these theories represent only a handful of the approaches used in the study of disasters, which is profoundly multidisciplinary, drawing on studies in psychology, sociology, social psychology, management science, actuarial studies, statistics and economics. Such a wide range of methods, approaches and perspectives presents both opportunities and large problems for those seeking to study, understand and explain policy disasters.

Bovens and 't Hart have attempted to link these specific disciplines and different objects of study to the various underlying 'philosophies of governance' which are implicit in the major frameworks we use to analyse policy problems (Bovens and 't Hart 1996: 101–108). In the process they have developed a comprehensive typology of different ways of seeing disasters – 'theoretical lenses' through which material and evidence may be structured and ordered to produce explanation (see Table 1.2) (Burrell and Morgan 1979; Golembiewski 1977). They distinguish between optimists, realists and pessimists.

Optimists, they argue, start from a belief that 'in principle a modern organiza-

Table 1.2 The structure of fiasco analysis

Philosophy	Optimists	Realists	Pessimists
Focus of study	Problem-solving	Managing competing values, institutional interaction	Coping with structural constraints
Typical 'cause' of disaster	Cognitive incompetence, information processing	Inadequate conflict resolution, organizational complexity	Dominant interests, system failure

Source: Bovens and 't Hart (1996: 101)

tion or a government is a powerful means for achieving the common good' (Bovens and 't Hart 1996: 95). Governments are seen as capable of pursuing their objectives rationally, through specialized hierarchies and the 'constant improvement of management and decision making' (*ibid.*). In such a view public servants are seen as essentially competent and well meaning. Failures of government in such a model are unusual, the result of political interference or individual error. Butler *et al.* (1994), for example, in their recent study of the Poll Tax fiasco in the UK, argue that the overriding of civil service advice and the dominance of politicians in the policy process were significant factors in creating the early, crucial failures in the design of this tax. A similar conclusion is reached by another recent study of the civil service role in the 'Arms to Iraq' affair (Foster 1996). From another angle, writers such as Irving L. Janis have stressed the risks of 'groupthink', arguing that 'the likelihood of failure is substantially less if sound procedures of information search, appraisal and planning are used' (Janis 1989: 4). In such a broadly 'Weberian' view of the policy process breakdowns are the exception, not the norm, and arise through departures from well-established administrative good practice.

This optimistic philosophy gives rise to a characteristic focus of study on governance as 'problem-solving' or decision. In such a view social problems are 'out there', more or less easily knowable and susceptible to a range of solutions, each of which has certain advantages and drawbacks, as well as (undefined) probabilities (Bovens and 't Hart 1996: 102). The government's task is one of defining the problem, generating options, evaluating them, implementing and then reviewing what has been done. Governing activity is seen as largely rational and voluntaristic. The goals of government are largely given, and choices are between the means of realizing them. Decisions are thus calculable in quantitative terms, and implementation is seen as a straightforward matter of effective control and good planning. In such a framework error is typically explained by poor training, personality and group pathologies, breaches of rational procedures or weaknesses in information flows.

Realists, however, start from a quite different philosophy, 'conceiving of public policymaking and governance as essentially fragile activities' (Bovens and 't Hart

1996: 97) and hence prone to failure. In this view public servants are more likely to be seen as individualistic utility-maximizers concerned with their own perks and privileges, or at best with advancing the cause of their departments in the great competition for political attention and resources. Such self-interested drives, however, are held in check by a range of procedures such as administrative controls and the conventions of democratic oversight and liberal constitutionalism – such as separation of powers, judicial review and the rule of law. Alternatively, public choice theory asserts that weaknesses tend to arise in the choice of activities which government undertakes, as much as in the methods used to undertake them. Accordingly, such theories seek to redesign institutions so that the social consequences of self-interest are minimized through widespread use of markets.

The realistic view tends to see policy-making as a complex social and political process involving competing values and ideologies, in which the ends of government action are eternally open to dispute, just as much as the means chosen to carry them out. Such a 'competing values' perspective requires constant cooperation and dialogue to make policy successful. Study thus tends to focus on 'distribution and redistribution, . . . and the selective uses and manipulation of information and other resources in the policy process' (Bovens and 't Hart 1996: 104). From this viewpoint failures in government spring from failure to agree on important issues or from the domination of decision by one, partial viewpoint – for example through corruption, clientilism, excessive secrecy or other breaches of agreed procedural norms.

An alternative realistic view sees government as existing within a wider web of networks and dependencies, such as agencies, client groups, the media and foreign governments. From such an 'institutional interaction' perspective, government activity consists not of decisions, but of constant bargaining within and through these networks. Policy thus unfolds iteratively, through a complex game played by individual and group protagonists. What government does is the result of complex and more or less impenetrable processes of institutional interaction. In its most extreme form, 'garbage can' processes occur, in which problems, solutions and actors coincide through a more or less arbitrary process (see Cohen *et al.* 1972). In some policy areas, however, well-established networks for processing issues may exist which render decisions more predictable. Such a focus thus studies the structures of competing organizations and the rules of the games they play, rather than the interests and values they seek to promote. Government is conceived of as highly complex and both internally and externally dependent, an 'organizational labyrinth'. Its effectiveness and legitimacy are thus seen as extremely fragile.

Those who share a *pessimistic* philosophy, by contrast, suggest that some policy areas are intractable or present unavoidably high levels of risk. On the one hand, Marxist theorists assert that fundamental inequality underpins the failures of the capitalist state, leading to overproduction, unemployment, fiscal crisis and instability. On the other hand, technological pessimists suggest that certain features of advanced technology cannot be made safe without a costly process of trial and error in which disasters will inevitably occur. However, without technological

15

progress, they argue, economic growth will stall. A stable economic future, they thus suggest, is 'risk prone' (Perrow 1984). Such views therefore tend to concentrate on the overall rationality of systems as a whole, within which individual episodes may be explained. The pessimistic view is therefore much more deterministic and sees disastrous episodes as part of a wider (or deeper) problem. The consequences of this structural weakness may be waves of disaster, which cumulatively undermine the legitimacy of the state as a whole. In such a model disastrous policy outcomes are often 'normal'.

This overview of the structuring of explanations of disaster may be criticized as an oversimplification of a range of complex and subtle analytical frameworks. It may also be criticized for artificially separating approaches which in practice are often used together, and for grouping together approaches which share assumptions at only the very highest level of generality. No doubt too there are important approaches which have not been included in this scheme. Each of these criticisms may be valid, yet the approach does clarify the relationship between normative expectations and empirical research foci, and shows how each tends to produce a particular bias in explanations of disaster. Explanations of disaster thus suffer from a similar irreducible contestability to that suffered by attempts to identify disastrous outcomes and responsibility for them. Starting from different opening assumptions, different analysts will describe the same problem in different ways; the difference in the explanation rests not on a disagreement about 'the facts', but the facts themselves may be a product of the methods used to arrive at them.

Blaming as a political process

Finally, Bovens and 't Hart argue that to label an event disastrous is also a political act, which may question the legitimacy of ruling groups or trigger demands for new resources, or for investigations which place leaders on the spot. The disaster label is a powerful political tool, which can be used to launch campaigns and advance political causes. Accordingly, in the real world of politics labelling events disastrous triggers inevitable conflict, in which the meaning of events is fought over through the studios of the television companies, through long months of public inquiry, in the parliaments and investigating committees. During this process blame is attributed, evaded, shrugged off, dispersed or taken on the chin.

As political scientists, however, we have some advantages which enable us to stand, if not above the fray, at least within it without ourselves becoming combatants by attributing blame for events. Our approach, however, does not claim to offer some objective, 'unbiased' account of disasters, but rather seeks to use the systematic methods of social science (including some of the perspectives outlined above) to illuminate understanding, conscious as we do so of the effects these methods may have on our understanding of events. Foremost amongst these methods is that of comparison.

Comparative analysis

In the cases which make up this book, each of our authors has worked with the framework of disaster analysis outlined above. Each chapter will begin by establishing the scope of the case to be presented and its claim to be considered disastrous, following this with a reconstruction of the case details. This process seeks to answer the following questions:

1   What grounds are there for claiming that the outcomes of this case are disastrous?
2   How bad was it?
3   Who or what was responsible?
4   How can it be explained?

The cases have been grouped into a number of categories to reflect as wide a range of the activities and predicaments of the western democratic state as it is possible to gather in a volume of this size and scope. We begin with the core functions of the nation-state: the maintenance of order is examined in two cases, one from Belgium, another from Holland. In the Belgian example (Chapter 2) Lode Van Outrive pursues the institutional origins of a constitutional crisis in the administration of justice, while Mark Bovens *et al.* (Chapter 3) examine a similar crisis, but through a detailed focus on the processes of media construction in the Netherlands.

We then examine three cases which, whilst still firmly located within the core functions of the nation-state, go beyond its 'night-watchman' role to examine failures in its wider 'welfare' functions. Rob Baggott's analysis of the early stages of the BSE crisis in the UK (Chapter 4) examines weaknesses in the protection of public health in the UK, Rob Sykes tracks the long standing failure of Italian regional policy for the *Mezzogiorno* (Chapter 5) and Wolfgang Seibel looks at the chronic impact of the rapid decision to merge the currencies of West Germany and the GDR (Chapter 6).

The next two cases study states in their international setting, but viewed from the perspective of domestic politics; both Pat Gray's account of the UK 'Arms to Iraq' affair (Chapter 7) and Eric Stern and Bengt Sundelius's account of the Swedish monetary crisis of 1992 (Chapter 8) chronicle severe shocks to dominant state strategies towards external threats.

We then move on to two studies of EU governance, with Ella Ritchie's account of the impact of the Common Fisheries Policy (Chapter 9) and Joanne van Selm-Thorburn and Bertjan Verbeek's study of the impact of disunity on EU strategy in the former Yugoslavia (Chapter 10).

In our conclusion Bovens *et al.* identify the common features underlying the explanations of disaster offered by our case authors and reflect on the causes of this apparent growth in disastrous policy-making.

We have selected cases which are more or less 'disastrous' on the criteria given above. Given the essentially contested nature of all disasters it is unlikely that we would have arrived at an uncontroversial listing. However, where there is doubt about the inclusion of a case, we decided to include some cases despite the fact that they might perhaps fall short of meeting all the characteristics one expects in disasters, on the grounds that these met sufficient of those characteristics to merit inclusion and that their absence would damage the representativeness of the book as a whole.

Note

1   There is an enormous amount of literature on outcome evaluation, as befits a fast-growing discipline whose focus is inherently critical of government. Important works addressing this topic include Carley (1980), Hogwood and Gunn (1984), Palumbo (1987), Power (1994) and Rist (1995). Later works show scepticism about the claims of evaluation to objectivity, a growing recognition of the inherent pluralism of methods of evaluation and increasing sophistication in the understanding of the effects of choosing different methods.

References

Adams, J. (1995) *Risk*, London: UCL Press.

Allison, G. T. (1971) *Essence of Decision: Explaining the Cuban Missile Crisis*, Boston, MA: Little Brown.

Beck, U. (1992) *Risk Society: Towards a New Modernity*, London: Sage.

—— (1995) *Essays on the Politics of the Risk Society*, New Jersey, CT: Humanities Press.

Bovens, M. and 't Hart, P. (1996) *Understanding Policy Fiascos*, New Brunswick and London: Transaction.

Burrell, W. G. and Morgan, G. (1979) *Sociological Paradigms and Organisational Analysis*, London: Heinemann.

Butler, D., Adonis, A. and Travers, T. (1994) *Failure in British Government: The Politics of the Poll Tax*, Oxford: Oxford University Press.

Carley, M. (1980) *Rational Techniques in Policy Analysis*, London: Heinemann.

Clarke, L. and Short, J. F. (1993) 'Social organisation and risk: some current controversies', *Annual Review of Sociology* 19: 375–399.

Cohen, E. A. and Gooch, J. (1991) *Military Misfortunes: The Anatomy of Failure in War*, New York: Vintage.

Cohen, M. D., March, J. G. and Olsen, J. P. (1972) 'A garbage can model of organizational choice', *Administrative Science Quarterly* 17 (1): 1–25.

Collingridge, D. (1992) *The Management of Scale: Big Technologies, Big Decisions, Big Mistakes*, London: Routledge.

Derthick, M. (1972) *New Towns in Town: Why a Federal Program Failed*, Washington, DC: Brookings Institute.

Doig, A. (1984) *Corruption and Misconduct in Contemporary British Politics*, Harmondsworth, Middlesex, and New York: Penguin.

Douglas, M. (1992) *Risk and Blame: Essays in Cultural Theory*, London and New York: Routledge.

Douglas, M. and Wildavsky, A. (1982) *Risk and Culture: An Essay on the Selection of Environmental Dangers*, Berkeley, CA: University of California Press.

Dror, Y. (1986) *Policymaking Under Adversity*, New Brunswick and London: Transaction.

Dunleavy, P. (1991) *Democracy, Bureaucracy and Public Choice: Economic Explanations in Political Science*, Hemel Hempstead: Harvester Wheatsheaf.

—— (1995) 'Policy disasters: explaining the UK's record', *Public Policy and Administration* 10(2): 59–64.

Dunleavy, P. and Weir, S. (1995) 'Media, opinion and the constitution', in A. Doig and F. Ridley (eds) *Sleaze: Politicians, Private Interests and Public Reaction*, Oxford: Oxford University Press.

Feldman, E. J. and Milch, J. (1982) *Technocracy Versus Democracy: The Comparative Politics of International Airports*, Boston, MA: Auburn House.

Fischer, F. (1990) *Technocracy and the Politics of Expertise*, London: Sage.

Foster, C. (1996) 'Reflections on the true significance of the Scott report for government accountability', *Public Administration* 74 (4): 567–592.

Gamble, A. (1988) *The Free Economy and the Strong State: The Politics of Thatcherism*, London: Macmillan.

Golembiewski, R. T. (1977) *Public Administration as a Developing Discipline*, New York: Dekker.

Gray, P. (1996a) 'When the minister won't resign', *Talking Politics* 9(2): 100–106.

—— (1996b) 'Disastrous explanations or explanations of disaster: a reply to Patrick Dunleavy', *Public Policy and Administration* 11(1): 74–83.

Habermas, J. (1976) *Legitimation Crisis*, London: Heinemann.

Hall, P. (1982) *Great Planning Disasters*, Berkeley, CA: California University Press.

Heidenheimer, A. J., Johnston, M and Levine, V. T. (eds) (1989) *Political Corruption: A Handbook*, New Brunswick and Oxford: Transaction.

Hogwood, B. and Gunn, L. A. (1984) *Policy Analysis for the Real World*, Oxford: Oxford University Press.

Hogwood, B. and Peters, B. G. (1985) *The Pathology of Public Policy*, Oxford: Clarendon Press.

Home Office (1994) *The Escape from Whitemoor Prison on Friday 9th September, 1994*, CM2741, London: HMSO.

—— (1995) *Review of Prison Security in England and Wales and the Escape from Parkhurst Prison on Tuesday, 3rd January, 1995*, CM3020, London: HMSO.

Hood, (1991) 'A public management for all seasons', *Public Administration* 69(1): 3–19.

Ingram, H. and Mann, D. (eds) *Why Policies Succeed or Fail*, London: Sage.

Janis, I. L. (1989) *Crucial Decisions: Leadership in Policymaking and Crisis Management*, New York: Free Press.

King, A. (1975) 'Overload: problems of governing in the 1970s', *Political Studies* 23: 284–296.

Lewis, D. (1997) *Hidden Agendas: Politics, Law and Disorder*, London: Hamish Hamilton.

McGrew, A. G. and Lewis, P. G. (1992) *Global Politics*, Cambridge: Polity Press.

Markovits, A. S. and Silverstein, M. (1988) *The Politics of Scandal: Power and Process in Liberal Democracies*, New York and London: Holmes & Meier.

Niskanen, W. A. (1971) *Bureaucracy and Representative Government*, New York: Aldine Atherton.

—— (1973) *Bureaucracy: Servant or Master?*, London: Institute of Economic Affairs.

Offe, C. (1984) *Contradictions of the Welfare State*, New York: Lexington.

Olson, M. (1965) *The Logic of Collective Action*, Harvard: Harvard University Press.

—— (1982) *The Rise and Decline of Nations*, New Haven, CT: Yale University Press.

Palumbo, D. J. (1987) *The Politics of Program Evaluation*, London: Sage.

Peirce, W. (1981) *Bureaucratic Failure and Public Expenditure*, New York: Academic Press.

Perrow, C. (1984) *Normal Accidents*, New York: Basic Books.

Pollitt, C. (1990) *Managerialism and Public Services*, Oxford: Basil Blackwell.

Power, M. (1994) *The Audit Explosion*, London: Demos.

Pressman, J. and Wildavsky, A. (1973) *Implementation: How Great Expectations in Washington are Dashed in Oakland*, Berkeley, CA: University of California Press.

Rist, R. C. (ed.) (1995) *Policy Evaluation: Linking Theory to Practice*, Aldershot: Edward Elgar.

Rosenau, J. (1980) *The Study of Global Interdependence*, New York: Nichols.

—— (1990) *Turbulence in World Politics*, London: Harvester Wheatsheaf.

Schwarz, M. and Thompson, M. (1990) *Divided We Stand: Redefining Technology, Politics and Social Choice*, London: Wheatsheaf.

Self, P. (1993) *Government by the Market? The Politics of Public Choice*, Basingstoke and London: Macmillan.

Shiels, F. L.(1991) *Preventable Disasters: Why Governments Fail*, Totowa, NJ: Rowman & Little-field.

Sklair, L. (1991) *Sociology of the Global System*, Hemel Hempstead: Harvester Wheatsheaf.

Tuchman, B. W. (1985) *The March of Folly*, London: Abacus.

Waters, M. (1995) *Globalisation*, London and New York: Routledge.

Wildavsky, A. (1988) *Searching for Safety*, New Brunswick and London: Transaction.

Part II

THE CORE FUNCTIONS OF THE STATE

2

THE DISASTROUS JUSTICE SYSTEM IN BELGIUM

A crisis of democracy?

Lode Van Outrive

Introduction

The discovery in August 1996 of inhuman and cruel treatment of children and even child murders revealed serious deficiencies in the Belgian police and judicial system and provoked a series of unusual mass demonstrations. Is this a real 'disaster' or 'fiasco'? How can the dysfunction of the Belgian justice system and its political context be explained? Was this an 'evolving' fiasco which can be explained by going back in time and by a process of 'backward mapping'? Why is Belgian democracy in crisis?

The crisis of the missing children and its aftermath

On 12 August 1996 a swimming pool attendant happened to notice a man dragging a young girl into a car near the baths where he was working. He noted the number plate of the car, and so the police found Marc Dutroux. A few days later they found the girl, Laetitia, still alive, but they also discovered another missing girl, Sabine. Later on in August and during September the police found the dead bodies of four other missing girls: Julie, Mélissa, An and Eefje. Soon it became clear that if thorough, professional investigations had been carried out earlier by the police and the magistrates the murders might have been prevented.

On 14 October 1996 Connerotte – a popular judge who was directing a successful police investigation – was removed from the case by the supreme court (the Cour de Cassation). Acting on a claim from Dutroux's lawyer, the supreme court judges had raised objections to the *juge d'instruction*, Connerotte, because he had attended a meal organized by an action group for parents of missing children. The two rescued girls and their parents were also at the meal.

Strikes by students and workers erupted in protest at this decision. Immediate demonstrations took place in front of the courts. In the ensuing media debate legal experts, including most magistrates and lawyers, defended the supreme court's decision, arguing that it was within the law. However, many intellectuals and ordinary people did not understand the decision and raised serious questions about the meaning of the law, the role of the courts, and the outlook and attitude of the judges, especially those sitting in the higher courts. Meanwhile, politicians also came under fire. Such upheavals would have been unthinkable in a normal climate of confidence in the justice system. As such, they were a symptom of a prolonged disease which had remained untreated for many years (Vandenbussche 1996: 111).

In October and November 1996 mass demonstrations took place all over Belgium. Pilgrimages took place to the scenes of the crimes. Huge numbers attended the funerals of the murdered children. On the initiative of the parents of the victims and the so-called 'white committees'[1] of ordinary citizens, more than 300,000 people marched silently through Brussels on 20 October: Flemish people and Walloons, representatives of the majority populations and of ethnic groups were all united once again as 'Belgians'. It was the first time that a demonstration of that size had been organized by anyone other than established political or trade union organizations. The slogans carried in the 'white march' demonstrated emotional solidarity with the parents of the missing children and also with the judges who were involved in the new investigation. They also combined many different complaints and issues. The higher court magistrates were the main targets, but also the government and the politicians, the justice system and the police. Some even expressed their fear that democracy was in danger and that the country faced a major crisis of legitimacy for its public institutions. The message of the demonstrations was clear: 'we are the people!' There were no longer any symptoms of 'Belgian mockery and cynicism' (Bovens and 't Hart 1996: 29); instead there was an emotional but sane and dignified *Volksempfinden*, or allocation of blame, a kind of 'repoliticization' of the system.

Official communications from the king's palace are very rare in Belgian history. In September 1996 King Albert II had held an audience with the parents of all the missing children and in a public communiqué sharply criticized the magistrates, the ministers and the government, and asked for greater internal and external controls on the justice system. The day before the white march, after a roundtable conference on child abuse and missing children, the king again publicly denounced the failures and the mistakes of the justice system, this time in even stronger terms. Because the king is not permitted to speak without first clearing matters with the government, some commentators interpreted these interventions as part of a strategy of political recuperation (Vandenbussche 1996: 117–133).

Another striking feature of the crisis was the flood of letters to the minister of justice. He received nearly 600 letters from private individuals; 2,200 schoolchildren from 152 schools also sent him letters, drawings and collages; nearly 100 petitions with some 90,000 signatures were delivered; 37 municipal councils and two provincial councils sent motions. All this was the result of initiatives taken by the most varied groups of people, whose demands were very similar to those advanced during the white march.[2]

Responsibility and blame

After a very emotional debate on 17 October 1996 the Lower House of Parliament decided to establish a commission of inquiry into 'the way the investigation by the police and judiciary has been conducted in the Dutroux–Nihoul case and related matters' (Chambre des Représentants de Belgique 1997). Different TV channels broadcast the sessions of the inquiry, except for those held behind closed doors. This was another unique experience – a parliamentary investigation almost as a form of national, public therapy. The commission published its report on 14 April 1997. The report contained many criticisms of police investigations and of the sluggishness of some magistrates. The commission also accused employees of the police and judiciary, by name, of a variety of mistakes and omissions. Many of those named then defended themselves by accusing each other, often contradicting themselves in the process. The police and the justice system seemed to lose all credibility. The structural conclusions of the Parliamentary Inquiry were as follows:

- *On the actions taken by the police*: in the *gendarmerie* (national police), relationships between officers in different sections were poor. There had been no real guidance given to the investigation, and officers in the national police had not communicated sufficiently well with other police forces. Some officers in these other forces had neglected the most elementary investigative tasks. Both logistical support and adequate supervision were lacking. The municipal police had lacked information and junior officers had worked without clear guidance. Senior officers of the different police forces had failed to collaborate. The absence of rules for proactive intelligence gathering and the use of special investigation techniques or for collaboration with informants had been a major handicap for the police.
- *On the actions taken by the judiciary*: there had been no respect shown – or consideration given – to the victims or the members of their families; assistance and advice had been neglected and their rights had frequently been ignored. The administration of justice was fragmented and this fragmentation prevented information flowing between different levels of the system. High staff turnover amongst *parquets* (the magistrates who manage and control police investigations) had disrupted the continuity of investigations. The organization of investigations was very weak and magistrates worked in a wholly reactive way. The *parquets généraux* (senior magistrates) did not really supervise the *parquets*; nor did they provide them with guidance on policy matters. The number of judges – and certainly of *juges d'instruction* (who decide on the use of special investigating methods and lead important criminal cases) – was too small and they lacked efficient logistical support.
- *On investigation procedures*: the general principles – relying on one-sided, secret, written procedures – were old-fashioned. A real adversarial system with well-regulated legal documentation was lacking. The inquiry recommended that

25

guidance to the police by the magistrates or the *juge d'instruction* was essential throughout the inquiry process.

The Dutroux–Nihoul inquiry merely repeated what previous commissions of inquiry had already said. Indeed, for many years parliament had been more clearly aware of the shortcomings of the police and the penal justice system than had the government.[3] A federal centre-left coalition agreement of 20 June 1995 had already paid a great deal of careful attention to the 'Renewal of Democracy and the Constitutional State'. That agreement, significantly enough, included subsections on 'An improved administration of justice' and 'Modernization and accountability of the courts'. It would seem that even the government had finally realized that the magistracy should no longer be left to its own devices and that the problems were more deep-rooted than ones of resourcing.

The coalition's reform programme was executed in slow motion, until the Dutroux affair galvanized the government and, most of all, the minister of justice. Reforms placed a high priority on the recommendations of the Dutroux–Nihoul Commission. The government strongly emphasized victim support, victims' rights and improvements to investigative measures in missing children cases. They also established a clearing house for information during investigations into missing children.

These measures may be seen as 'rituals of reassurance and purification' ('t Hart 1993: 43). Governments in such circumstances need to

> be seen in overall control of the situation to avoid (more) massive, unfore-seen and uncontrollable public reactions. They want to reassure the public that every conceivable effort is being made to get to the root of the problem, and seek to provide reassurance that a crisis situation will not be abused for partisan political purposes . . . but in many cases follow by statements or actions which do just that.
>
> ('t Hart 1993: 43)

The investigation of other potential victims and of criminal paedophile networks (the Nihoul case) – as well as of the possible shielding of those accused by powerful patrons – is still under way. The investigation into the disappearance of Loubna – a girl missing since 1992 – was reopened in February 1997, following pressure from the media and campaign groups on behalf of the parents of missing children. After only a few days the police found the dead body of the girl, and another scandal broke about past failings of the police and the magistrates. Clearly the early investigations of missing children had been very badly executed and young lives could have been saved.

A policy failure is the creation of the language used to depict it, and its identifi-cation is a political act, not just a recognition of fact (Edelman 1988: 31). The media played a full part throughout in the construction of interpretations of these events. From the end of August 1996 onwards the media reported daily on the activities of the police and the judges, as well as on the reactions of intellectuals, journalists, politicians, ordinary members of the public and the parents of the victims (Bovens and 't Hart 1996: 10). At the same time the media were busy uncovering (and systematically revisiting) many other scandals. In all these earlier scandals key members of the Belgian elite had been implicated: deputy prime ministers, ministers and other politicians, higher civil servants, lawyers, and important commercial and industrial actors.[4]

If definitions of disaster exist, it seems that the functioning of the Belgian justice system corresponds perfectly to them. It clearly involved: failure against implicit and explicit objectives; perception as "disastrous" by a wide range of opinion; a falling short of what is achievable, even from a pessimists viewpoint; intensive or extensive disruption of social and political processes; and significant loss of control' (Gray 1996: 77). In view of the many warning signs about the justice system, it could also be seen as a disaster which was both foreseeable and avoidable, and one where events were substantially traceable to the actions or inactions of policy-makers. The events described above seem 'likely, given current trends, to remain judged as disastrous, and [to] form part of a chain of consequences which reaches far beyond the immediate policy arena' (*ibid.*: 78).

Explanations of the crisis

Although there is widespread agreement that the events described above were disastrous, analysis has produced many contrasting explanations.

Socio-economic conditions

Difficult socio-economic conditions were important as a background to these events. Large factories (les Forges de Clabecq, Renault Vilvoorde and others) had closed. Unemployment was still rising; the official figure of 13 per cent probably masked a rate of nearly 25 per cent. To reach the so-called 'Maastricht criteria' for European Monetary Union the government had cut the welfare budget, especially in the health sector. All this served to create an atmosphere of insecurity and a climate of decline. Demonstrations by workers in front of the courts denounced redundancies and restructuring, increased competition, cuts in welfare, unemployment and social exclusion. It may indeed be possible to argue that complaints against the justice system reflected a dysfunction of the wider society (Cartuyvels and Mary 1997: 122–123).

Benign neglect

A frequently adopted 'face-value approach' argues that professional politicians had neglected issues involving the police and the justice system (Huyse 1996: 196–199). It would be more accurate to accuse the different governments, ministers and party leaders, because parliamentarians had warned several times –

starting in the 1980s – of problems with the justice system (Van Outrive 1996: 371–375). The early policy statements of the centre-right government had made no special reference to penal or judicial policy; nor had much interest been shown over the previous two decades. During debates in parliament nothing was said about such policies, not even by the socialists, despite their having made some provision for them in their election programme (Fijnaut 1982: 93–98). It was only after numerous critical Parliamentary Inquiries that the government finally took the issue seriously and published its 'Pentecost Plan' on 5 June 1990. In the introduction to the plan, however, the government noted that the Belgian judiciary was of 'high standing', and that problems were often the result of misunderstandings or abuses of the system.

Various excuses for this neglect of the justice system may be advanced: the problems could not be handled due to the schisms between ethnic, socio-economic and ideological groupings which affect Belgian politics; public debt, unemployment and social security were the most pressing questions to be dealt with by the government at the time; private troubles (with justice) do not easily become public issues; the magistrates traditionally play 'dumb'; politicians were out of touch with the 'real world'; early warning systems which enabled communication between the citizens and the politicians were no longer working; there was no longer a culture of debate in the wider society and even the academic world kept silent (Huyse 1996: 20–23).

Another explanation for this neglect was given on several occasions by the minister of justice, who argued that legislation had not responded to the evolution of Belgian society and had not been adapted to new social problems. Notwithstanding the development of legislative activity from an almost artisanal activity to one more akin to mass production, only small steps had been taken and no big structural reforms or changes to underlying concepts had occurred (De Clerck 1997a: 7–10; 1997b: 41–43; 1997c: 24–29). However, after the impressive reaction of 'civil society' to the Dutroux affair the prime minister and the minister of justice were obliged to admit publicly to this neglect and to promise improvement.

Lack of opportunities

Some arguments drew attention to the lack of opportunities in the past to change the justice system. In Belgium, big changes were always triggered by 'accidents'. Although many criticisms had been made of the legal system in the past, a major event like the Dutroux–Nihoul case had been lacking (Huyse 1996: 27–29). A series of murderous raids had been carried out between 1982 and 1985 by the so-called *Bande de Nivelles*, killing twenty-eight people. Some observers spoke of terrorism, even 'right-wing terrorism'. The whole of Belgium had been not just worried by the attacks, but increasingly impatient when no apparent progress was made by inquiries, amidst evidence of conflicts between the different police forces and magistrates, the sudden removal of personnel, the disappearance of documents and witnesses, and clues about the involvement of the extreme right – which were not followed up. The Belgian people were certainly scared at that time, but there had been no emotional revolt like the one that occurred after the child murders. Of course, in 1996 the involvement of innocent children and the conviction that they could have been saved made appeals to the people's emotions more effective. However, perhaps it is still necessary to explain why the killing of twenty-eight people by the *Bandes de Nivelles* did not provoke the same spontaneous organization of 'white' committees. Moreover, a lack of opportunity for such powerful collective reactions is not a reason for the dysfunction of the police and the justice system.

Evidence of dysfunction

A rare survey among magistrates shows 'a poignant lack of material means to function' (Christiaensen *et al.* 1992: 220–222). The backlog of cases before the courts has been traced back to the poor quality of many of the magistrates, the growing volume of cases brought to court, the growth in the number of appeals, the shortage of judges and their out-of-date working conditions and procedures (Van Delm 1993: 33–39).

Highly complex, excessive and obscure legislation and procedures can undoubtedly lead to difficulties in enforcing the law. Extensive and complicated procedures leave room for all kinds of disputes, often resulting in criminal proceedings being dropped as a result of lapse of time. This seems to be particularly the case for financial and economic matters. The wealthy, assisted by highly qualified and sharp lawyers, make the most of this. Barring a few exceptions, the police and the courts have not achieved any results after political assassinations, cases of terrorism with right-wing overtones, fiscal fraud and corruption by important political figures. In many cases there was no outcome, there were no verdicts or arrests, or, at very best, there were outcomes which seemed dubious (Van Bosbeke and Willems 1990). In these circumstances suspicions began to grow that important channels of communication linked policemen, magistrates, lawyers, politicians and industrial or commercial interests. However, an explanation is still needed as to why, despite this change in public perception, failure persisted and reform proposals failed.

The changing role of the press

The role of the press has also been used to explain why no real changes were made to the judiciary. Until the end of the 1980s the Belgian press was strongly linked to the big political parties. The leaders controlled their press. However, relations between the media and the political parties – indeed, between the media and political authority generally – have changed. Financial crises and threatened bankruptcies placed important newspapers in the hands of private entrepreneurs. A marked trend towards commercialization developed. The consequence was

strong competition between the most important newspapers and weekly maga-
zines. Sensational news, and particularly news of scandals, became an important
weapon in this struggle for readers. The alliance with the traditional political
parties became much looser and dissident voices came to be heard (Deltour 1996:
159–161).

In the 1990s scandals gained growing attention from the public through the
media. 'It is increasingly difficult for the judiciary – which is supposed to tackle
political *tangentopoli* (the state of bribes) – to let justice take its course . . . the judiciary has to face the retrospective indignation of some police officers and
journalists. In recent months they have tightened certain controls to such an extent
that others can find it hard to prove suddenly that they have *mani puliti*, or clean
hands. Any journalist can come up with a list of 20 "scandals" of a financial,
economic but also political nature: "Scandalitis" – every day has its own
scandal. . . . In that climate, allegations can turn into proof, investigative activities
become accusations and suspicions outright judgements' (De Moor 1994a: 12–17;
author's translation).

The media played not only the role of newsmaker, but also that of mediator
between the authorities and the population, including the parents of the child
victims, because of the decline in intermediate bodies such as political parties,
unions and other traditional associations (Le Paige 1997: 221–231). Important
politicians – and some higher magistrates – became more and more angry about
the role of the media (Deltour 1996; Huyse 1996: 203–204), accusing them of
sensationalism, provocation, bias and exploitation of leaks about ongoing investigations (Le Paige 1997: 215–228). However, despite this even more critical – but
also now politically criticized – role of the press, reforms were still not forthcoming.
Why?

The politicization of the justice system

Alongside negligence, the politicization of the entire justice system, including the
police, is frequently mentioned as the cause of its weakness. Belgium, in this view,
is another example of a 'partyocratic regime'; political power in Belgium is identified with traditional political parties whose leaderships control appointments
(Delwit 1997: 160). After the Dutroux affair an avalanche of letters on this theme
written by ordinary people was published in the newspapers (Tanghe 1997:
110–123). Such a negative view of the system was able to thrive in an environment
of structural politicization of the magistracy. When a politician was involved in a
criminal case, people compared the political colour of the person charged with
that of the judge, and noted the tendency for nothing to come of trials where the
colours matched (Deltour 1996: 25). Indeed, barring some recent exceptions, the
political hue of every magistrate is more or less publicly known.

The minister of justice is responsible for the quality of the judiciary
(Vandenberghe 1981: 52), and the law requires an impartial appointments system.
However, the lists of candidates for appointment are agreed in advance by the

leaders of the main political parties. The members of other elected bodies system-atically followed these agreements and party directives. 'The party-political influence is hence no longer the work of individuals, but of well equipped party structures' (Huyse 1985: 124). This arrangement was motivated by wholesome philosophical and ideological pluralism, by the withdrawal of selection and promotion from previous corporatist arrangements. There were, however, some risks in the system of patronage for judicial appointments: 'Long political negotia-tions and delays in appointments with resulting backlog in judicial proceedings; a loss of quality and of course the politicization of the judiciary itself' (*ibid.*: 124–128). Although it is not certain that this politicization of the courts' decisions occurs in all cases, obviously the perception that the possibility exists suffices to arouse mistrust. Lawyers blame the loss of a case on party politics; politicians, on the other hand, hint at power and influence – 'Judges were no longer beyond suspi-cion' (*ibid.*: 128).

Up to now it has been the case that the great many advisory bodies through which promotions in the magistracy take place cannot guarantee quality either. Procedures are not open, and seniority is an important factor, as is the support of political patrons. The leading journalist De Moor recently bemoaned the lot of candidate judges:

> How long will candidate judges . . . have to go on gathering the necessary
> votes in the provincial council and the court in order to be appointed? . . .
> Many first presidents, presidents, vice-presidents and chamber presidents
> of the courts bear personal blame for the humiliating agony that is killing
> off the judiciary.
>
> (De Moor 1994b: 30–31)

When the citizens complain about the politicization of the magistrates they blame the politicians, but it is even worse for the magistrates, who are considered political opportunists and hence incompetent. When citizens no longer respect the magistrates they no longer trust the justice system, and in the end they mistrust everything. Justice is associated with corruption, complicity, incompetence, with 'I don't give a damn' (Tanghe 1997: 39–40, 47–48). From time to time there is clear evidence of such politicization: services rendered to – or protective relations with – politicians; the obvious discontinuance of an investigation; but also the taking up of a conservative stance in social matters. Thus, the left-wing terrorists of the *Cellules Communistes Combattantes* (CCC) in Belgium were dealt with suspiciously quickly, while the presumed right-wingers are still at liberty. There are also judges who will systematically give property rights preference over the right to strike. In one jurisdiction, large chemical companies are acquitted of environmental crimes for the most diverse reasons, whereas other courts would sentence them (Huyse 1994: 102–104). Some observers even go further, suggesting the existence of secret societies and clubs, linking legal, commercial and political interests. As De Moor recently put it:

In order to understand an investigation, sentence or arrest it is sometimes not unwise to colour the organisational chart of the court and the table of lawyers with their political-ideological tendencies, without forgetting their membership of certain service clubs. While the Christian Democrats still reign in some courts, the liberals, often within the confines of their lodges, make a grab for power. . . . Talking of which, should magistrates, like some other professionals, not have the decency to stay away from all those clubs and associations in which the contacts with society are in any case restricted to dining and conniving?

(De Moor 1994b: 30)

It is perhaps too simplistic to argue that the political parties in Belgium have a mistaken and unhealthy grip on judicial power and that this easily turns into *docile au prince, terrible au justiciable!* (gentle to the prince, terrible to those seeking justice). More generally, the politicization of the judiciary is not a sufficient factor to explain the deficiency, the stagnation, the immobility and even the dysfunction of the system in the past (Delwit 1997: 171). The hypothesis that politicization automatically means stupidity and incompetence is very doubtful. Even the existence of a partially politically recruited and promoted judiciary does not hinder innovation, and such magistrates may work together with elected representatives to create an administration of justice that matches the needs of the actual society, that is more democratic, more transparent and, even, more efficient. But that is not what happened.

Absence of control

A significant problem, however, is sometimes held to be that of the *independence* of the judiciary vis-à-vis the legislature and the executive. Under-regulation, which gives the judges ample discretion, almost automatically causes the latter to make pseudo-political decisions. In such cases, the judge may be promoted to acting legislator and important political problems come to be dealt with in ordinary courts of law, the State Council or the Court d'Arbitrage (Huyse 1994: 105–107).

Senior magistrates took the opportunity provided by the discussion about the failures of the justice system to insist on the importance of the separation of the three powers: legislative, executive and judicial. In doing so, they argued that all external control on the judiciary was wrong, that justice had to be a 'serene island' in the wider society. In such a view there is no reason for any accountability to anybody (Tanghe 1997: 38). This long-standing debate continued particularly over the role of the public solicitor. Opponents of the notion of a wholly independent public solicitor, such as the Flemish Magistrate's Association, argued, for example, that 'The world of politics has a more sensitive finger on the pulse of society than an aloof magistracy' (Magistratuur en Maatschappij 1994 : 11) and hence that a degree of political oversight was essential. But why did the judiciary reject such outside control? Why was the refusal accepted and how could it come to block reforms?

Dominant interests

On 16 May 1987 the keynote speaker at a seminar in Leuven addressed the so-called 'unease' over the administration of criminal justice.

> It is being said everywhere, in many different ways, that penal law is in crisis. . . . The smaller the degree of politicization within a certain problem area, the bigger the influence of those working in this area on the formulation of problems and policy-making in this field. Lawyers or penal experts tend to monopolise the field and close ranks. Applied to penal law, this means that those who belong to the 'implementing staff' are awarded a monopoly in penal policy-making within the margins they have been granted by the political institutions.
>
> (Dupont, 1987: 395–398)

So we come to the fundamental questions: who has an interest in the 'status quo' and what kind of interests are involved? Do politicians, magistrates and other categories of important people share common interests? Did they act to defend their interests? An interesting hypothesis could be that there is a conglomeration of people – some call it a 'caste' – belonging to the political world, the world of the judiciary and practitioners of the law (mostly, but not exclusively, lawyers), as well as to the academia, and in top jobs in industry and commerce. All these people not only need each other from time to time, but, more importantly, share the same opinion on law and the administration of justice and have the same very authoritarian ideas about the way their own universe and those of the other elites and of the ordinary people should function. Debate or dissenting opinions are hardly tolerated, if they are tolerated at all.

In the Belgian parliament and in government not only are there too many jurists and practising lawyers, but many of them belong to the more conservative elite professional groups and factions of the political parties: they play an important part in the Christian Democrat Party, among the conservative liberals, the nationalists, the extreme-right parties and even the reformist Social Democrats. They form a majority. Their leaders accumulate a governmental or parliamentary power base with one another through the political parties, so that they can exercise enormous control over 'political personnel', both within and outside parliament.

The great majority of the magistrates, and certainly those who occupy key positions in the justice system, owe their power to their nomination by important political leaders. It is not at all certain that they forget this all the time. An analysis of the sentences passed by the average judge, for example, shows a considerable number of 'extra-legal considerations' affecting sentencing (Tanghe 1997: 76).

One might imagine that intellectuals, most of all law faculty professors, would have enough autonomy to function as an innovating force in law and justice. Some may very well do so, but only if they do not share a purely technical conception of the law and if they are not themselves important practising lawyers, as is very often the case.

Finally, the world of practising jurists and lawyers is dominated by those lawyers with the most wealthy clients. They are splendid masters at manipulating legal procedures. Well-to-do or moneyed industrial or commercial interests are allowed to abuse the procedural rules and the courts in their own interests through the long and complicated way many cases come to court, the arbitrary division of labour between the judges and the courts, and the lack of quality control; there is also an extreme formalism and, finally, an enormous lack of transparency (Schoenaerts 1995: 97, 100, 105, 109, 215). Lawyers seek out breaches of procedural rules committed by ordinary police officers and judges during the instruction of cases, and exploit them to win their case. Important judges agree to play the game with them (Tanghe 1997: 131–132).

Still more important is the fact that all these people share the same monopolistic conception of the justice system. The law is not seen as the law of society, but as their monopoly. They have a kind of superiority complex, a notion of sovereignty that suggests they can dispose of the law, like the sovereigns during the *ancien régime*. Legal aid has to be considered as a market product and has to remain the monopoly of the professional group of 'experts' or licensed lawyers. They believe that it is even wrong to take account of the conceptions, the judgements, the feelings and the consciousness about legal matters within the wider society. They conceive the law and the administration of justice to be matters of deduction from big principles and certainly not as a matter of induction, of integration of divergent social viewpoints in a kind of equilibrium (Tanghe 1997: 149). All this combines with a very ritualistic, symbolic, legalistic, robotic, formalist and positivist conception of the law, wrapped in a language inaccessible to the common person (Cartuyvels and Mary 1997: 102–110). The rule of law has to be applied whatever the human and social circumstances may be. They believe that they have to protect the constitutional state (*l'état de droit*), which is (wrongly) associated with 'democracy'. Because of their interaction with the other members of the upper classes – the financial, economic, professional, political and higher administrative classes – they have become a major threat to the constitutional state and to democracy (Tanghe 1997: 33–34,167).

Reflections: when the judiciary slips, does democracy fail?

> Fiascoes only start to provide a challenge to the system when they occur more frequently, inflict cumulative damage, and pose legitimacy problems for policy makers and perhaps the political regime as a whole.
>
> (Bovens and 't Hart 1996: 105)

In recent years, the Belgian parliament has produced many critical inquiry reports and proposed many changes to the police and the justice system. Many party leaders have managed to drag their feet on legislative follow-up. Even when a new centre-left government announced a plan for widespread change – in July 1995 – implementation was restricted to new declarations about action plans until the tragic events of the end of August 1996 pushed matters forwards. The parliament was itself hindered by the 'partyocratic' system in playing its required role within a democratic regime. The government even felt safe enough to declare in a candid way that there had been some negligence concerning the judiciary. As we have seen, the government had been warned over many years about the dysfunction of the system, but did nothing. If the democratic institutions can no longer provide a check on executive action, democracy is in danger.

For many years pressure groups in the field of criminal justice did not really exist. Any attempts to organize interest groups within the magistracy were nipped in the bud either by the attorney-general or by the president of the Courts of Appeal. This is changing: magistrates (particularly young ones) are now allowed more or less to organize themselves, and they do so effectively. But some important senior judges still object to this exercise of a democratic right and are successful in using subtle sanctions against it (Tanghe 1997: 34–41).

And what about the 'white movement'? It is still not clear what will happen to this exercise in repoliticization and 'participative democracy'. White committees still function in different places in the country. On 22 June 1997, the first anniversary of the disappearance of the two children, further demonstrations took place. Journalists were in a hurry to report that the demonstrations were no longer significant and that the movement was in decline. Some important politicians became openly nervous and critical about the white movement and started to accuse it of some 'brown' (fascistic) characteristics. So it is possible that this not very well-organized movement will fail to reach the core of the political decision-making process and will be unable to achieve a response from the top politicians, because of the arrogance and the cynicism of the latter, and their impotence to bring in workable reforms. Or perhaps it is because there are no longer any bridges – intermediary organized bodies – to link not only the middle and upper classes, but also the intellectuals and ordinary people, with the political authorities (Hooghe 1997: 16–17).

We have described the absence of a democratic culture within the justice system: the democratization movement in society has left it largely untouched. Proposals for the reorganization of the administration of justice have been reduced to 'more of the same': more personnel, more technical means, more management. It is by no means clear that the media can continue to play a significant role in the new democratization process. The 'fourth estate' suffers considerably from increased competition for readers, competition that forces it to bring in more sensational news more quickly and to become less critical about sources. Previously, the media were controlled by political leaders. More recently, important politicians have taken every opportunity to blame them, and to reduce their credibility and hence their importance in influencing the political decision-making process.

Efforts to bring about changes in the judiciary seem to take the form of an incoherent gathering or a half-finished project. Even more striking is the fact that the government – and, under its command and control, the parliament – is now reinforcing a repressive penal approach to these deep-seated problems, whilst avoiding fundamental rethinking of the role and functioning of the judiciary, even though the whole system is old-fashioned, inefficient and without inspiration (Cartuyvels and Mary 1997: 110–123). Meanwhile, public legal aid – an excellent way of monitoring an unjust and partial administration of justice – is still lacking. *Vox populi?* I don't think so. Rather, *vox beati possidenti* (the voice of holy vested interests). Shouldn't democracy and justice serve the interests of the citizens in search of justice, instead of those of the lawyers, magistrates or other privileged people?

Notes

1 The term 'white' was used to denote neutrality and the absence of party colours.
2 Analysis undertaken by the Law and Society Research Group of the Department of Penal Law and Criminology, University of Leuven, on behalf of the minister.
3 Every 'scandalous event' in Belgium seems to provoke the setting up of a special commission of inquiry. From March 1980 to July 1997 ten different inquiries were set up by parliament.
4 The still unsolved murder of an important politician; the Agusta and Dassault bribery cases and the suspect financing of political parties; stories of money laundering and corruption involving politicians; billions of Belgian francs of public money wasted in fake development programmes; cases of fraud involving subsidies and doubtful bankruptcy; blocked investigations into the corruption of politicians and senior civil servants; also the leaking of the diary of an ex-secretary of one of the major political parties, which mentioned all kinds of dubious arrangements; exposure of a public investment project as a cover for the diversion of funds to offshore islands; at least three magistrates jailed, charged with corruption; an international fiscal fraud involving a bank and members of the Belgian upper class (*De Morgen*, 19 February 1997).

References

Bovens, M. and 't Hart, P. (1996) *Understanding Policy Fiascoes*, New Brunswick: Transaction.
Cartuyvels, Y. and Mary, P. H. (1997) 'Crise de la justice: et au delà?', in Y. Cartuyvels, F. Delperée, P. Delwit, C. De Valkeneer, C. Doutrelepont, G. Haarscher, J. Kotek, H. Le Paige, P. H. Mary, C. Panier, V. Paulus de Chatelet, F. Ringelheim, M. Uyttendaele and J. Vogel *L'Affaire Dutroux – la Belgique malade de son système*, Brussels: Interventions-Editions Complexe.
Chambre des Représentants de Belgique (1997) *Enquête parlementaire sur la manière dont l'enquête, dans ses volets policiers et judiciaires a été menée dans 'l'affaire Dutroux–Nihoul et consorts'*, Brussels, 713/6 -96–97: 1–310.
Christiaensen, S., Claes, P. and Dupont, L. (1992) 'Knelpunten betreffende het functioneren van het strafrechtelijk vooronderzoek – samenvattend verslag van een

empirische studie' [Bottlenecks in the functioning of preliminary criminal inquiries – summary of an empirical study], *Panopticon* 13 (3): 222–225, 236–239.

De Clerck, S. (1997a) 'Minister van justitie De Clerck over gerecht en politie' [Minister of justice De Clerck on police and justice], *Politeia* 3 (10): 7–10.

—— (1997b) 'Toespraak' [Speech], *Vlaams jurist vandaag* 4 (1–2): 41–43.

—— (1997c) 'Grenzen aan het recht' [Limits of the law], *Tijdschrift-juridisch cahier* 5 (2): 24–29.

De Moor, F. (1994a) 'Zo staan de zaken' [That is how things are], *Knack magazine*, 30 March: 12–17.

—— (1994b)'Beschuldigde sta op – het gerecht is de instorting nabij' [Will the accused rise – the court is close to collapse], *Knack magazine*, 30 November: 30.

Deltour, P. (1996) *Man bijt hond* [Man bites dog], Brussels: Icarus Standaard Uitgeverij.

Delwit, P. (1997) 'Politisation, dépolitisation, répolitisation. Les partis politiques et la société belges', in Y. Cartuyvels, F. Delperée, P. Delwit, C. De Valkeneer, C. Doutrelepont, G. Haarscher, J. Kotek, H. Le Paige, P. H. Mary, C. Panier, V. Paulus de Chatelet, F. Ringelheim, M. Uyttendaele and J. Vogel *L'Affaire Dutroux – la Belgique malade de son système*, Brussels: Interventions-Editions Complexe.

Dupont, L. (1987) 'Polemische bespiegelingen over strafrechtshervormingen' [Polemic reflections on penal law reforms], *Panopticon* 8 (5–6): 395–398.

Edelman, M. (1988) *Constructing the Political Spectacle*, Chicago, IL: Chicago University Press.

Fijnaut, C. (1982) 'Partijpolitiek en strafrechtelijk beleid' [Party politics and penal policies], *Panopticon* 3 (2): 93–98.

Gray, P. (1996) 'Disastrous explanations – or explanations of disaster? A reply to Patrick Dunleavy', *Public Policy and Administration* 11 (1): 74–81.

't Hart, P. (1993) 'Symbols, rituals and power: the lost dimensions of crisis management', *Journal of Contingencies and Crisis Management* 1 (1): 37–50.

Hooghe, M. (1997) 'Over de politieke slagkracht van nieuwe sociale bewegingen' [On the political strength of new social movements], *Samenleving en Politiek* 4 (6): 9–17.

Huyse, L. (1985) 'Politieke benoemingen in de magistratuur. Een probleemformulering' [Political appointments in the magistracy. The formulation of a problem], *Panopticon* 6 (2): 124–128.

—— (1994) *De politiek voorbij. Een blik op de jaren negentig* [Past politics. A look at the nineties], Leuven: Kritak.

—— (1996) *De lange weg naar Neufchâteau* [The long way to Neufchâteau], Leuven: Uitgeverij Van Halewijck.

Le Paige, H. (1997) 'Les média et les "dysfonctionnements"', in Y. Cartuyvels, F. Delperée, P. Delwit, C. De Valkeneer, C. Doutrelepont, G. Haarscher, J. Kotek, H. Le Paige, P. H. Mary, C. Panier, V. Paulus de Chatelet, F. Ringelheim, M. Uyttendaele and J. Vogel *L'Affaire Dutroux – la Belgique malade de son système*, Brussels: Interventions-Editions Complexe.

Magistratuur en Maatschappij [Magistracy and Society] (1994) 'De efficiëntie van de justitie' [The efficiency of the judiciary], *Colloquium*, 16 December: 11.

Schoenaerts, B. (1995) *De Belgische justitie – een kafkaiaanse nachtmerrie – analyse en remedie* [The Belgian justice system – a Kafkaesque nightmare – analysis and remedy], Gent: Mys & Breesch, Uitgevers.

Tanghe, F. (1997) *Het spaghetti-arrest – Recht en democratie* [The spaghetti-decree – law and democracy], Antwerpen Baarn: Hadewijch.

Van Bosbeke, A. and Willems, J. (1990) *Kirchen an Co – het blauwe netwerk* [Kirchen and Co – the blue network], Brussels: Uitgeverij EPO.

Van Delm, J. (1993) *Justitie in opspraak – de verloren eer van het Belgische gerecht* [Justice discredited – the lost honour of Belgian justice], Antwerpen: Standaard Uitgeverij.

Van Outrive, L. (1996) 'The political role of the judiciary: the Belgian case', *Res Publica* 38 (2): 371–384.

Vandenberghe, H. (1981) 'De politisering van de magistratuur' [The politicization of the magistracy], *CEPESS-bladen* 4: 52.

Vandenbussche, F. (1996) *Meisjes verdwijen niet zomaar – de zaak-Dutroux: het falen van de Belgische justitie en politie* [Girls don't disappear just like that – the Dutroux affair: the failing Belgian justice system and police], Utrecht-Antwerpen: Kosmos-ZK Uitgevers.

THE MASS MEDIA AND POLICY DISASTERS

The IRT disaster and the crisis in crime-fighting in the Netherlands

Mark Bovens, Paul 't Hart, Sander Dekker, Gerdien Verheuvel, Eline de Vries

A disastrous fight against organized crime

It all began with a simple press release. On 7 December 1993 it was announced that an interregional criminal investigation team (IRT), established in 1989 to fight organized crime in the Netherlands, was to be disbanded. The controversy that ensued in the wake of IRT's dissolution resulted in banner headlines about police involvement in drug trafficking, a major Parliamentary Inquiry and a crisis in the criminal investigation system.

The Parliamentary Inquiry into investigation methods used to combat organized crime revealed that the Dutch police authorities had not only authorized the importation into the country of hundreds of tons of drugs (many of which found their way to the streets), but in some cases also financed criminal investigations with the revenues of illegal transactions. Extensive use had also been made of criminals as informers, who were often paid substantial sums or were allowed to keep the revenues of their illegal transactions. There had been no systematic discussion, authorization or monitoring of these very controversial police methods. The criminal investigation process involved many different organizations. As a result, jurisdictions and responsibilities were diffuse, communications faulty, and the criminal investigation system was afflicted by bureaucratic infighting, leaks to the press and personal conflicts. Finally, administrative, legal and political authorities had great difficulties in exercising control. Police investigators often operated on their own and in secret. By the mid-1990s, the Dutch fight against organized crime had come to be regarded as a major policy disaster.

Policy disasters, however, unlike natural disasters, cannot be observed by the use of our senses alone. Policy disasters are construed. They require the revelation and interpretation of facts and figures. Interpretation, in its turn, requires frames of references, scripts and arguments. Moreover, the construction of policy disasters is a highly political activity since it always involves the attribution of accountability and blame (Bovens and 't Hart 1996). In western societies the media are pivotal in this process.

The analysis in this chapter first introduces the main events of the case and describes it as a policy disaster. Second, we present some general thoughts on the dynamics of mass media reporting of controversial policies. Using work by Vasterman and Aerden (1995) on publicity waves, we formulate some expectations about the intensity, focus, normative content and political significance of media reporting in the first six months of the public scandal about crime-fighting methods. These are then checked against evidence obtained from a content analysis of newspaper reports on the affair, and the main findings are presented. The chapter ends by discussing some questions about the role of the media in the construction of policy disasters raised by this chapter.

The crisis of crime-fighting in the Netherlands

The historical context

In the three decades after the Second World War the crime rate in the Netherlands was low compared to that of neighbouring countries. Consequently, crime-fighting was largely a depoliticized affair. For many years the Dutch police came close to the ideal image outlined for it by one of the fathers of the Dutch police system, the nineteenth-century liberal statesman Thorbecke, who wanted 'a police that is seen and heard of as little as possible' (Rosenthal *et al.* 1987). The major challenges for the Dutch police in this period lay in the maintenance of public order (anti-authoritarian youth culture, new social movements) rather than in combating crime. The police were even urged to downplay their repressive role and to expand their involvement in various forms of social assistance. They were to become more tightly integrated into local community structures ('Projectgroep Organisatiestructuren' 1977).

Things started to change in the early 1980s. Drug abuse, the drug trade and drug-related petty crime became the focus of public concern. Steep rises in major crime statistics attracted political attention, with some types of crime having increased tenfold over the previous decade. In 1985 a new plan by the Justice Ministry put crime-fighting back on the agenda of the police and the criminal justice system (Ministry of Justice 1985). The plan advocated a dual policy. Day-to-day petty crime (shoplifting, burglaries) was to be the focus of broad-based local-level prevention efforts. Organized crime (drug trafficking, money laundering, fraud) was to be dealt with by a centralized repressive effort.

The successor to this policy, announced in 1990, was couched in alarmist terms (Ministry of Justice 1990). This argued that the criminal justice system faced a discrepancy between the increasing scale of serious crime and the system's ability to apprehend, try and incarcerate criminals. This endemic performance shortfall was considered a threat to the system's legitimacy. The report highlighted the shortcomings of the system in dealing with organized crime. Criminal investigation tasks accounted for only 15 per cent of police personnel strength, with 70–80 per cent devoted to the maintenance of order and social assistance activities (Hoogenboom 1994: 21). Police investigators and public prosecutors lacked the requisite specialized expertise in accounting, computing, environmental and fiscal law. Their information about the organization and modus operandi of criminal groups was patchy. The then minister of justice, Hirsch Ballin, embarked on a personal crusade to increase police effectiveness and declared a 'war on crime'.

The institutional context

In the peculiar institutional setting of the Dutch police system, implementing a war on crime was a hard task. While during the 1980s criminal groups increased their scale of operation to regional, local and international levels, under the 1957 Police Law the Dutch police force was still organized principally on a local basis, with 148 local forces and a national police comprising seventeen districts.

Moreover, there was a complex authority and accountability system (Rosenthal 1984). A functional division was made between public-order maintenance and crime-fighting activities. The police were answerable to the local burgomaster for the former; the public prosecutor – an official based in the national public prosecutor's office within the Ministry of Justice – was in charge of the latter. When it came to the overall administration of the police force, another distinction was made. The 148 local forces were administered by the burgomasters in conjunction with the Ministry of the Interior, whereas the national police force was administered directly by the Ministry of Justice. To keep the system together at the local level, the burgomaster, the local public prosecutor and the police chief were supposed to liaise regularly in what was called 'triangular consultation'. There were, however, major local differences in the extent to which these triangles performed a substantive policy function. In practice, the police chief, rather than his two bosses, was the dominant force in the network, because of his control over information given to the others and disagreement between them on the priorities for the allocation of police capacity (Albert 1994).

The 1957 Police Law was a compromise in an ongoing controversy about the nature and organization of policing in the Netherlands, which merely continued after its adoption. To some extent, the dispute was about diverging philosophies of policing. The public-order perspective sees the police force as a pragmatic, community-oriented peacekeeper. It favours a local approach: local police forces administered by local authorities. In contrast, the criminal justice perspective views the police primarily as upholding the rule of law in as uniform a way as possible throughout the country. It emphasizes the crime-fighting role of the police and favours a national police force. These philosophical differences were institutionalized in competing organizational clusters: the public-order approach was advocated by the municipalities and their patron at the national level, the Interior Ministry, whereas the Justice Ministry and the public prosecutor's office championed the criminal justice approach. They were locked in a bureaucratic-political stalemate, which was reproduced in parliament.

Reform proposals to tighten up the system one way or the other initially failed to solicit enough support. Yet the pressure to improve police organization continued to build until the growing concern about the rise in crime played into the hands of the advocates of the criminal justice perspective. The stalemate was finally broken when – during the formation of a new cabinet following a general election in the spring of 1989 – the decision was finally made to reform the police. However, yet again the newly proposed Police Bill contained elements of compromise. It did not propose a uniform national police force; instead, the two existing types of forces were to merge into twenty-five regional forces. The dual authority system was left largely intact, but the administration of the force was given to the burgomaster of the biggest city in the force's region, leaving his colleagues in smaller towns with only their authority for the maintenance of public order. The chief public prosecutor was given a role as co-administrator of the regional force. The major decisions about the allocation of money and manpower were now made by the 'triangle' of the central city in the region, consisting of the burgomaster, chief prosecutor and the regional police chief. This system came into effect in January 1993 and was supposed to solve the problems of scale, size and coordination that had undermined the crime-fighting capacity of the old system.

The major weak spot of the new system was held to be the limited potential for democratic control of the police. Since Holland does not have a regional administration, there was a mismatch between the scale of the new police system and the scale of representative government. In the old system, local councils had a substantive role in police oversight, with their link to the burgomaster as the main reference point. Given the diminished role of all the burgomasters (and thus all local councils) but one in every region, it was alleged that the system suffered from a 'democratic deficit' (see Cachet *et al.* 1994).

The crime-fighting process

The day-to-day practice of organized-crime investigations by these teams, and other detective units and special investigation forces (notably the customs service and the fiscal investigation service), evolved largely independently of the legal reform process. Anticipating the police reorganization, the Justice Department had already taken the initiative to intensify inter-force cooperation by forming so-called interregional criminal investigation teams (IRTs; *interregionale rechercheteams*). These were to be elite units devoted exclusively to the fight against large-scale organized crime. They were to contain the necessary mix of police and technical professionals, organized on an appropriately large scale to enable the effective preparation of cases against major criminal gangs. One such team, established in January 1989, involved collaboration between the Amsterdam, Haarlem, Utrecht and Hilversum police forces. There were others in other parts of the country.

These teams were focused on penetrating the core of criminal organizations.

They operated in the strictest possible secrecy, and explored new tactics to obtain information about the organization and modus operandi of major Dutch drugs importers in particular. These included the use of electronic surveillance equipment, phone tapping, undercover agents and paid informers. Although, formally, the public prosecutor should have had a key role in supervising the investigation process, in practice individual policemen of crack units within the IRTs were given or acquired considerable discretion in the use of investigation tactics. The perceived need for secrecy to protect the safety of informers was a major reason for a policy of compartmentalizing operational information pursued by some police investigators, even up to the point of not informing their superiors of what exactly they were doing. Also, some 'hands-on' public prosecutors who were deeply involved in IRT operations sometimes withheld information from their colleagues and superiors.

While this, in itself, was a risky way of operating, its vulnerability was increased by a number of factors, including:

- the absence of a legal framework regulating the use of intrusive surveillance and other investigation tactics – this created a considerable risk of prosecutions based on information obtained by the use of these tactics being thrown out in court;
- a lack of a clear investigation policy within the public prosecutor's office, and, consequently, large differences between the supervisory styles employed by different prosecutors;
- pervasive speculation about 'moles' in the police leaking information to the targets of major criminal investigations, as well as speculation about the use of 'counter-surveillance' by criminals;
- tense relations between the constituent forces making up the IRTs, stemming from deep-rooted historical and cultural barriers to intensified inter-force cooperation.

In summary, the Dutch police were trying hard to become more effective in the fight against crime, driven by a wave of public and political concern about the rise in crime. This struggle took place in the context of a police system which was still organized largely at the local level, which featured a highly complex and ambivalent authority and accountability structure, and which lacked a consistent policy on how intensive investigation methods should be used to combat serious crime.

The IRT disaster

In Table 3.1, an outline is provided of the main events that caused the issue to flare up. The public controversy about crime-fighting methods started on 7 December 1993, when the Amsterdam police 'triangle', consisting of Amsterdam burgomaster Van Thijn, Chief Public Prosecutor Vrakking and Police Commissioner Nordholt, announced the dissolution of the IRT, citing its use of inappropriate and unacceptable investigation methods as the main reason. It soon transpired that interpersonal and inter-force relations within the team had been highly strained, with hardline pragmatists in Utrecht and Haarlem opposing the more rule-bound and traditional force in Amsterdam. Refusals to share information were common; mutual distrust was high. On 8 November 1993 a newly appointed team leader, Van Kastel, had submitted a damning report to his Amsterdam superiors, alleging that factions within the team were involved in operations that violated criminal investigation codes. His main worry was the use by factions within the team of the so-called Delta method, which involved the use of informants in providing the police with information about drug smuggling operations. Informants were monitored by the police but otherwise left free to act, in order to enable the informer to rise up the criminal hierarchy. Moreover, the informer was allowed to keep most of the money paid to him by the criminal organization and part of it was used to finance secret police operations. In the process, the police allowed large quantities of drugs to reach the streets. Following consultation with the ministers of justice and home affairs, the use of the Delta method was terminated on 15 November 1993.

Table 3.1 Chronology of the IRT affair

Date	Event
25 January 1989	The IRT is formed.
29 March 1993	Coordination of the IRT is handed over by the Utrecht police to the Amsterdam police, under the control of chief inspector Van Kastel.
8 November 1993	The so-called 'Van Kastel report' appears. It is highly critical of the IRT's modus operandi, especially the so-called Operation Delta.
15 November 1993	The public prosecutor's office terminates Operation Delta; consultation with ministers of justice and home affairs.
7 December 1993	Press announcement that the IRT is dissolved. The Amsterdam police cite the 'use of inappropriate and unacceptable investigation methods', as the main reason.
15 January 1994	Van Thijn (former mayor of Amsterdam) becomes minister of home affairs.
22 January 1994	Media report on corruption in the Amsterdam police. Amsterdam police commissioner Nordholt calls his Utrecht colleague Wiarda's allegations 'infamous'. Wiarda denies having made the allegations.
23 January 1994	Wierenga commission established by the ministers of home affairs and justice.
24 March 1994	Wierenga report. No evidence of corruption within the Amsterdam police force. The real reasons behind the dissolution of the IRT were, according to the commission, tensions within the Amsterdam public prosecutor's office and the unwillingness of the Amsterdam force to cooperate with other forces. Chief prosecutor Vrakking, attorney-general Van Randwijck, and commissioner Nordholt are held responsible. Prime minister Lubbers and Van Thijn immediately announce that the resignation of these officials is out of the question.
7 April 1994	First IRT debate in parliament. Motion concerning parliamentary inquiry into investigation methods. Ministers of justice and home

	affairs promise to hold urgent meetings to review the performance of those officials involved.
3 May 1994	National elections. Political clashes between Hirsch Ballin and Van Thijn.
20 May 1994	News reports of a continuing 'crisis of authority'. Official dissolution of the government pending formation of a new coalition. Parliament demands a second debate.
25 May 1994	Second IRT debate. Motion declares that Hirsch Ballin and Van Thijn should abstain from further involvement in the affair.
27 May 1994	Resignation of Hirsch Ballin and Van Thijn.
1 June 1994	Parliamentary working group preliminary inquiry into investigation methods established.
21 October 1994	The working group recommends a full Parliamentary Inquiry be held.
6 December 1994	Parliamentary Inquiry into investigation methods officially established (the Van Traa Commission).
end December 1994	Parliament demands clarification on alleged drug trafficking. Minister of justice Sorgdrager misinforms parliament following press revelations concerning controlled drugs, as a result of Haarlem public prosecutor Van Veen's failure to pass on information to her.
April 1995	Investigation by the Internal Affairs Branch into the Haarlem CID's involvement in drug trafficking.
1 September 1995	Start of public hearings by the Van Traa Commission.
October 1995	Controversy over the size of the 'early retirement' package offered to attorney-general Van Randwijck.
1 February 1996	Publication of report by the Van Traa Commission signals an 'institutional crisis' in crime-fighting and calls for restrictions on various special investigation methods.
25 March 1996	Cabinet response to the inquiry report rejects some of the most restrictive policy proposals.
May 1996	Parliamentary debate on the inquiry report. Controversy erupts about the absence of resignations following publication of the report. Key proposals of the Van Traa Commission accepted.
September 1996	Ministry of justice publishes 'implementation plan'.

The announcement in December of the dissolution of the IRT did not specify the Delta method episode because it was deemed too risky to publicize it. However, the announcement triggered a media-amplified war of words between Commissioner Nordholt and his Utrecht colleague Wiarda. Wiarda went on record on 22 January 1994, claiming that the main cause of the team's problems had not been the use of controversial methods but corruption within the Amsterdam force, which meant that any information shared by his men found its way to the opposing side. Nordholt denied the charges, accused Wiarda of disloyalty, and repeated his reasons for dissolving the team but again did not mention the highly confidential facts contained in the Van Kastel report. He was backed up by his erstwhile political superior, former Amsterdam burgomaster Van Thijn, who found himself in an awkward transition role, having become minister of home affairs only a few days earlier, following the death of the previous incumbent.

The Wierenga inquiry and its aftermath

Faced with an increasingly nasty scandal, the two ministers in charge of the police, Justice Minister Hirsch Ballin and Home Affairs Minister Van Thijn established an independent commission led by the burgomaster of the city of Enschede, Wierenga. Its report appeared on 24 March. It argued that the decision to abolish the team had been wrong and that no illicit methods had been used – again without any mention being made in the report of the Delta method. However, immediately following the report's publication, the press reported, from insider sources, that there had been 'controlled traffic' in large quantities of drugs. During the parliamentary debate about the Wierenga report on 7 April 1994, the ministers were instructed to take measures to clean up the mess.

The constitutionally prescribed dissolution of the cabinet in anticipation of the 3 May national elections provided little relief for the two ministers, who by then had developed serious personal and political disagreements, precluding any forceful joint intervention. The new parliament kept up the pressure. On 25 May it judged that too little action had been taken and accepted a motion calling on the two ministers to abstain from any further involvement in the affair, turning it over to the prime minister. The result of this parliamentary pressure was the resignation of Hirsch Ballin, followed the same day by that of Van Thijn.

An institutional crisis

Parliament subsequently started its own investigation into the affair, which was elevated in December 1994 to the status of a formal Parliamentary Inquiry with quasi-judicial status and procedures. Its televised hearings in the autumn of 1995 caused the affair to resurface in the public domain and revealed much deeper problems in the fight against organized crime than the internal squabbles of a single investigation team. During its investigations it became clear, for example, that even after the termination of the Amsterdam–Utrecht IRT the Delta method continued to be used by other police units well after its abolition in Amsterdam, and that far larger quantities of more serious drugs had been brought into the market in this way than had originally been thought.

In February 1996 the inquiry report was published amidst a blaze of publicity. Its main conclusion was that crime-fighting in the Netherlands was crippled by a threefold institutional crisis (*Enquêtecommissie Opsporingsmethoden* 1996: 420-422):

- *A crisis of norms.* Police and prosecutors were operating in a legal and normative vacuum left by the government and the legislature. Consequently there was widespread uncertainty and ambiguity about the appropriateness of various investigation methods, which left room for strongly divergent interpretations by various police units and public prosecutors.
- *A crisis of organizations.* Crime-fighting tasks, responsibilities and capabilities were divided across a large number of organizations, without a clear division

of labour or effective coordination arrangements existing between them. This set the stage for controversies about who was responsible for what.

- *A crisis of authority.* Public prosecutors had in effect lost their grip on the criminal investigation activities of the police. This was largely because the public prosecutor's office failed to produce a coherent and consistently implemented policy on investigation methods. The problem was exacerbated by the divided police authority structure.

No single actor or agency was held responsible for the development of this crisis. The inquiry report pointed to a combination of factors, including overzealous detectives and public prosecutors, a disorganized team structure, bad management at senior levels in the police force and the public prosecutor's office, a lack of accountability of the police vis-à-vis its superiors, and legislative negligence. The report contained harsh criticisms of many of the key agencies and officials involved, but did not explicitly call for the resignation of ministers or other personal sanctions against officials. In his public statements immediately following the publication of the report, the inquiry chairman nevertheless made it clear that he thought that various of the main actors, especially in the police and public prosecutor's office, should be punished. When it came to the prospects for ending the crisis, the inquiry warned that it could not be resolved by a limited number of dramatic decisions. Instead the report proposed a wide-ranging package of legislative, administrative and organizational reforms.

The parliamentary debate about the inquiry report became somewhat of an anti-climax. Most of the reform proposals were quickly accepted and the Justice Ministry was instructed to prepare an implementation plan. Most of the debate focused on two issues: the desirability of sanctions against officials and the report's proposed legal ban of some of the most sensitive investigation methods. To the dismay of the inquiry chairman, parliament was reluctant to instigate tough sanctions against the major protagonists. In the end, Interior Minister Dijkstal announced a system for the rotation in office of police chiefs. Within the Justice Department, several key officials had been ushered out during or following the inquiry, largely under pressure from the justice minister, who felt she had not been properly advised by her most senior civil servants.[1]

And the war against crime? It continued to excite the public imagination. At the end of 1996 the 'trial of the century' was held, of a leading Dutch drug 'baron' pursued by the IRTs. Much of the action in court centred on the admissibility of evidence obtained through the use of controversial investigation methods. This gave rise to a publicity war between the media-conscious team of top-notch defence lawyers and the public prosecutor's office, which even employed the services of an expensive PR consultant during the trial period. Meanwhile, media revelations of investigation scandals continued, particularly about the sometimes bizarre operations run by a duo of special investigators in the Haarlem CID, who – in the spirit of the Delta method – had been deeply involved in the setting up of transcontinental drug smuggling routes using criminal informers. This eventually led to a criminal prosecution for perjury committed while they were being interviewed by the commission of inquiry.

A policy disaster?

There is no doubt that the IRT case and the crime-fighting problems it revealed qualify as a major policy disaster as defined by Bovens and 't Hart (1996) and in most of the chapters in this volume. The political perception of failure was widespread and the damning conclusions of the Parliamentary Inquiry met with universal approval. Many negative events were noted and attributed incontrovertibly to failures of individuals and organizations within government. Most painfully, it became clear that under the eyes – if not the direct supervision – of the Dutch police many tons of drugs found their way on to the streets of Holland and other European countries. Moreover, as noted in the inquiry report, the IRT affair was the trigger to much more than the failure of a programme or a policy. It revealed serious shortcomings in the effectiveness and legitimacy of some of the core agents and institutions of the Dutch *Rechtsstaat*, including the police, the public prosecutor's office and the Department of Justice. Even though the initial corruption charges later proved to be unfounded, press reports and inquiry findings revealed that many officials had shown bad judgement and a lack of prudence, and that the state's crime-fighting fortress had been built on institutional quicksand. Finally, the public scandal aroused by the revelations virtually paralysed significant portions of the criminal justice system for months on end in an atmosphere of uncertainty and mutual recrimination. Through the politicization of its most advanced methods, the war against crime suffered a major blow, no doubt to the advantage of the very targets of those methods.

The mass media and policy disasters

As noted in the introductory chapter to this volume, it is important to understand why some social problems, policy controversies and failing programmes come into the limelight and enter collective memory as 'disasters' and others do not. The Bovens and 't Hart (1996) scheme of fiasco construction was introduced there to help make sense of the political selectivity of disaster construction. The Bovens and 't Hart study focused strongly on the types of arguments used in the construction of policy disasters and did not deal with the question of those who are involved in that process. In this chapter we seek to fill part of this gap. We look at an important arena of public debate and political interaction, namely the mass media. Specifically, we are interested in the dynamics of media attention towards alleged policy disasters: how does media coverage of the nature, causes and political repercussions of negative events develop over time, and how does it vary between different news sources?

Today, the mass media provide a pivotal forum for political sense-making and mass mobilization (Chaffee 1975). Their role in the political agenda-setting process has been well documented (Cobb and Elder 1972; Nimmo and Sanders 1981; Kingdon 1984; Rochefort and Cobb 1994). Many policy-makers take what is in the media as an indicator of the public agenda at large and use this to focus their legislative and administrative agendas. At the same time, their awareness of the power of the news media has prompted policy-makers to try to influence the content of news reports to suit their political or agency needs. Likewise, journalists may be acutely aware of the political significance of their reporting activities. They may actively seek to influence public perceptions and confront authorities with their findings and opinions. Yet they are often careful not to antagonize owners, financiers and influential political gatekeepers. The media, in short, have become an integral part of the political arena where policies are made, evaluated and reformed, with newsmakers often more aptly characterized as players than as spectators (Kennamer 1992; Spitzer 1993).

According to some, the news media have closely followed, if not led, the general tendency in western societies to expect more of government and at the same time to become more critical of its actual performance. Sabato (1991), writing on the American situation, has characterized the evolving role of the press in relation to government by using a canine metaphor. Before Watergate, the US press corps acted as the president's 'lapdog': docile, uncritical, willing to oblige. The conspicuous success of *Washington Post* investigative journalists Woodward and Bernstein in putting the Watergate scandal on the political agenda, ultimately bringing down president Nixon, heralded the era of the press as 'watchdog', the media as guardians of the integrity of governmental power, proactively scrutinizing the conduct of public affairs for signs of failure and wrongdoing. The subsequent flow of incidents of red tape, waste, abuse and scandal, combined with the ever increasing speed and competitive pressures of the modern news business, are said to have pushed the watchdog role of the press beyond the limits of propriety. Currently, political reporters roam government offices and political corridors as if they were 'junkyard dogs', aggressively seeking any form of political dirt available, and not hesitating to put up a vicious fight to get it.

While the junkyard dog image may be slightly overblown, and is certainly not readily applicable to most European countries, it probably does convey a general trend towards more proactive, more critical reporting of government conduct. In the study of political scandals, for example, muckraking journalism time and again proves to be vital in bringing to light improprieties, misconduct and other forms of government failure (see Markovits and Silverstein 1988). In the Netherlands, most of the national policy disasters in the 1985-95 period that led to major and quasi-judicial Parliamentary Inquiries started with press reports or leaks to the press (Bovens and 't Hart 1993).

To understand how the process of disaster construction in mass media reporting takes place, we use the work of Vasterman and Aerden (1995) about publicity waves. According to them, there is a distinct pattern to media coverage about major public events, which, as we argue here, may lead us to understand media-driven politicization of government performance better. Vasterman and Aerden discern four phases in publicity waves:

1   *Identification*: a new phenomenon is discovered and a news theme is created (labelled). Journalists will then proceed to search for related news and will be sensitized to observe new events through the newly created common filter. There is great pressure on journalists to be in on the potential scoops under the new theme, and the temptation to go with speculation and rumour is large.

2   *Extension*: the news theme constitutes a widening umbrella under which many related subjects are placed. The original theme acquires a much wider scope. Incidents are increasingly treated as part of a broader trend and interpreted accordingly. More and more incidents are treated in this way and there will be a distinct impression that the phenomenon itself – rather than just media attention to it – is on the increase. Calls for action increase.

3   *Reaction*: gradually the news becomes dominated by the reactions of authorities and other interested parties, who may seek to escalate or de-escalate the publicity wave. Stories and reports deal less and less with the original phenomenon and more with its wider impact. Reporting tends to branch out ever more widely in a search for further expansion of the news theme.

4   *Extinction or renewal*: in the case of extinction, the news theme is exhausted, and both reporters and stakeholders turn their attention gradually to other matters. In the case of renewal, the original news theme is superseded by a related and equally tantalizing theme that arouses new waves of reporting activity and socio-political responses.

Below, we apply this process model to the mass media coverage of an important part of the IRT disaster in the Netherlands, and use content-analysis techniques to see whether actual press reporting matches the four-stage logic of the model. The general expectation is that the publicity wave model describes the dynamics of media reporting of the IRT case. This general prediction can be specified in terms of three expectations. First, we expect the *intensity* of media coverage of the IRT case to follow the pattern of identification, extension, reaction and extinction/renewal. Second, the *focus* of media coverage should expand over time, stabilize and subsequently decrease. In visual terms, the model predicts that both the intensity and the focus of media coverage will have the shape of an inverted U-curve. Third, the model implies that media coverage is increasingly targeted on the role and responsibility of higher level actors. Going beyond the model, we look at media reporting of the activities of political accountability fora during the period under study. If the media do play a political agenda-setting role, we may expect to see that parliament targets the same problems and actors for its critical attention as do the media, e.g. by following the logic of the 'publicity wave'.

Constructing a policy disaster

The following analysis of the IRT case is based on a content analysis of four Dutch newspapers, two main national dailies (*NRC-Handelsblad* and *De Telegraaf*) and two local newspapers from Amsterdam (*Het parool*) and Utrecht (*Utrechts nieuwsblad*). The latter were chosen because of their proximity to the two main policing and political-administrative arenas pitted against each other following the dissolution of the interregional team. For practical reasons, the analysis has remained confined to the first major IRT crisis period. All papers were fully checked for news articles (not editorials) on the case, from 7 December 1993 (the date of the dissolution announcement) to 28 May 1994 (one day after the resignation of the ministers). This period was divided into six equal time periods of roughly one month. It is important to keep in mind the key events taking place during each of these periods:

- *Period 1* (7 December 1993–4 January 1994): crisis trigger; initial responses from all sides; media offensive.
- *Period 2* (5 January 1994–2 February 1994): corruption charges against the Amsterdam police; calls for inquiry.
- *Period 3* (3 February 1994–3 March 1994): Wierenga Commission conducts its investigation; press leaks.
- *Period 4* (4 March 1994–1 April 1994): Wierenga report published; first parliamentary debate.
- *Period 5* (2 April 1994– 30 April 1994): ministers of home affairs and justice to take measures; national elections; growing tensions between ministers.
- *Period 6* (1 May 1994– 28 May 1994): growing dissatisfaction with lack of follow-up; second parliamentary debate; ministerial resignations.

Each article was retrieved and filed. The headlines and contents of the articles were coded using a codebook based on a further operationalization of the main hypotheses. Careful checks were made to ensure that articles were coded consistently.[2]

Patterns of media coverage: intensity, focus, targets

Looking at the evolution of media coverage during the period under study, we find that it matches the predictions of the publicity wave model only to a certain extent. The *intensity* of media reporting on the case is depicted in Figure 3.1. The combined number and length of the articles do evolve, but do not fully fit the predicted inverted U-shape. Most notably, media attention decreased during the third month, when the Wierenga Commission was conducting its highly confidential investigation. In fact, to prevent press leaks and counter-surveillance by organized crime, the commission set up offices and conducted its interviews in the closely guarded, sound-proof headquarters of the Dutch intelligence service. It is, however, also remarkable that media coverage decreased in the hectic sixth month of the crisis, when the parliamentary drama unfolded, suggesting that at least some form of saturation if not extinction of the affair took place (media attention was to be renewed with vigour more than a year later, during the public hearings of the Parliamentary Inquiry).

The *focus* of media coverage shifted in different ways. First of all, Vasterman and Aerden's (1995) assertion that, over time, different items will be connected to the emerging news theme was indeed borne out in this case. Tables 3.2 and 3.3 show the attention paid to different aspects and sub-stories in the headlines and articles, respectively. The emphasis in the headlines shifts from the dissolution of the team towards the corruption allegations, then highlights the Wierenga Commission and its preoccupation with the appropriateness of investigation tactics, and then turns toward the question of ministerial responsibility. When one looks more closely at the actual content of articles, a roughly similar pattern emerges. The pattern is weaker because full articles are obviously less selective than headlines and allow journalists to touch upon multiple themes. Most remarkable in Table 3.3 are the upsurge and then extinction of the corruption issue, and the gradual onset of ministerial responsibility.

Within the overall criminal investigation scandal theme there were distinct sub-

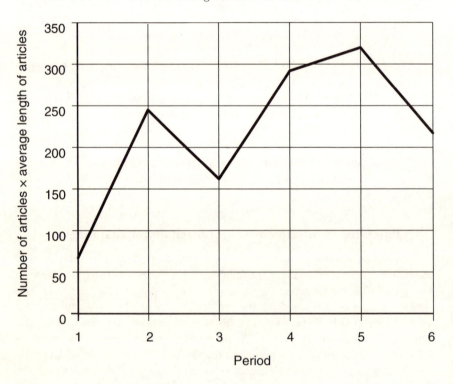

Figure 3.1 Intensity of newspaper coverage of the IRT affair

Table 3.2 Newspaper headline coverage of the IRT affair

	Percentage of articles per period containing the headline item					
	Period %					
	1	2	3	4	5	6
Dissolution of IRT	25	5	0	5	2	0
Corruption	0	31	14	0	1	0
Investigation methods	15	4	16	17	11	1
Trial consequences	15	5	20	1	4	0
Inter-force relations	0	8	6	2	1	4
Internal affairs investigation	0	9	10	2	2	0
Wierenga Commission	0	7	0	19	6	0
Ministerial responsibility	0	1	0	9	12	37
Relations between Van Thijn and Hirsch Ballin	0	0	0	0	5	8
Decline of trust in police	0	1	0	1	1	0
Administrative measures	15	4	4	3	6	8
Sanctions against personnel	5	1	6	14	21	4
Others	25	22	25	26	30	37

controversies. The initial scandal dealt with a range of operational police issues (investigation tactics, corruption, implications for ongoing trials). Later on, another appeared, centring on the political issue of who controlled the police. This agenda shift comes out in the comparison of the period during which each actor held media attention. As Table 3.4 shows, media reporting of the crisis went

Table 3.3 Newspaper article coverage of the IRT affair

	Percentage of all articles in each time period containing the subject item					
	Period %					
	1	2	3	4	5	6
Dissolution of IRT	80	80	73	61	23	27
Corruption	10	77	41	31	6	3
Investigation methods	90	45	67	65	39	14
Trial consequences	55	15	37	0	7	1
Inter-force relations	20	54	22	30	14	25
Internal affairs investigation	0	46	33	8	7	4
Wierenga commission	0	30	35	76	50	45
Ministerial responsibility	0	15	6	33	38	70
Relations between Van Thijn and Hirsch Ballin	0	0	0	0	7	42
Decline of trust in police	5	5	4	6	7	5
Administrative measures	25	30	18	9	22	48
Sanctions against personnel	20	11	14	36	38	40
Others	25	22	24	41	41	41

Table 3.4 Local, national, police and other actors in newspaper coverage of the IRT affair

	*Average number of actors per article, in each period**					
	Period					
	1	*2*	*3*	*4*	*5*	*6*
Local	1.05	0.78	0.86	0.50	0.36	0.38
National	0.05	0.97	0.29	1.23	1.41	1.74
Police	0.75	0.80	0.78	0.47	0.39	0.42
Other	0.70	1.30	0.71	1.56	1.57	1.97

Note:
*For example, in period 3 an average of 0.86 local actors were mentioned per article

through a process of 'nationalization', with the importance of coverage of national actors increasing significantly over time. There was also a clear widening and 'politicization' of the disaster. The bottom part of the table indicates that attention to police actors decreased while that to other, predominantly political, actors (ministers, parliamentarians, the investigation commission) increased.

In examining the third aspect of the publicity wave model – media portrayal of the roles and responsibilities of key actors – we looked at three variables. These include the media's overall evaluation of policy outcomes, its attribution of those outcomes to the decisions and actions of policy actors rather than impersonal forces, and its assignment of blame to individual officials. Table 3.5 provides the results of this analysis of media content.

In the upper row, the proportion of articles containing negative judgements seems to suggests that the media were all but united in their depiction of the case as a fiasco. It has to be observed, though, that the percentages relate to the total number of articles coded, including those without any evaluative content whatsoever. If, however, we take as our starting point only the evaluative articles, the percentages go up to 71, 90, 100, 93, 85 and 94 for the six periods, showing an almost universal condemnation of the events.

Table 3.5 Layers of fiasco construction by newspapers in the IRT affair

	*Percentage of articles per period containing a layer of fiasco construction**					
	Period %					
	1	*2*	*3*	*4*	*5*	*6*
Negative assessment of outcome	35	46	55	59	40	52
Human actors involved	20	14	20	50	36	52
Blaming individuals	5	20	33	60	49	66

Note:
*In period 2, for example, 20 per cent of the articles blamed specific individuals

From the second row it appears that – especially following the publication of the Wierenga report – the tendency to view the course of events as having been predominantly influenced by identifiable policy actors increased. Most conspicuous, however, are the findings with respect to blaming in the third row of Table 3.5. They reflect a progressive tendency to blame individual policy-makers. The only exception is period 5, which reflects the fact that this was the time when the ministers were preparing to take the remedial action demanded by parliament. When they appeared to be less than vigorous in doing so, they became the target of scathing media opinions, as evidenced by the furthest right column of Table 3.5.

Table 3.6 also reveals that, although it was the police chiefs making much of the noise in the initial period, Utrecht Commissioner Wiarda escaped relatively unscathed, whereas his Amsterdam colleague Nordholt began to face a media backlash following the Wierenga report's conclusion that the decision to dissolve the team had been unnecessary. The other main effect of Wierenga's actions was to put a significant portion of the blame for the IRT fiasco on officials in the public prosecutor's office, who had kept a relatively low profile in the early stages of the crisis. The Amsterdam chief prosecutor and attorney-general came under serious criticism, which eventually resulted in the latter's highly publicized early retirement.[3]

Accountability fora

The final issue examined concerned the extent to which the activities of accountability fora such as local councils and parliament coincide with the thrust of media reporting and evaluation as it develops over time. Overall, it seems to be the case that they do coincide. Figure 3.2 shows that it took accountability fora some time to respond to the surprise news of the dissolution of the team and the internal

Table 3.6 Attribution of blame in the IRT affair

	Period %					
	1	*2*	*3*	*4*	*5*	*6*
Burgomaster of Amsterdam	5	1	0	3	2	3
Burgomaster of Utrecht	0	1	0	0	0	0
Public prosecutor of Amsterdam	5	0	2	20	13	12
Management of the IRT	0	1	12	3	0	0
Amsterdam head of police	5	8	4	22	12	18
Utrecht head of police	0	8	6	7	2	1
Minister of home affairs	0	1	4	10	15	45
Minister of justice	0	5	2	20	19	44
Prime minister	0	0	0	8	7	0
Attorney-general of Amsterdam	0	0	10	19	12	11
Wierenga Commission	0	0	0	8	7	0
Others	0	4	14	18	19	16

Note:
*For example, in period 4 the minister of justice is blamed in 20 per cent of articles

police battles that lay at its heart. Yet they were fully engaged in period 3, and parliament succeeded in pressurizing the minister of justice to set up the Wierenga investigation. The commission was given time to conduct its business, but when its report came, parliament seized on it and played a highly visible role in escalating the affair to the level of a major political scandal, which reached an initial climax in the resignation of two cabinet ministers.

Conclusions

There appears to be little room for doubt that the mass media were important players in the policy disaster that was triggered by the surprise dissolution of the interregional investigation team. The sheer intensity of media coverage and its consistently critical assessment of police practices and judicial policy contributed to the atmosphere of political crisis which developed and spun out of control in the spring of 1994. Media-amplified leaks of confidential police information played an important agenda-setting role and contributed to the deepening of the disaster. During the subsequent expansion of the crisis in 1995 and 1996, the media would again play this role, even to the extent of raising questions as to whether some media were misused by criminals in possession of confidential police information stolen or leaked from police stations and public prosecutor's offices.

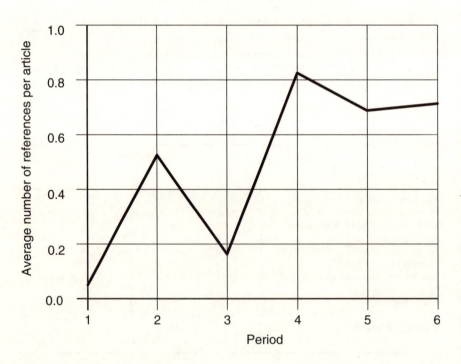

Figure 3.2 Actions of accountability fora as portrayed in the press during the IRT affair

The limited scope of this case analysis does not allow for generalizations to be made about the applicability of the publicity-wave model of media behaviour to policy controversies. To the extent that we were able to test the model's predictions, we found mixed results. A conceptual problem with the model is that it does not specify the temporal limits of the phases. Is a publicity wave a matter of days, weeks, months or years? Are all phases presumed to have a similar duration? How, in fact, can one establish the occurrence of a publicity wave without bending the time frame so as to fit the predicted inverted U-curve pattern? One may look upon the period under study here as a separate case where a full sequence of identification, extension, reaction and renewal is supposed to be found. However, one can also argue that these six months were just part of a more protracted publicity wave regarding organized crime and criminal justice policy in the Netherlands that continued until well after parliament had dealt with the inquiry report in the spring of 1996.

Another important area that needs to be tackled is the interplay between media activities and the strategic manoeuvring of players involved in policy disasters and political scandals. The publicity-wave model implicitly portrays the journalist as a quasi-autonomous actor competing in the market for news. Individually and collectively, journalists may decide that a particular story strikes a chord and is worth pursuing. The reality of the IRT affair and other policy disasters is that part of the spectacle is produced by the elites themselves. Either overtly, through offensive or defensive public statements, or covertly, by off-the-record briefings and the leaking of confidential information to the press, policy-makers and bureaucrats feed the media frenzy. They may do so because they are intent on exploiting the crisis atmosphere, but they may well feel they have little choice. They are caught up in the self-sustaining dynamics of the politics of blaming that may arise following some initial revelation about damage, wrongdoing or other evidence of potential policy disasters. The media are part and parcel of this politics of blaming, but may be better characterized as a co-player than as an arbiter. In this process, journalists and policy elites do not operate in separate worlds. They interact, and may even align with each other.

Notes

1   Sorgdrager was herself politically vulnerable because she had been a top official in the public prosecutor's office before assuming a cabinet position in the summer of 1994.
2   Initial probes revealed that the intercoder reliability fell below the threshold of 0.75. The codebook was amended accordingly, bringing the intercoder reliability up to the 0.80–0.95 range.
3   The retirement occurred after protracted negotiations between the attorney-general and the minister of justice. The media got wind of the suggestion that a retirement bonus of well over 1 million guilders was involved, and seized upon this to create another story line connected to the case.

References

Albert, H. J. (1994) *De ongelijkzijdige driehoek, zwolle, tjeenk willink,* Arnhem: Gouda Quint.

Bovens, M. A. P. and 't Hart, P. (1993) 'De sociale constructie van beleidsfiasco's', in M. van Twist and O. van Heffen (eds) *Beleid en wetenschap: Hedendaagse bestuurskundige beschouwingen,* Alphen aan den Rijn: Samsom.

——(1996) *Understanding Policy Fiascoes,* New Brunswick: Transaction.

Cachet, A., Muller, E. R., van der Torre, E. J., Verberk, M. P., van der Sluis, A. and Wolberink, M. M. E. (1994) *Politiebestel in verandering: verhoudingen tussen politie, bestuur, justitie en gemeenteraad onder de oude en nieuwe politiewet,* Arnhem: Gouda Quint.

Chaffee, S. H. (1975) *Political Communication: Issues and Strategies for Research,* Beverly Hills, CA: Sage.

Cobb, R. W. and Elder, L. D. (1972) *Participation in American Politics: The Dynamics of Agenda Building,* Boston, MA: Allyn & Bacon.

Enquêtecommissie Opsporingsmethoden, Opsporing Gezocht (1996) The Hague: SDU.

Hoogenboom, B. (1994) *Het politiecomplex,* Arnhem: Gouda Quint.

Kennamer, J. D. (1992) *Public Opinion, the Press, and Public Policy,* Westport, CT: Praeger.

Kingdon, J. W. (1984) *Agendas, Alternatives and Public Policies,* Boston, MA: Little Brown.

Markovits, A. S. and Silverstein, M. (1988) *The Politics of Scandal: Power and Process in Liberal Democracies,* New York and London: Holmes & Meier.

Ministry of Justice (1985) *Samenleving en criminaliteit,* The Hague: SDU.

——(1990) *Recht in beweging,* The Hague: SDU.

Nimmo, D. D. and Sanders, K. R. (1981) *Handbook of Political Communication,* Beverly Hills, CA: Sage.

'Projectgroep organisatiestructuren, politie in verandering' (1977) The Hague: Ministerie van Binnenlandse Zaken (unpublished).

Rochefort, D. A. and Cobb, R. W. (1994) *The Politics of Problem Definition: Shaping the Policy Agenda,* Lawrence, KS: University of Kansas Press.

Rosenthal, U. (1984) 'The bureaupolitics of policing: the Dutch case', *Police Science Abstracts* 12: 1–14.

Rosenthal, U., 't Hart, P. and Cachet, A. (1987) *Politiemanagement: een politiek-bestuurlijke visie,* Arnhem: Gouda Quint.

Sabato, L. J. (1991) *Feeding Frenzy: How Attack Journalism has Transformed American Politics,* New York: Free Press.

Spitzer, R. J. (1993) *Media and Public Policy,* Westport, CT: Praeger.

Vasterman, P. and Aerden, O. (1995) *De context van het nieuws,* Groningen: Wolters-Noordhoff.

Part III

THE 'WELFARE' STATE

4

THE BSE CRISIS

Public health and the 'risk society'

Rob Baggott

Introduction

The BSE crisis clearly illustrates the multilevel and multifaceted nature of policy disasters.[1] Over and above its effect on the beef industry and the potential implications for human health, the crisis had an adverse impact on the fortunes of the Major government, further undermined the UK's relationship with Europe and exposed flaws in the operation of European Union institutions. This chapter focuses upon the development of the crisis, up to the official announcement in March 1996 of a possible link between BSE and its human equivalent, Creutzfeldt-Jacob disease (CJD).[2] The so-called 'beef war' that developed in the aftermath of the March announcement is excluded from this analysis and remains for others to explore.

This analysis is in three main parts. First, the outcomes of the actions of the UK government are evaluated in order to establish the 'disastrousness' of British policies in this domain. In particular, claims made by various stakeholders and analysts about the costs (and benefits) associated with the policy are carefully scrutinized. There then follows a section outlining the specific criticisms of the UK's management of the crisis and the early involvement of European Union institutions. The third and final task is to place these outcomes, events, actions and criticisms in the context of broader explanations of policy disaster.

A policy disaster?

According to Bovens and 't Hart (1996), the first task when analysing policy disasters is to assess 'how bad is bad'. Policy disasters are not merely negative events; they are perceived as going beyond the pale of acceptability. It is therefore important to evaluate in a critical manner the negative consequences of the policy. It is also crucial to look for positive expectations and outcomes that might have motivated policy-makers to take a particular course of action.

The costs of dealing with the BSE crisis prior to March 1996 were already substantial: £147.8 million was accounted for by expenditure on research, compensation and advertising, miscellaneous government costs and farmers' losses (Anand and Forshner 1995). Following the March announcement, a number of predictions emerged regarding possible future costs. These varied considerably but were in a different league from those hitherto incurred, largely because of the costs of eradication.

Based on the assumption that the entire British herd would be destroyed, it was estimated that compensation for farmers, the restocking of herds, the value of lost sales and unemployment costs amounted to £35.2 billion (Coyle 1996). This was certainly an over-estimate. Beef exports were double-counted in the figures for lost sales. Unemployment costs were also exaggerated, as it was assumed that all workers in the industry would fail to find alternative employment. Another estimate, based upon similar assumptions about the extent of the cull, was much more conservative, at £15 billion, with continuing costs of up to a £1 billion a year (*Economist* 1996). Nevertheless, those who opted for the lower estimate conceded that the effect on the economy would be significant. Financial experts predicted a £6–7 billion increase in the trade deficit, a fall in national income of around 1 per cent and a rise in inflation of up to 1.5 per cent (Coyle 1996; *Economist* 1996; Keegan 1996).

Comprehensive figures relating to the actual (as opposed to the estimated) costs of the crisis have not yet emerged. However, from the information available it appears that the original estimates exaggerated the actual economic costs of the crisis, largely because of the decision not to cull the entire British herd. The revised cost of the culling and compensation programme over a three-year period was £3.59 billion. The latest available figures show that in the 1996/97 financial year, the total cost – including compensation to farmers, payments to slaughterhouses and renderers, costs of storage and incineration, and aid to renderers and abattoirs – was just over £1.5 billion (of which the EU's net contribution was £28 million (Hansard 1997).

The impact of the crisis on the British economy was moderated by the European Union's contribution to the compensation package for farmers and its intervention in the beef market. In addition, domestic sales of British beef products began to recover slowly in the latter part of 1996, largely because of falling prices. Yet, by December 1996 sales of fresh beef were still down 13 per cent on the previous year, while sales of 'non-fresh' beef products, including burgers and pies, were 38 per cent lower (P. Brown 1997a). Official figures, from the Ministry of Agriculture Fisheries and Food (MAFF), the Scottish Office, Agriculture, Environment and Fisheries Department, the Northern Ireland Department of Agriculture and the Welsh Office (1997) revealed a fall of 29 per cent in UK beef production and a drop of between 15 and 20 per cent in average UK beef consumption in 1996 compared with the previous year. The market price of cattle also fell by 14 per cent in this period. Furthermore, the export ban imposed by the European Union remained in place, at a cost to British beef exporters of over £0.6 billion a year (exports accounted for approximately 20 per cent of sales prior to the ban). European beef sales also remained depressed – six months after the crisis broke, sales were down approximately 15 per cent – underlining the point that significant costs were borne by producers on the continent as well as in the UK.

The actual impact of the crisis on the wider British economy is difficult to calculate. Some indicators show an improvement in 1996 compared with 1995 (Office for National Statistics 1997). Government borrowing fell from £35.1 billion to £24.8 billion in this period. But because of the range of factors involved, it is impossible to establish with any accuracy what this figure would have been in the absence of the BSE crisis. The balance of trade in goods deteriorated over this period, from a deficit of £11.6 billion in 1995 to an estimated £12.5 billion in 1996. But again, given the multiplicity of factors which impinge on this statistic, the precise impact of the crisis is difficult to measure.

Notwithstanding these problems of measurement, it seems fairly clear that the economic impact of the crisis was less extreme than some of the original predictions. However, other costs – omitted from economic calculations – must also be taken into account. First, there is the cost of human and animal suffering. Between 1986 and 1996, 163,216 cases of BSE were confirmed. The number of actual cases of BSE in this period is believed to be higher than this – because of deliberate under-reporting and subclinical infection.[3] As far as human suffering is concerned, the full extent of the BSE/CJD connection is not yet known. In the UK, up to December 1997, there were 23 confirmed cases of 'new variant' CJD (vCJD) – the type believed to be associated with BSE in cattle. Recent research has established strong similarities between the two diseases (Collinge et al. 1996), but the discovery of cases of vCJD in Germany and France (which so far have recorded very small numbers of BSE cases) has raised doubts about the epidemiological link between BSE and vCJD (Chazot et al. 1997).

Because of uncertainties about the extent of infection in cattle, the contamination of the food chain and the possibility of transmission to man, the ultimate impact of the crisis in human terms is difficult to predict with any accuracy. Estimates of the total number of people likely to be affected by vCJD vary widely. The most comprehensive study so far has identified a low limit of seventy-five individuals and an upper limit of 80,000 (Cousens et al. 1997). The human suffering of victims and their relatives has a cost. But this is difficult to quantify even if more exact estimates on the likely prevalence of the disease were available. Over and above this, there are the costs of caring for victims in the latter stages of the illness. These would be substantial if the higher estimates of prevalence proved to be correct.

A further cost to take into account is the declining public trust in government that has arisen from the BSE crisis. Specifically with regard to the BSE issue, surveys indicated a high level of public distrust. In an ICM poll on behalf of the *Guardian* newspaper in April 1996, 73 per cent of respondents felt that government knew of the risk involved and tried to hide it (Linton and Bates 1996). Other surveys revealed similar findings: 70 per cent of respondents in a poll conducted by the Consumers' Association in June 1996 thought that government had withheld information about BSE, while in a survey conducted by the Rowntree Reform Trust in September of that year, three-quarters of the public reported that they did not trust the government to tell the truth about beef (Pudephatt 1996). However, despite these findings it is difficult to assess the contribution of this particular crisis to the decline in public trust of government. The British Social Attitudes survey, reporting fieldwork completed prior to March 1996, found that 'the British public appears now to have less confidence in the ability of the political system to respond to its wishes than has ever been recorded before' (Curtice and Jowell 1996). This declining faith was undoubtedly influenced by a range of factors present in the 1990s, including other political scandals and fiascos, such as the 'Arms to Iraq' affair (see Chapter 7) and allegations of 'sleaze' in British government.

Given that the costs of the crisis are already high (and may turn out to be even higher), it may seem odd to ask if the policy pursued yielded any benefits. Yet on closer inspection it certainly did have a number of short-term advantages. Both the UK government and the European Union bought time by their actions, and postponed the full-blown crisis for at least five years (see European Parliament 1997). Their policies of reassurance and misinformation temporarily staved off the collapse in confidence in the beef industry. Although an explicit cost–benefit assessment by government was conspicuously absent, it seems that the desire to maintain faith in the product – and, by implication, confidence in government's handling of the issue – was the key aim or 'benefit' (Anand and Forshner 1995). The potential costs of inaction, though large, were regarded as uncertain and long term. Risks were therefore taken because – in economists' terminology – the expected costs of inaction were outweighed by the relatively high and immediate short-term benefits of continued political power and industrial profitability.

In summary, a simple appraisal of costs and benefits confirms that in terms of both socio-economic indicators and political legitimacy the policy adopted had disastrous consequences. Even if the most pessimistic of the predictions regarding vCJD fail to materialize, even if the link between BSE and CJD remains unproved, the costs of the crisis – in terms of the market intervention, the collapse in consumer confidence, the culling scheme and the costs to farmers, the meat industry and taxpayers – far outweigh the short-term benefits of the approach pursued by the UK government and European Union institutions.

A disastrous policy process?

A number of alleged errors, misjudgements and miscalculations were identified at each stage in the policy process, both within the UK government's handling of the issue and in the response of the European Union institutions.

UK government: the politics of expertise

The UK government was criticized for failing to heed early warnings about BSE and for being unwilling to investigate the problem further in the initial stages. It was also accused of manipulating and suppressing research into the cause, prevalence and transmission of BSE. Specific worries about cross-infection through recycling animal waste as feed were raised as long ago as 1979. The Royal Commission on Environmental Pollution warned about the 'the risk of transmitting disease-bearing pathogens to stock and thence to humans' (Royal Commission on Environmental Pollution 1979: 150). However, it did not recommend that the practice be banned. As will become clear, this initial warning was reconstructed many years later by the media, in a way which added to the blame being heaped on government.

When the first case of BSE was confirmed in 1986, the Ministry of Agriculture, Fisheries and Food (MAFF) was criticized for its sluggishness in seeking out further independent research and expert advice about the transmissible nature of the disease. It assumed that the disease was very similar to scrapie,[4] which had existed in sheep for hundreds of years without causing apparent harm to other animals or humans. Subsequently the ministry did seek external advice, but chose generalists rather than experts in the field of spongiform diseases. Indeed, the Southwood Committee – a working party set up in 1988 to advise ministers on the issue – effectively admitted its own lack of expertise by recommending the establishment of a further advisory committee on research. The membership of this second committee, the Spongiform Encephalopathy Consultative Committee – chaired by Dr D. A. J. Tyrrell – did include experts in the field of transmissible encephalopathies. So did its permanent successor, the Spongiform Encephalopathy Advisory Committee (SEAC), chaired initially by Tyrrell and from 1995 by Professor J. Pattison. At the same time, however, both committees excluded those who took alternative views on the causal mechanisms of the disease or who were outspoken critics of government policy. In this sense the Tyrrell Committee's membership was narrow, perhaps a mistake in view of the lack of consensus in this field of scientific research (see Lacey 1994). A further point is that the terms of reference of the Tyrrell Committee were deliberately narrow, focusing on research rather than policy advice in a broader sense.

Significant delays were identified in establishing these advisory committees, receiving their advice and publishing reports. The Southwood Committee was established in May 1988, nearly eighteen months after the first BSE case had been confirmed. Southwood himself was reported as being critical of the delay (*Observer* 1990). The Southwood Committee met infrequently over a long period (Lacey 1994). Although it issued a number of interim recommendations – which were accepted by government – the final text of the report was not issued until February 1989. The Tyrrell Committee report was also subject to delay. Though its work was completed by June 1989 at the latest, its report was not completed until January 1990 (*ibid.*). In its defence, MAFF denied that the delay in publication had impeded the research into BSE and that it had not wished to publish the report before the resources were available to implement it (Agriculture and Health Committees 1996b: 172).

Other delays were also highlighted. Research into vertical transmission of BSE (from cow to calf) was delayed for nine months. It has been argued that MAFF was reluctant to fund research into this possible link because of the implications for eradication policy (Lacey 1994). A project eventually began, and reported that 7–8 per cent of calves born to mothers in the later stages of BSE will go on to develop the disease, though only 1 per cent of calves born to infected mothers will do so (Anderson *et al.* 1996). Others have claimed that pressure was exerted on the research community not to pursue particularly controversial projects, especially on the nature of the link between BSE and CJD (Dealler 1996). While this is difficult to prove, MAFF certainly sought to exert tight control over the research process. It achieved this through control over research funding and in view of its sole ownership rights over the brains of cattle diagnosed with BSE. Notably, a recommendation by the Tyrrell Committee that there should be a random survey of cattle brains at slaughter was not taken up. Such a survey would have revealed the extent of unrecognized infection in cattle entering the food chain and was therefore highly controversial. However, it should be noted that the Tyrrell report did not give this research high priority, making it easier for MAFF to argue that it was unnecessary.

Besides skewed membership selection and tactical delays, the politics of expertise in this case may also have involved deliberate attempts to suppress research findings. For example, in 1997 it was revealed that research into the possible BSE infection of dogs had ceased six years earlier (P. Brown 1997b). MAFF had often denied that BSE could be transmitted to dogs. It defended its decision not to pursue research on the grounds that there was no health risk to the British public even if dogs were infected (as they are not part of the human food chain) and that there would be a public outcry if such experiments were conducted. In fact, other experiments on dogs have gone ahead despite public criticism and often without public knowledge. And, on the first point, though dogs are not part of the human food chain, evidence regarding transmission (particularly relating to infection through bovine offal in pet food – banned in 1990) would have had wide implications for the public perception of risk, thereby undermining the market for beef products.

Critics of the UK government believe that evidence regarding the possible transmission of BSE to humans was deliberately withheld and that statistics were manipulated to convince the public that beef products were safe (Lacey 1994; Dealler 1996). Lacey (1994) maintains that the BSE statistics were 'massaged' – by transferring cases to earlier years – in order to support the MAFF line that the epidemic was under control. Furthermore, the procedure for diagnosing BSE was altered in February 1992 and official claims that these changes resulted in an improvement of diagnosis were disputed (*ibid.*).

UK government: the politics of implementation

The UK government has been accused of errors of omission and commission when formulating specific policies on BSE/CJD. First, it did not make BSE a notifiable disease until June 1988, almost eighteen months after the first confirmed case. Second, it was slow to introduce the ruminant feed ban (cattle, sheep and deer were not allowed protein derived from other animals). This was introduced in July 1988 – yet six months earlier MAFF had accepted that ruminant-derived meat and bonemeal (MBM) was the only viable explanation for the disease (Agriculture and Health Committees 1996a). MBM was still permitted for pigs and poultry feed until 1992, allowing cross-contamination of ruminant feed both in feed mills and on farms. Eventually, MBM was banned completely from farms in 1996. A related issue is the cross-infection of non-ruminants with contaminated bovine offal. Until a statutory ban was imposed in 1990, the only means of preventing this was a voluntary agreement by the feed manufacturers not to include certain offals – known as SBOs[5] – in animal feed.

Third, the UK government was slow to ban the use of SBOs in food for human consumption. The offal ban was eventually introduced in November 1989, having been announced five months earlier. The House of Commons' Agriculture Committee (1990a) was critical of this delay, notwithstanding MAFF's argument that essential consultation and further research prevented earlier implementation.

The ban did not initially apply to cattle aged under 6 months (maternal transmission not being regarded as a possibility at this time by MAFF), though this was extended to all cattle in 1994. But even before this evidence became available there had been warnings about the possibility of maternal transmission. The Agriculture Committee (1990a) called, unsuccessfully, for the offal ban to be extended to all cattle, including calves. It also believed that farmers should be discouraged from breeding from animals whose dams had been affected by BSE, though it did not support the slaughter of all calves from BSE-affected cows. The scientists on the Tyrrell Committee did not support a breeding ban either, although there was some dispute over the precise wording of their advice to ministers on this issue (Agriculture Committee 1990b).

The relatively low level of compensation offered to farmers for BSE-infected cattle was heavily criticized. A compensation scheme was introduced in August 1988, under which farmers were paid 50 per cent of the market value of each animal. This was widely seen as inadequate, giving little incentive for farmers to keep animals out of the food chain (though visibly affected animals were excluded from August 1988). Reportedly, members of the Southwood Committee argued for 75 per cent compensation (*New Statesman and Society* 1989). Eventually, in February 1990, MAFF announced that it would compensate farmers for 100 per cent of the market price: the number of BSE cases rose from over 7,000 in 1989 to over 14,000 in 1990. In its report the House of Commons' Agriculture Committee (1990a) observed that the public might have been reassured had full compensation been introduced earlier.

Although it was critical of several aspects of government policy, the Agriculture Committee concluded that in general the response had been acceptable. It contrasted the handling of the BSE crisis with the salmonella in eggs issue of the late 1980s, remarking that departmental coordination and the use of independent scientific committees had led to improvements (Agriculture Committee 1990a). The committee applauded the fact that ministers had gone beyond the scientific advice in some areas: first, on the matter of the feed ban (which pre-empted Southwood's report: the committee only later endorsed an indefinite ban) and, second, with regard to the offal ban (Southwood initially recommended a ban on offal in baby food only). However, the Agriculture Committee's broad support for the government's approach was at odds with some of the serious criticisms it identified in its report. Furthermore, the committee did not foresee that many of its important recommendations, particularly those relating to tracking systems,[6] would be ignored.

A number of failures were later identified at the policy implementation stage. The feed ban imposed in 1988 was widely flouted, as is reflected in the finding that 28,000 of the 160,000 cases of BSE confirmed by 1996 occurred in animals born after 1988 (Stekel *et al.* 1996). This was blamed largely on the continued use of contaminated feed (Wilesmith *et al.* 1992), though vertical and even horizontal transmission were possible factors. Many feed-compounders apparently ignored the relevant regulations (Lacey 1994). This is hardly surprising given the lack of policing and the absence of legal and financial penalties – which were not introduced until 1996.

There was evidence of poor enforcement of standards in abattoirs. Several reports condemned hygiene standards in British abattoirs in connection with the BSE regulations, and with regard to food hygiene generally. In November 1994, 30 per cent of slaughterhouses in England and Wales scored less than 50 out of 100 points for meat hygiene standards (Macintyre 1996). In September 1995, 48 per cent of slaughterhouses inspected by the State Veterinary Service failed to meet the 1989 SBO regulations (Hansard 1995). This proportion fell to 34 per cent when the exercise was repeated a month later. By February 1996 only 6 per cent failed to reach the required standard. In 1996 four abattoirs were fined for not applying the rules designed to curb the transmission of BSE to humans (C. Brown 1996). There was understandable concern that the failure of abattoirs to maintain standards was leading to the contamination of carcasses. This was coupled with anxiety about cross-contamination at other stages in the food production and rendering processes.

The European dimension

European Union institutions, though often cast in the role of broker between the UK and other European governments on the BSE issue, eventually became implicated in the mishandling of the crisis. The European Parliament's inquiry into BSE focused particularly on the Commission's role in closing off sources of information about the problem. According to this inquiry, no effort was made to find out more about the link between BSE and CJD, and when concerns were raised within the Health Directorate (DGV), research was thwarted (European Parliament 1997: 24). Moreover, the inquiry judged that between 1990 and 1994

BSE veterinary inspections were suspended by DGVI (the Agriculture Directorate) under pressure from the UK government. It also found that the Commission deliberately downplayed the BSE problem in an effort to avoid disruption to the beef market. It found clear documentary evidence of efforts by the Agriculture Directorate to close down discussion in the Scientific Advisory Committees and prevent the matter from entering the public domain (ibid.: annexes 20–2).

The Commission and the Council were criticized for failing to adopt effective policies to prevent health risks (European Parliament 1997). Yet some steps were taken. BSE was designated a disease notifiable to the European Commission in 1990. The European Commission implemented a series of restrictions on British beef products, including a ban on bovine offal, in 1990. In the same year 'bone in beef' exports to the Community were limited to farms which had not had a confirmed case of BSE in the previous two years. In 1994 this time limit was extended to six years. In the following year it was restricted further, with only beef from cattle aged 30 months at slaughter being permitted for export to member states in 'boned' form. In 1996 all beef exports from the UK were banned, including the export of live animals. Earlier, in 1989, the Commission had intro- duced a ban on UK exports to other member states of live cattle born before 1988 (and offspring of suspected BSE cases). In 1990 this export ban was extended to cattle aged 6 months or over. Finally, the European Commission introduced a series of restrictions and, later, a complete ban on the use of MBM feed.

Indeed, these actions led some British politicians to argue that the Commission was being aggressive, dictatorial and over-responsive to the interests of continental beef producers, particularly the French farmers. However, until 1996 the Commission resisted policies that would impose higher costs on the UK (and the wider European) beef industry, and the rendering and feed industries. For example, in 1990 suggestions that British beef should be exported only in a deboned form were fiercely contested at senior levels within the Agriculture Directorate (European Parliament 1997: annex 18). Eventually a selective ban on 'bone in beef' was implemented later that year. The Commission did not act to ban the export of meat and bonemeal from the UK until 1996 – it had considered such action as early as 1989 – and did not ban the use of mammal proteins in feed for ruminants until 1994 (a practice banned in the UK in 1988).

Explaining the BSE disaster

The consequences of the BSE crisis were undoubtedly adverse. Furthermore, alle- gations of policy errors and misjudgements were not without foundation. Most criticisms were made at the time, rather than with the benefit of hindsight. Important warnings were therefore simply not heeded. Nevertheless, one must understand that policy disasters are subject to a process of perception and construction (Bovens and 't Hart 1996). It is not enough to detail costs or provide evidence about errors of judgement. One must also seek to explain how policy disasters emerge and why they are interpreted as such. This section attempts to explain the BSE crisis using four different approaches: ideological, institutional, socio-cultural and media-centred.

Ideological explanations

One way of understanding the BSE crisis is to explain events with reference to dominant ideologies. The term 'ideology' in this sense means more than party-political ideology. It also includes the assumptive world of the political actors involved, e.g. the policy-maker's subjective understanding of their environment, and the values and assumptions they hold (Murray-Parkes 1971; Young 1977).

The ideologies of policy-makers involved in the BSE crisis predisposed them towards a particular response. In the case of the British governments of Thatcher and Major, the response was strongly influenced by a deregulatory philosophy (Gifford 1996). The Thatcher government did not pursue the previous Labour government's efforts to tighten up regulations on animal feed and sought to reduce the costs on the rendering industry (Agriculture and Health Committees 1996b). The Major government subsequently claimed that Labour's draft regulations related to salmonella and would have been ineffective in tackling BSE (which at the time had not been identified), whereas other stakeholders believed the regulations would have helped prevent other transmissible diseases such as BSE.

The emphasis upon deregulation placed a greater burden of proof on those who desired further controls in this field, reinforcing a key aspect of British science policy culture identified by Wynne (1996). In addition, the Conservative government's support for commerce and private enterprise added weight to the arguments of economic interests keen to avoid further regulation. As a consequence, the precautionary principle of public health – particularly relevant to cases where the potential costs of inaction are high and scientific outcomes uncertain – was not upheld.

As far as the European Union institutions were concerned, the philosophy of deregulation was not a key factor. But the dominant institutions in the governance of the BSE issue – in particular the Agriculture Directorate within the European Commission – were clearly guided by an assumption that produced a similar policy response. This core assumption was that the management of the market – and, by implication, the protection of the short-term interests of the beef and related industries – was paramount (European Parliament 1997: 22).

Institutional explanations

Institutional explanations focus on the way in which particular interests and types of expertise are incorporated within the policy process. One important line of research in this tradition can be found in studies of policy communities and networks (Richardson and Jordan 1979; Marin and Mayntz 1991; Marsh and Rhodes 1992). In this case, a relatively closed and enduring network of public and private stakeholders seems to have been in place. Within the UK government and European Union institutions, producer interests were in a much stronger position than those concerned with the promotion of health and the protection of consumers. In the UK, the policy was managed largely by MAFF, along with an array of national agencies and local authorities. The Department of Health was very much the junior partner in the management of the policy, in spite of the apparent joint venture between itself and MAFF in recent years. As Winter noted, 'a joint venture does not necessarily imply an equal partnership, and most would agree that MAFF is the lead department within the joint policy community' (Winter 1996).

The implication is that producers dominated decision-making in this policy arena. MAFF operated in a closed policy network, along with the representatives of the beef and related industries. Consumer and health interests were much more at arm's length. MAFF also operated in a closed scientific community. Many of the scientific experts used by the ministry were either directly employed by it or contracted to it in some other way. MAFF selected its advisors in a way which promoted a consensus view consistent with government policy. Moreover, the policy was developed in a secretive way, with information being kept out of the public domain.

This dominance of closed networks was similarly evident within the European institutions involved in the BSE issue (European Parliament 1997). First, the Agriculture Directorate, like its British counterpart, had a close relationship with producer interests. Second, these interests, along with representatives of the UK government, were able to infiltrate and pressure European institutions from within. For example, pressure was exerted through the Scientific Veterinary Committee (ScVC), a body consulted by the Commission on the matters affecting animal health. Usually the Commission bases its legislative proposals on the opinions of this committee, though it may go beyond its recommendations if it thinks fit. It appears that the ScVC view was shaped largely by a subgroup specifically devoted to the BSE issue (*ibid.*: 10). This subgroup was dominated by UK government nominees (for a time it was chaired by a former advisor to MAFF) and reflected the MAFF position. The administrative support for the subcommittee was undertaken by a temporary Commission official who was formerly a MAFF civil servant. Not only were the Commission and its advisory committees 'colonized' by those who reflected the UK government's stance, but there is also evidence that the Commission gave in to direct lobbying from the British government on a number of occasions. One such issue was the suspension of BSE-related slaughterhouse inspections between 1990–94, a direct response to pressure from the UK's chief veterinary officers (*ibid.*: 9).

Furthermore, as in Britain, decision-making at the European level was highly secretive. Discussions took place behind closed doors, often without minutes. As the European Parliament's inquiry into the affair noted, the scientific committee system was opaque, complex and anti-democratic (European Parliament 1997:

35). Moreover, as was noted earlier, the Commission made a deliberate attempt to curtail public debate on the issue.

The BSE case reflects the wider dominance of technocrats within the policy process. According to Fischer (1990), politics has become a technologically oriented task. Consequently, the expertise of technocrats is a key resource in governance. They may be used to give legitimacy to decisions made by government (Barker and Peters 1993). However, problems arise when experts differ in their views. Where scientific consensus breaks down, government must choose its advisors carefully to support its chosen position. The result is an artificial 'scientific consensualism' (Anand and Forshner 1995). There is much evidence of this in the BSE case. Scientists who were critical of government were excluded from advisory bodies. Those with expertise that might have led to a more cautious policy – such as experts in risk management, for example – were not involved in the machinery of policy advice.

Social and cultural theories

The BSE crisis can be comprehended in terms of broader social and cultural perspectives. For example, Beck's (1992) work on the 'risk society', the role of science in government and the public's view of science is particularly relevant to this case. According to Beck, technological progress is increasingly overshadowed by a growing awareness of the risks associated with wealth production. Society has to face these problems and manage the risks involved. However, these risks are of a different magnitude from those which have previously accompanied economic development. Modern risks are potentially catastrophic, are not confined to particular sections of the population (though there may well be class differences in exposure to risk) and are not limited in terms of their duration.

Growing awareness of these risks has wide implications. Scientific knowledge is of little help in predicting the extent and duration of such hazards. As a result, its legitimacy is weakened, thereby undermining in turn the authority of government in situations where policy is based on scientific advice. Instead of believing the 'fiction' of a single scientific rationality, the public becomes increasingly aware that there are competing rationalities and expertise that adopt different perspectives (see Collingridge and Reeve 1986; Rudig 1993). Indeed, survey evidence indicates that the public are suspicious of scientists and scientific advice, though there are considerable variations between countries (Topf 1993).

The BSE case exemplifies the dilemmas of the risk society. The unpredictability and uncertainty associated with the disease have exposed not only the inability of scientists to comprehend what is going on, but also the level of disagreement among experts on this issue. As a result, the authority of scientific advice has been undermined and the legitimacy of public policy challenged. Government initially sought to deal with the problem through the machinery of scientific advice, emphasizing the expertise of those scientists who supported a minimal interventionist approach. But this was unsustainable – the risks were no longer, in Beck's terminology, 'latent'. It was therefore forced into measures which were 'unnecessary' on narrow scientific grounds, but which were nevertheless required to restore public confidence.

Media-centred explanations

The media often play a key role in the construction of policy disasters. One must therefore examine why the BSE issue arrived on the political agenda and how the media portrayed the response of government. The media has taken a great interest in the BSE issue. It is easy to understand why. Health issues are at the top of the public agenda. Food scares potentially affect us all and make good copy. In the sense that coverage attracts readers and viewers, the media's interest in the BSE (and other food safety issues) has therefore been shaped by commercial considerations. But government also encouraged media interest by its attempts to suppress information and present a rosy view of the situation.

Media interest in BSE has been present from the point at which the government admitted its existence in 1986. Ten years on, following the March 1996 announcement, the issue dominated news coverage for over a month and continued to be a live issue throughout the spring and summer of that year. In the intervening decade, the coverage of BSE waxed and waned. The main triggers for publicity were: the publication or leaking of new scientific evidence on BSE transmission; the UK Parliamentary Inquiry of 1990 (the hearings and the final report); details of poor implementation; and government announcements with regard to both official reports on BSE and the introduction of new regulations.

The UK government was criticized for its poor handling of the media on this issue. Certainly, MAFF (and the Department of Health) adopted a complacent tone. Some of the steps taken by ministers to reassure the public, such as the 'Gummer-burger' (where the agriculture minister, John Gummer, publicly fed a beefburger to his young daughter), look even more ridiculous in hindsight than they did at the time. It is difficult to disagree with Anand and Forshner's (1995) point that the government failed to come to terms with the reality that the media was an active stakeholder in the BSE debate, and that poor media relations contributed to the unfavourable treatment of the government's handling of the issue and, it may be added, the level of public distrust.

The media have consistently criticized the government's handling of the BSE crisis and other food scares, such as salmonella in eggs, listeria and, more recently, a serious outbreak of *E. coli* in Scotland (see Pennington Group 1997), and have done much to undermine public faith in the government's handling of the issue. But was the media coverage of the government's management of the issue balanced and fair? In particular, was government blamed unfairly for the errors identified earlier?

The media's treatment of the issue failed to emphasize the scientific uncertainties associated with BSE. Some coverage has been sensationalist, uncritically endorsing the views of those predicting catastrophe (Agriculture Committee

1990a). The costs of the crisis were also exaggerated to some extent, as noted earlier – though it has to be acknowledged that the uncertainty involved with regard to the economic and human consequences left enormous scope for 'guesstimates'. Furthermore, alternative theories about the cause of BSE were largely ignored by the media, even though they implied equally forceful condemnation of government policy. For example, Purdey (1996) identified organophosphates as a possible factor in the onset of BSE. The fact that this theory has not received greater attention is due to some extent to media disinterest, and perhaps also to the power of the chemical and pesticides industries.

The media's reporting of the unfolding of the BSE crisis has tended to assume perfect information and foresight among political actors. Apart from suggestions of conspiracy, based on an assumption that MAFF has been a prisoner of the food and farming industry, little effort has been made to analyse policy errors and explain them in context. There has been little analysis of the options open to decision-makers, and the media has to some extent operated with the benefit of hindsight. At times this has led to an oversimplistic construction of events, where errors are exaggerated and crude explanations gain credibility. One example of this was the way in which the media consistently referred to the Royal Commission on Environmental Pollution's 'prophetic warnings' about BSE. As was noted earlier, the report did express some concern about the transmission of diseases between animals and man, but it did not make any recommendations save to *encourage* the recycling of poultry waste as cattle feed.

In the face of an emerging public scandal, media coverage tends to become motivated by the need to find someone to blame (Markovits and Silverstein 1988). If it is already unpopular for other reasons, the government is an ideal target (Bovens and 't Hart 1996). The responsibility of others who may have contributed to the problem – scientific advisors, the farming and food industries – may be downplayed. Hence government, rather than the rendering industry or the feed mills, is primarily blamed for allowing feed to be contaminated, and government, rather than the abattoirs, is held responsible for poor hygiene standards. The Thatcher and Major governments, by their responses to the BSE problem, undoubtedly contributed to this focused blaming, but it is important that other actors should not be absolved of responsibility.

Finally, the European Union's intervention in the issue was treated in different ways by the British media. Some, particularly the tabloid press and the Conservative sections of the 'quality' press, took the line that Europe was interfering unnecessarily in a domestic issue. This type of coverage later became particularly intense during the 'beef war' of 1996. The liberal 'quality' newspapers and the broadcast media, on the other hand, tended to take the view that Europe was something of an 'honest broker', arbitrating between the UK and European partners. The revelations of the European Parliamentary Committee, referred to earlier, indicated that both perspectives were inaccurate.

Conclusion: learning lessons

Bovens and 't Hart (1996) acknowledge that some manifestations of policy failure are so powerful that little scope is left for debate about whether or not a policy disaster has occurred. The tragic cases of those affected by CJD, particularly the younger victims of the new variant of the disease, the suffering of BSE-infected cattle and of the farmers whose livelihoods have been ruined create an understandable urge to allocate blame. In many ways, government is an ideal target for these feelings. This chapter has not tried to absolve government of blame, nor has it sought to paint a more optimistic picture of the consequences of the crisis. Rather, it has set out to correct some misconceptions and has sought to place events in a broader context so that they may be better understood.

There are a number of lessons to be drawn from the BSE case. Ideological and institutional explanations of the crisis highlight a number of factors. These include excessive secrecy in government, narrow scientific advice, the dominance of short-term commercial considerations, the low priority given to consumer and health interests, the inappropriate application of deregulation, and poor coordination of enforcement agencies. These are general problems of governance, which may need to be addressed in order to prevent other policy failures in the area of public health and safety.

The BSE case also reveals the process through which events come to be labelled as disasters. Like other food safety issues, BSE was extremely attractive to the media. As a result, the media played a key role in highlighting alleged policy errors, predicting disastrous consequences of policy and attributing blame. In consequence, complex issues and events were sometimes reduced to a fairly simple level, facilitating the labelling of the crisis as a 'classic' policy disaster. Again, this is not to deny that mistakes and misjudgements were made. The key point is that other serious policy failures may avoid being characterized as 'disasters' simply because the issues they raise are less attractive to the media.

Finally, the BSE crisis exemplifies the wider problems and dilemmas facing policy-makers in modern societies. As the public becomes more aware of the risks involved in wealth production, in particular those risks that are potentially catastrophic, it is likely that government institutions (and their scientific advisors) will be exposed to challenge and criticism on their handling of such issues. Moreover, the credibility, and perhaps also the authority, of government bodies may be further undermined in the future, as they increasingly come to be perceived as 'disaster prone'.

Notes

1   BSE (bovine spongiform encephalopathy) is a progressive neurological disorder of cattle which is ultimately fatal. It has a long incubation period, of between two and eight years, and is believed to be caused by unconventional infectious agents known as prions.

2   Creutzfeld-Jakob disease is a disease in humans similar to BSE in cattle; until recently, it affected around 20–30 elderly people in the UK each year. Recently a new variant has been discovered which appears to have a shorter incubation period and affects younger people.
3   Subclinical infection is where an infection exists but the sufferer shows no sign of illness.
4   Scrapie is a form of spongiform encephalopathy that occurs in sheep.
5   SBOs (specific bovine offals) include the brain, spinal cord, thymus, spleen, intestines and tonsils of cattle.
6   Another way of maintaining public confidence in British beef, both at home and abroad, would have been to introduce a tracking system, so that the history and move-ment of infected animals could be traced. The need for such a system was recognized in the late 1980s. If the worst happened and vertical transmission (cow to calf) and hori-zontal transmission (within the herd) were found to occur, efficient eradication could take place only if animals were properly certified. In addition, the existence of such a scheme would help maintain public confidence in the product and reassure importers in other countries, as well as protecting animal and public health. The Agriculture Committee (echoing a recommendation of the Southwood Committee) urged the government to set up a comprehensive system of identification, but only Northern Ireland took up this initiative.

References

Agriculture Committee (1990a) *Bovine Spongiform Encephalopathy: 5th Report of the Agriculture Committee, Session 1989/90* (HC 449), London: HMSO.
—— (1990b) *Bovine Spongiform Encephalopathy: 5th Report of the Agriculture Committee, Session 1989/90, Minutes of Evidence* (HC 449), London: HMSO.
Agriculture and Health Committees (1996a) *Bovine Spongiform Encephalopathy (BSE) and Creutzfeldt-Jakob Disease, Minutes of Evidence* (HC 331), Memorandum Submitted by the Ministry of Agriculture Fisheries and Food, London: HMSO.
—— (1996b) *Bovine Spongiform Encephalopathy (BSE) and Creutzfeldt-Jakob Disease, Minutes of Evidence* (HC 331), London: HMSO.
Anand, P. and Forshner, C. (1995) 'Of mad cows and marmosets: from rational choice to organisational behaviour in crisis management', *British Journal of Management* 69(4): 221–233.
Anderson, R., Donnelly, C., Ferguson, M., Woodhouse, E., Watt, C., Udy, H., Mawhinney, S., Dunstan, S., Southwood, T., Wilesmith, J., Ryan, J., Hanville, L., Millerton, J., Austin, A. and Wells, G. (1996) 'Transmission dynamics and the epidemiology of BSE in British cattle', *Nature*, 29 August: 779–788.
Barker, A. and Peters, B. G. (1993) 'Science policy and government', in A. Barker and B. G. Peters *The Politics of Expert Advice*, Edinburgh: Edinburgh University Press.
Beck, U. (1992) *The Risk Society*, London: Sage.
Bovens, M. and 't Hart, P. (1996) *Understanding Policy Fiascoes*, New Brunswick: Transaction.
Brown, C. (1996) 'Abattoirs flout mad cow rules', *Independent*, 19 December: 9.
Brown, P. (1997a) 'Beef sales slump puts revival claims in doubt', *Guardian*, 21 January: 9.
—— (1997b) 'Report on BSE in dogs suppressed', *Guardian*, 29 April: 6.
Chazot, G., Brouselle, E., Lapres, C., Blattler, T., Aguzzi, A. and Kopp, N. (1997) 'New variant of CJD in a 26 year old French man', *Lancet* 347, 27 April: 1181.

Collinge, J., Sidle, K., Meads, J., Ironside, J. and Hill, A. (1996) 'Molecular analysis of prion strain variation and the aetiology of new variant CJD', *Nature* 383, 24 October: 685–686.

Collingridge, D. and Reeve, C. (1986) *Science Speaks to Power*, London: Pinter.

Cousens, S. N., Vynnycky, E., Zeidler, M., Will, R. G. and Smith, P. G. (1997) 'Predicting the CJD epidemic in humans', *Nature* 385, 16 January: 197–198.

Coyle, D. (1996) 'The economy feels the strain', *Independent*, 23 March: 3.

Curtice, J. and Jowell, R. (1996) 'The sceptical electorate', in R. Jowell, J. Curtice, A. Park, L. Brook and D. Ahrendt *British Social Attitudes 1995/6*, Aldershot: Dartmouth.

Dealler, S. (1996) *BSE – the Search for the Truth*, London: Bloomsbury.

Economist (1996) 'Cash for cows', 30 March: 29–30.

—— (1997) 'The other BSE scandal', 22 March: 25–26.

European Parliament (1997) *Report on Alleged Contraventions or Maladministration in the Implementation of Community Law in Relation to BSE*, Committee of Inquiry into BSE, European Parliament Session Documents DOC-EN/RR/319/319544 and DOC-EN/RR/319/319579.

Fischer, F. (1990) *Technocracy and the Politics of Expertise*, London: Sage.

Gifford, C. (1996) *Deregulation, Disasters and BSE*, Nottingham: European Labour Forum.

Hansard (1995) *Weekly Hansard: House of Commons* 267(1703), 20–24 November: 192–193.

—— (1996) *Weekly Hansard: House of Commons* 280(1730), 24–27 June: 190.

—— (1997) *Weekly Hansard: House of Commons* 292(1753), 17–21 March: 717–718.

Keegan, W. (1996) 'BSE could scupper Tory poll chances', *Observer*, 24 March: 1.

Lacey, R. (1994) *Mad Cow Disease: a History of BSE in Britain*, St Helier: Cypsela.

Linton, M. and Bates, R. (1996) 'Public suspects beef cover up', *Guardian*, 3 April: 1.

Macintyre, D. (1996) 'Germans hit hopes of end to beef ban', *Independent*, 5 April: 1.

Marin, B. and Mayntz, R. (eds) (1991) *Policy Networks: Empirical Evidence and Theoretical Considerations*, Boulder, CO: Westview Press.

Markovits, A. S. and Silverstein, M. (eds) (1988) *The Politics of Scandal: Power and Process in Liberal Democracies*, New York and London: Holmes & Meier.

Marsh, D. and Rhodes, R. A. W. (1992) *Policy Networks in British Government*, Oxford: Oxford University Press.

Ministry of Agriculture Fisheries and Food, Scottish Office Agriculture, Environment and Fisheries Department, Northern Ireland Department of Agriculture and Welsh Office (1997) *Agriculture in the UK 1996*, London: Stationery Office.

Murray-Parkes, C. (1971) 'Psycho-social transitions: a field of study', *Social Science and Medicine* 5: 102–115.

New Statesman and Society (1989) 2 June: 17.

Observer (1990) 'The rot in John Bull's beef', 20 May: 19.

Office for National Statistics (1997) *Economic Trends* 520, March.

Pennington Group (1997) *Report on the Circumstances Leading to the 1996 Outbreak of Infection with E. Coli O157 in Central Scotland: The Implications for Food Safety and the Lessons to be Learned*, Edinburgh: Stationery Office.

Pudephatt, A. (1996) '£20 billion has been wasted . . .', *Independent*, 15 November: 18.

Purdey, M. (1996) 'Mandarins who fail to ask the right questions', *Parliamentary Brief* 4(6), May: 36–39.

Richardson, J. J. and Jordan, A. G. (1979) *Governing Under Pressure: The Policy Process in a Postparliamentary Democracy*, Oxford: Martin Robertson.

Royal Commission on Environmental Pollution (1979) *Agriculture and Pollution*, Cmnd 7644, London: HMSO.

Rudig, W. (1993) 'Sources of technological controversy: proximity to our alienation from technology', in A. Barker and B. G. Peters *The Politics of Expert Advice*, Edinburgh: Edinburgh University Press.

Stekel, D. J., Nowak, M. A. and Southwood, T. R. E. (1996) 'Prediction of future BSE spread', *Nature* 381, 9 May: 119.

Topf, R. (1993) 'Science, public policy and the authoritativeness of the governmental process', in A. Barker and B. G. Peters *The Politics of Expert Advice*, Edinburgh: Edinburgh University Press.

Wilesmith, J. W., Ryan, J. B. M. and Hureston, W. D. (1992) 'BSE: case control studies of calf feeding practices and bone meal inclusion in proprietary concentrates', *Research in Veterinary Science* 52: 325–330.

Winter, M. (1996) 'Intersecting departmental responsibilities, administrative confusion and the role of science in government: the case of BSE', *Parliamentary Affairs* 49(4): 550–565.

Wynne, B. (1996) 'Patronising Joe Public' *Times Higher Education Supplement*, 19 April: 13.

Young, K. (1977) 'Values in the policy process', *Policy and Politics* 5: 1–22.

5

ITALIAN PUBLIC POLICY AND THE SOUTHERN QUESTION

Policy disaster or political disaster?

Robert Sykes

Introduction

This chapter focuses on attempts by postwar Italian governments to deal with the so-called 'Southern Question' (*questione meridionale*) via public policy intervention.[1] Despite some forty years of concentrated government intervention specifically targeted at its economic development, the south of Italy, or *Mezzogiorno*, still lags far behind the rest of the nation.[2] Although Italy now rates among the world's seven most industrialized economies, with aggregate growth rates which match or exceed those of other European Union states (Padoa-Schioppa Kostoris 1993), the *Mezzogiorno* still has significantly lower levels of per capita gross domestic product (GDP), consumption and employment than the rest of Italy and the rest of Europe.[3] If we also consider criteria normally related to economic development, such as poverty, social exclusion and vulnerability to crime, the essential dualism of Italy's economy and society between the Centre-North, on the one hand, and the South, on the other, is clearly apparent (Apicella 1996; EUROSTAT 1996a, 1996b; Leonardi 1995; Mingione and Morlicchio 1993; Organization for Economic Cooperation and Development 1996).

Insofar as this dualism persists, is it the result of failings of economic development policy intervention or are other factors responsible? In other words, does this continuing dualism represent a 'policy disaster', or might other explanations which consider, for example, the role of the national political system and the key political parties, regional and local government, and the role of the mafia offer a better understanding of the endurance of the *questione meridionale*? This chapter will seek to show that whilst, in its own terms, economic development policy for the South is characterized by failure, this failure needs to be set in the context of the broader failings of the Italian political system and of key players and institutions within it at both national and local levels. These systemic failings are now the focus of various attempts to reform the Italian political system.

79

A policy disaster?

In what senses might Italian public policy towards the economic development of the South be disastrous? First, we need to clarify the term 'policy disaster'. Bovens and 't Hart (1996) have suggested four levels of definition of a policy fiasco or disaster, all of which are open to interpretation and contestation. The crucial point is that policy disasters are socially and politically constructed phenomena: views differ on what constitutes a disaster, whether and in what ways policy intervention was involved, which actions and processes were implicated in the 'disastrous' chain of events and, finally, whether any or all of these actions were avoidable or blameworthy. In the case of national economic development policy for the South of Italy, whilst it may initially appear that 'policy disaster' is an appropriate description, as will become clear, not all stakeholders would agree with this assessment. Also, the significance of public policy intervention is arguable, and the consequent allocation of blame for the failure, and thus its explanation, is rather more complex than it first seems. We will return to these issues at the end of the chapter. First, we suggest in what ways, and by whom, economic development policy for the South might be deemed 'disastrous'.

Measures of disaster?

As a number of analysts have pointed out, whilst national public policy for the South may have had some effect in changing the economy of these regions, it has failed to develop an autonomous and competitive industrial base there (D'Antonio 1991; Del Monte and Luzenberger 1989; Giunta and Martinelli 1995; Leonardi 1995; Martinelli 1985). The *Mezzogiorno* still has a structurally dependent economy, accounting for only 29 per cent of Italy's total employment, yet 54 per cent of its unemployment. The *Mezzogiorno*'s levels of consumption are sustained by large transfer payments via the state. Although this is difficult to verify, it seems that transfers to the South by central government account, on average, for about 60 per cent of GDP since the 1950s. Indirect and direct income support accounts for approximately half the South's GDP, and the Bank of Italy estimates that approximately four-fifths of the country's total public deficit is attributable to the South.[4] These facts have led one analyst to conclude recently that 'the larger macroeconomic imbalances of the Italian system can be attributed, directly or indirectly, to underdevelopment in the South and to the draining of national wealth that support for consumption in the South inflicts on the rest of the country' (D'Antonio 1991: 402).

The 1996 levels of GDP per capita in the South are still significantly below those for the rest of Italy and, indeed, for most other areas of Europe. All of the southern regions of the South are well below the EU average, ranging from Abruzzi-Molise (87 per cent), Sardegna (77 per cent) and Puglia (74 per cent), to Sicily (71 per cent), Campania (69 per cent), Basilicata (66 per cent), and, with one of the lowest rates for the whole of the EU, Calabria (60 per cent) (EUROSTAT

1996a).[5] Similar disparities exist in unemployment rates. Campania (22.8 per cent), Calabria (21.9 per cent), Sicilia (21.7 per cent) and Sardegna (20.1 per cent) had some of the highest unemployment rates for the whole of the EU in 1996.[6] Indeed, these rates conceal even higher rates of unemployment for women and young people in the South: examples are female unemployment rates of 34.8 per cent in Campania and 33.2 per cent in Sicilia, and youth unemployment rates of a massive 68.7 per cent in Campania and 60.6 per cent in Calabria (EUROSTAT 1996b). The policy of transforming the South's economy from its dependence upon agriculture towards an advanced industrial economy has been scarcely more successful. Some 17 per cent of all jobs in the South are still in the agricultural sector (7.8 per cent in the centre-North), whereas only some 11.8 per cent are in some form of industrial employment, as compared with 26.4 per cent in the centre-North (D'Antonio 1991: 403).

If one turns from purely economic criteria to the measures usually associated with economic development, such as poverty, housing conditions, access to education and educational achievement, health and overall quality of life, recent studies confirm that residents of the urban centres of the South, such as Naples, Palermo, Catania and Messina, still fare much worse than the rest of Italy (Mingione and Morlicchio 1993). CIPE, the government commission on poverty in Italy, found in 1988 that, whereas the incidence of poverty was less than 9 per cent in the Centre-North, the poverty rate rose to more than 26 per cent for the whole of the South, with an incidence of more than 35 per cent in Calabria (Ginsborg 1994: 239–241).

Disastrous for whom?

Alongside this 'balance sheet' of failure we should consider alternative readings of what has happened in the South. When set alongside patterns of economic and social dualism in other countries, such as Portugal and Greece, it might be argued (1) that development in the *Mezzogiorno* has been at least as successful as in these countries and (2) that the policy measures used in Italy were matched by similar regional development policies elsewhere in Europe. Furthermore, it is clear that some regions of the *Mezzogiorno* have begun to show signs of significant economic development. In particular, the Abruzzi, Molise, Puglia and, to a lesser extent, Sardinia have all shown signs of economic growth, especially in the small and medium-sized business sector (Leonardi 1995). Some parts of Basilicata, Sicily and Puglia have also begun to develop a more dynamic base to their agricultural sectors, though overall such areas retain more in common with their southern neighbours than with more prosperous regions to the North.

There is another sense in which some do not regard public policy for the South as disastrous: many southerners have benefited from these interventions at a personal or family level. For example, the creation of large firms in Naples, Taranto and elsewhere provided jobs for some southerners, if only for relatively few and for limited periods. Similarly, and though at enormous cost to the national economy, transfer payments have provided a significant source of income to many southern families and, indeed, levels of consumption of food and non-food products are now at or near levels for the North. Emigration, an important indicator of economic underdevelopment, has now effectively stopped (Ginsborg 1994; Leonardi 1995).

There are two other 'stakeholders' who are unlikely to regard southern public policy as disastrous: the mafia and the dominant postwar political elite led by the Christian Democrats. The role of these two groups, separately and together, will be discussed more fully below. Suffice it to say that both groups have benefited enormously, financially and politically, from southern public policy. Not only have the various mafia-type groups managed to divert and/or control funds intended for southern economic development, but they have also managed to influence the local administrative structures and schemes charged with managing and delivering such policy. In addition, southern public policy intervention has been a significant part of the Christian Democrat Party's strategy to secure votes and a national power base for much of the postwar period.

So the question of whether public policy for the South has been disastrous thus turns out to be more difficult than it might first seem. Before we can attempt to answer the question posed at the beginning of this chapter, however, we need to have a clearer picture of what forms government interventions actually took.

A history of reform efforts

Although the *questione meridionale* has been with Italy in various forms since the mid-1800s, this chapter focuses only on national public policy in the postwar period (Bevilacqua 1993; Bagnasco 1977). Even then, the problem of summarizing such a long period means that only the most important features can be mentioned. Whilst many aspects of Italian public policies have had a southern dimension, the main focus here will be upon economic development policy. In the formal policy context described, the main actors were central government, the various 'parastatal organizations', regional government (from the 1970s onwards) and local government administrators. Informally, as will later be explained, the Mafia and similar organizations were just as crucial as these actors in determining the outcomes of policy.

The 1950s: 'pre-industrialization'

The most important development for subsequent southern public policy was the formation in 1950 of the *Cassa per il Mezzogiorno* (Fund for the South). In the 1950s, the Cassa's role was to develop the agricultural sector and to build up the region's economic infrastructure (Martinelli 1985; Sassoon 1986; Ginsborg 1990). This so-called 'pre-industrialization' policy was supposed to create the conditions for subsequent spontaneous economic growth through industrialization in the South; 60 per cent of the Cassa's funding went to the construction of roads and aqueducts and to land reclamation during the 1950s (Graziani 1972). In this period the *Mezzogiorno* saw very significant increases in agricultural productivity. This, however, was mainly due to the migration of large numbers of southern rural inhabitants to the North to work for low wages, and in often appalling conditions, in the booming economies of Turin, Milan and other northern cities (Ginsborg 1990; Sassoon 1986; Graziani 1972).

In the South, manufacturing industry was largely unchanged during this period – investment and productivity remained low, whilst they climbed rapidly in the North and centre of Italy. Nevertheless, the 1950s saw a net increase of 13 per cent in such employment in the South (Martinelli 1985). As Graziani (1972) points out, this growth needs to be set in the context of two other factors. First, the growth in southern manufacturing employment was based upon a small expansion in regional income funded by public transfers, generating an increase in consumer demand, which, in turn, was largely met by labour-intensive southern firms. Second, the increase must be set alongside the depopulation due to agricultural underemployment of southern rural areas and the massive migration from the South either to foreign countries or to the North (Furlong 1994: 239–246; Ginsborg 1990: 210–253; Graziani 1972: 371–391).

Two public institutions (*enti pubblici*) came to have a major significance in public policy for the South: IRI (*Istituto per la Ricostruzione Industriale*, the Institute for Industrial Reconstruction) and ENI (*Ente Nazionali Idrocarbi*, the state hydrocarbons company). These two, along with the Cassa and other agencies, formed a type of state intervention in industry and beyond, the so-called 'parastatal' system, which was to dominate southern policy through the late 1950s and 1960s.

The 1960s: state-sponsored industrialization

By the end of the 1950s the Italian government's economic policy for the South shifted towards industrial development. The Cassa began to concentrate activity on the following priorities: location incentives such as tax relief: grants and subsidized interest rates to private firms investing in the South; consortia of local governments for the promotion of industrial development in particular areas; public works programmes; and requirements for public industries to locate in the South. Public policy sought to attract private investment to the South and to use state-run industries, such as petrochemicals and steel production, set at various locations around the *Mezzogiorno* to attract further small and medium-sized enterprises to the region. In this process the IRI and ENI were centrally important. Very large projects such as the Italsider steelworks near Taranto (IRI) and the large refineries in Sicily (ENI) were supposed to develop the South's economy. Though technologically advanced, these schemes were largely unconnected to the rest of the South's economy and provided few jobs in the local areas, earning themselves the title 'cathedrals in the desert' (Del Monte and Giannola 1978; Martinelli 1985; Sassoon 1986; Graziani 1972).

Between 1960 and 1969 the share of national public investment in the South was above 30 per cent, most of it in steel and petrochemicals. The net increase in manufacturing jobs in the period 1959–69 was 5.5 per cent, only half that of the previous decade. The traditional industries experienced a net loss in employment in the 1960s. Furthermore, as more advanced and competitive northern firms came to dominate the southern market, the less efficient but employment-providing local firms were decimated. Unemployment continued to be a major problem in the South, and the government also sought other ways of tackling it besides industrialization. One of these was the expansion of central and local government. By the end of the 1960s about 30 per cent of southern wages and salaries came from employment in public administration, whereas the Italian average was 20 per cent. On the other hand, industrial wages and salaries were 47 per cent of all incomes in Italy overall, but in the South the figure was only 33 per cent (Sassoon 1986: 57).

Another way in which the state intervened was via welfare provision. A central feature for the South was the provision of disablement pensions, the number of which increased enormously in the 1960s. As Ascoli and others have pointed out (Ascoli 1987; Ferrera 1984), these pensions were used as a way of buying off social and political discontent in the *Mezzogiorno* related to the lack of employment and economic development. Initially such pensions depended upon certification by a doctor, but in 1969 a new Pensions Act introduced new rules for disability pensions, including the provision that medically documented physical invalidity was no longer required for the receipt of a disability pension. Residence in an 'economically disadvantaged area', i.e. an area of chronic high unemployment (viz the South), became a basis for application for a disability pension.

The 1970s: crisis and change

In the early 1970s the Cassa was integrated into the Interministry Committee for National Economic Planning and newly created regional governments took over some of the fund's functions. Indeed, regional and local administration of national policy became increasingly important from this point onwards. Whilst the core of southern industrial policy remained the provision of financial incentives and subsidies, these became more widely spread in the 1970s. Large corporations were supposed to submit their investment plans for the scrutiny and approval of the Interministry Committee. Other large projects were to be jointly developed by local governments and private corporations. A new tax-abatement scheme was also introduced, which gave a 100 per cent relief from social security payments for any new job created in the South (Del Monte and Luzenberger 1989).

One result of this policy turn was a second wave of manufacturing investment in the South between 1970 and 1973. Unlike the pattern of investment in the 1960s, which complemented investment in the North and was largely based on heavy industry, the pattern in the 1970s was essentially a substitute for investment in the North. The response by the Italian state and private industry to the 'hot autumn' of industrial unrest in 1969 was to shift investment and production from the North to the South, where union organization was much weaker, wages and salaries lower, and the workforce less resistant to new production techniques. Consequently, investment in the South between 1970 and 1973 reached 38 per cent of the total for Italy (Martinelli 1985; Sassoon 1986). This was the period when the completion of the Taranto and Naples steel complexes occurred, but investment also occurred in modern manufacturing sectors such as electronic and electrical machinery. There was a substantial increase in southern manufacturing employment (5.5 per cent over four years), most of which was in these new industries.

From 1973, along with most other western capitalist economies, Italy experienced the worst economic downturn since the war. The response of Italian capital was to decentralize production still further and close down production facilities. Perhaps the most disastrous response for the South, however, was the drop in investment, which fell back to pre-1960s levels. The steel and chemical industries under public control experienced a major crisis, leading them to withdraw investment in the South, and private corporations which had so recently begun to invest heavily in the South also reduced their investments and activities. Southern unemployment rates became nearly double those of the North, Northern-based firms withdrew and many of the traditional industries closed (Sassoon 1986). Some specific measures were designed to help the South. A new Act (No. 183) was introduced which simplified application procedures for firms wishing to gain support for southern investment and gave full payroll exemptions for workers hired by manufacturing firms. Overall, however, it may be said that policy for the South after 1975 became considerably weaker and even more disorganized.

Two other developments of public policy in the 1970s need to be mentioned here. One is the *Cassa Integrazione*, a fund subsidized by the central government which allowed workers being temporarily laid off to receive an income at or about their normal earnings level when in employment. This scheme was used by firms, with government agreement, to reduce their redundancy costs and to buy off industrial discontent. Though originally supposed to apply for the first six months of redundancy, the scheme became increasingly permanent, with obvious implications for spiralling public expenditure. Though used initially in the North, the scheme became widespread in the South in the 1970s. The other aspect was the massive increase in welfare-state expenditure and provision in the late 1970s. Formally, a comprehensive range of welfare facilities was provided for all Italian citizens. Actually, provision and access varied widely between the centre-North and the South. Funds were not forthcoming from central government for the regions or communes to carry out their responsibilities. Houses and schools were not built. Only some regions, usually in the centre and the North, actually delivered most of the services required by law (Saraceno and Negri 1994). In short, another public policy development reinforced the dualistic character of Italian society.

The 1980s and 1990s: deregulation and policy termination

Although the Italian economy as a whole began a process of rapid recovery and expansion from the middle of the 1980s, the South gained relatively less from this new 'economic miracle'. The policy of active state intervention to encourage private industrial development, coupled with large state projects, in the South was gradually replaced in the 1980s with a package of demand-side measures such as wage subsidies, unemployment benefit and pensions. The *Cassa Integrazione* took on an ever-increasing significance in the South as firms laid off more workers. However, public policy specifically for the South of the sort seen between the 1950s and 1970s gradually disappeared and ultimately ended during the 1980s and 1990s.

Through the late 1980s and 1990s Italian governments began to employ the deregulation strategy found elsewhere in Europe. Publicly owned firms were sold off, and the *enti pubblici* were prepared for break up and sale. Intervention in the *Mezzogiorno* passed increasingly to the European level, as the region became one of the European Union's Objective 1 regions for assistance through the Community's Structural Funds. Finally, in 1993, the remaining 'southern' schemes were terminated, and policy for the region became part of the more general economic and social policy remit of various departments.

Explaining the plight of the South

How can these policies and their outcomes be explained? Three models of explanation will be considered and assessed. The first of these refers to certain structural characteristics of Italian politics which, together, may usefully be captured in Pasquino's (1989) term 'party government'. The second approach focuses upon the role of criminal organizations such as the mafia in structuring the economy and politics of the South. The final approach focuses on the dominant culture of the *Mezzogiorno* and the absence of what is called 'social capital'. We will summarize each approach in turn before suggesting how they might help in understanding the role of public policy for the South.

'Party government'

Postwar Italian politics is characterized by a number of features which are of particular significance to politics and policy in the South. These structural features centre on the domination of government by the Christian Democratic Party and the associated system of *partitocrazia*. Pasquino (1989) has coined the term 'party government' to characterize public policy processes and practice in postwar Italy. By this term he means that (1) all the most important government decisions are made by persons elected on a party basis or by people nominated by and responsible to these elected persons; (2) policies are decided within the governing party or after negotiations with governing coalition partners; and (3) the most important actors, such as ministers and prime ministers, are chosen by the parties. The Christian Democratic Party's sole domination of Italian governments lasted from 1945 until 1981, and, after 1981, the Christian Democrats (DC) still had a major role in the five-party coalitions until 1992. The party managed this domination not only through its ability to secure votes in parliamentary elections, but also through its control of the office of prime minister, which it held for almost all of the postwar period . The DC thus managed, in its own words, to 'occupy' the state and effectively became the 'state party' for much of the postwar period. In the immediate postwar period this hegemony was based upon two linked strategies: to present the DC as the bastion of anti-communism, and to present it as the party of Roman Catholicism (Furlong 1994; Ginsborg 1990; Pasquino 1996). It was during this period that it established a core electoral base in the South, which it was to depend upon in the next forty-plus years. Securing the support of the South was fundamental to DC's electoral strategy and, thus, to its policy concerns in the various governments which it dominated until the 1990s. As various analysts have shown, this one-party dominance has been at the heart of the special character of Italian postwar politics and policy (e.g. Furlong 1994; Ginsborg 1990; Hine 1993; Leonardi and Wertman 1989; Pasquino 1996). Allum expressed it as follows: 'without their success in the South, the Christian Democrats would never have become the dominant party in the country, nor would it have been able to conserve that primacy' (Allum 1981: 314).

This political edifice, with the DC at its head and the *Mezzogiorno* as a key constituent of the political settlement which underpinned it, provided the context which all political actors had to operate within until it finally began to collapse in the 1990s. Not only the political parties, but also bodies such as trades unions, religious organizations, popular movements and even individuals have been constrained to engage in a process of politicized exchange and negotiation in order to secure their desired outcomes from the political system. What distinguishes this 'bargained pluralism' from other pluralist systems, however, is both the degree and the quality of politicization of the processes of interest aggregation and articulation (Hine 1993). The mechanisms of exchange and negotiation are only partly those of a combination of electoral politics and interest-group pressure upon elected politicians found elsewhere: in Italy the dividing line between politics and civil society has become virtually obliterated. Whilst the DC may have been the initiator and prime beneficiary of this system, it became a framework within which the making and delivery of public policy by all groups took place. It is this system which has been called *partitocrazia*.

The term '*partitocrazia*' refers not simply to the way in which public policy in Italy is the result of negotiation between the major parties in government, but also to the politicization of the administrative apparatuses which make up government at central, regional and local level. Almost all government institutions (one notable exception being the Bank of Italy), near-government or parastatal institutions (such as IRI and ENI), and even the state-controlled television stations (RAI) have been involved in a distribution of jobs based upon nominations from political parties. This process of *lottizzazione* created and sustained a political system, especially but not exclusively in the South. The result has been described as an *archipelago* state, 'a federation of institutions, a field in which different institutional strategies are exercised and developed' (Donolo 1980:165). Policy and policy implementation are mediated through a complex system of institutions within which actors from large private companies and individual citizens must seek to secure their ends on the basis of political bargains. The typical form this has taken is clientilism.

Clientilismo is integrally related to one-party domination and *partitocrazia* (Furlong 1994: 15–18; Ginsborg 1994: 83–86). Though it has its traditional roots in the bargains made by individuals or families with a local power broker or patron in return for payment in cash or kind, modern Italian clientilism primarily involves the political parties. Typically, in return for votes, local and regional government officials associated with the parties intervene on behalf of their clients to smooth the way of planning applications, speed up benefit negotiations or health treatment, etc. This process is interwoven with the process of coalition-building in order to retain power by Italian governments. As Ranci summarizes it, 'a regime of fragmented negotiations between local and central authorities has permeated both the public administration and the political arena, making clientilist intermediation the most incisive way to obtain public benefits' (Ranci 1994: 273).

The mafia and the political economy of the Mezzogiorno

The interconnections between Italian politics and organized crime are still being revealed, but it now seems clear that such connections have been a hidden but nevertheless important feature of postwar Italian politics and society (Findaca and Constantino 1994; Ginsborg 1990, 1994). The crucial issue is how the mafia has both provided a socio-economic and political context for Southern policy from the 1950s onwards, and, in relation to the institutions of national and local government and government policies, succeeded in framing the political economy of the *Mezzogiorno* since then.[7] Cesoni (1995) has recently reviewed the various analyses of the mafia's multiple roles in the South, and she points to the central significance of the relationship between Mafia-type organizations (MTO) and southern political and administrative structures.[8] The seminal works of Arlacchi (e.g. 1980, 1983) and Dalla Chiesa (1976) have been the focus for subsequent works, which, for our purposes, may be summarized as follows.

MTOs were crucially transformed in the 1960s and 1970s from their traditional role as mediators in the rural economy of the South, to that of active and autonomous entrepreneurs in the developing capitalist economic structures (Cesoni 1995: 53). This transformation was based upon two factors: the development of the European illegal drug market, which generated enormous profits for the MTOs, and access by the MTOs to the public-sector economy, including special schemes for the South and emergency schemes such as the funding for social and economic regeneration following the 1980 earthquake in Campania. The modern 'mafia economy' is certainly based upon a wide range of illegal activities such as tobacco smuggling, drug trafficking, extortion, illegal gaming, prostitution, sale of stolen and counterfeit goods, and so on (Cesoni 1995: 65–73). This gives such organizations enormous economic power. Yet it is in terms of the penetration of legitimate economic and political activity, based upon this economic power, Cesoni and others argue, that the true significance of the MTOs resides. Not only do these organizations use physical violence and the threat of such violence to demand protection payments from legitimate businesses, but they also use the money gained from their illegal activities to intervene in activities such as building, transport and tourism. This they do both by influencing and manipulating existing businesses, and also by setting up enterprises of their own which then compete in the legitimate markets for labour and for contracts (Cesoni 1995:70–73). In short, and as Arlacchi has influentially argued, the Mafia and other MTOs now exist as entrepreneurs and enterprises in their own right, rather than simply as criminal organizations affecting the legitimate private and public sectors of the economy (Arlacchi 1983).

It is from these economic activities, illegal, quasi-legal and legal, that the MTOs derive their power. It is also, according to Cesoni, the basis of their broader legitimation: 'legitimation from below, through the distribution of revenues and control of the labour markets which they operate; legitimation from above, thanks to the mechanisms of politico-economic exchange which they have developed with certain politico-administrative sectors' (Cesoni 1995: 73; my translation). Furthermore, this economic power is translated into political power, which, in turn, is used to accumulate further economic advantage, and so on. Cesoni argues that it is the activities of the MTOs in the public sector – that is, the economy which is managed and formally controlled by central and local government – which are the most important in qualitative terms. The 'political market', as she terms it, is based upon exchange between government officials, who receive votes and/or payment, and the MTOs, who in return secure impunity from legal investigation and effective control of the public sector economy (*ibid*.: 75). There exists, according to this analysis, a reciprocity between the interests and activities of the MTOs and the government officials at national and, principally, local level who are charged with deciding and administering public-sector schemes. In the *Mezzogiorno* the MTOs thus represent one of the two poles of employment, economic redistribution and revenue, alongside the local and national state. Rather than being subject to the criminal perversion of their activities by the Mafia and other MTOs, in this view the officials of government charged with control of the public sector in the South have played an active role, based upon shared interests, in developing and sustaining the 'mafia phenomenon'. This, she concludes, is one of the reasons why the MTOs have for so long managed to escape serious governmental attack, protected by the 'law of silence'.

The culture of the Mezzogiorno

The third approach is represented by a number of writers who share a focus on the characteristic cultural norms which, they argue, distinguish the *Mezzogiorno* from the rest of Italy and which, in turn, are said to provide the key to understanding the failure of the southern economy to develop, the continuing power of the Mafia and similar organizations, and the overall dualism of Italy's economy, society and politics.

Banfield (1958) used the term 'amoral familism' to characterize the social norms of the *Mezzogiorno*, which, he argued, impeded economic and political development there. This referred to the 'inability of the villagers to act together for their common good or, indeed, for any end transcending the immediate, material interests of the nuclear family' (Banfield 1958: 10). In short, the explanation of the 'backwardness' of the *Mezzogiorno* lay in the cultural character of its society.

More recently, Putnam *et al.* (1992) has developed the notion of 'social capital' in an attempt to explain the differential effectiveness and outcomes of regional and local government in Italy and, indirectly, its persisting economic and political dualism. His study, carried out over some twenty years and involving all twenty Italian regions, correlates the differential performance, politically and economically, of these regions with different sets of norms which, he argues, typify the central and northern regions, on the one hand, and the South, on the other. In the former, a civic culture incorporating 'social capital' exists; in the latter, it does not. Indeed, the study suggests that the correlation is so strong that it may be used as a very significant explanatory factor in the differential performance and economic development of centre-northern regions and those of the South. So what are these characteristic norms; what is 'social capital'? Social capital refers to the features of trust, social norms and networks which characterize social organizations such that they can achieve ends which, in their absence, would not be achievable by individuals working on their own. A social group or collectivity which possesses trust between its members can work collaboratively to pursue shared ends. The absence of such mutual trust means that individuals or families must pursue their own immediate ends in competition with others, creating a kind of 'prisoner's dilemma' situation. Putnam argues further that these cultural characteristics were, very largely, set in the historical past of the different regions as far back as medieval times and, it would appear, will be very difficult to change (*ibid.*: 131–162).

Leonardi, one of Putnam's research associates, has recently developed further the notion of social capital as an approach to understanding the dualism of Italy, and in a somewhat less culturally determinist manner. He suggests that whilst the Centre-North regions of Italy have developed economies characterized by market rules and socially oriented norms, the South has been dominated by non-market rules and individually oriented norms (Leonardi 1995: 172–174). In the South, two types of capitalism have resulted: state capitalism and criminal capitalism. The role of the mafia and similar organizations must, in his view, be incorporated into any understanding of the economic development of the *Mezzogiorno*.

Most interestingly, Leonardi's analysis, whilst referring initially to the notion of social capital, moves away from Putnam's form of civic culture explanation towards a broader analysis based upon the importance of political actors, policy instruments and institutions, and the character of local political economies: 'the real challenge to development is posed by the structure of public policies. If policies are not well designed to take advantage of local physical and human resources, they will not work' (Leonardi 1995: 176).

Policy disaster or political disaster?

Any assessment of the success or failure of public policy for the South needs to take account not only of the policies themselves and the political processes by which such policies were developed and administered, but also of the socio-economic context within which the polices were applied. It would appear that the special policy interventions to resolve the 'Southern Question' between 1957 and 1993 were fundamentally part of the structure and processes of 'party govern-ment' we have set out above. The Christian Democrat-dominated system of *partitocrazia*, with its attendant clientilist practices and party-political bargaining, provided the broad structural framework for public policy for the South. Nevertheless, this structural political framework provides only part of the explana-tion for this policy's failings. It seems increasingly clear that policy for the South was in many senses 'appropriated' by various illegal and quasi-legal bodies of a mafia type in the South. This was done in such a way that the official objectives of public policy were at best subordinated and at worst perverted to serve the interest of such groups and their allies in central and local government offices. Thus the 'failure' of such policy substantially to achieve its outcomes in terms of economic development and the eradication of social and economic dualism must be set alongside the economic and political benefits derived from such schemes by the mafia, by corrupt local officials and by the political parties. This informal 'political market', to use Cesoni's (1995) term, served, for most of the postwar period, to bolster a political system at both regional and national level which, though formally illegal and illegitimate, was regarded by various significant stakeholders as legitimate because they benefited from it. It is in this socio-economic and polit-ical context that we should recognize the importance of norms and mores in the South: what Putnam *et al.* (1992) call an absence of 'social capital' and Banfield (1958) calls 'amoral familism' should rather be interpreted as forms of relatively rational response to a social, economic and political system which evidently, to local people, did not correspond to the formal-legal norms and procedures of the Italian state. Thus the lack of 'social capital' noted by Putnam as an absence of mutual trust and collective orientation in southern regions should be seen as part of a *different* socio-cultural environment rather than as simply a *defective* one.

To speak of a 'policy disaster' in this complex socio-economic and political situ-ation may therefore seem misleading. The argument of this chapter suggests an alternative reading. If disaster it was and is, then perhaps we should see it as a political, rather than a policy, disaster. The term 'political disaster' here relates to the significance of public policy for the South in the context of a crisis of the overall political system in Italy.

The evidence on the socio-economic outcomes of public policy in the South is likely to be considered by most Italians as indicating failure on almost all counts.

When we turn to other criteria of a policy disaster, such as the existence of strong beliefs about who is responsible or what is to blame, the picture is less clear.

Whilst government policy-makers and local-government policy administrators are implicated in these failings, so also are the mafia-type organizations and even the culture of the *Mezzogiorno*, we have suggested. The picture becomes even more blurred when we ask the question 'which specific actions of policy agents contributed to the disaster?' Whilst we have suggested that the alliance of interests between government officials and mafia-type organizations has consistently served to frustrate the formal policy aims of southern policy, it is virtually impossible to identify specific agents and actions. Consequently, allocating blame for these policy failures is likely to be an essentially contestable exercise.

Public policy for the South may, however, be regarded as disastrous in another sense. The enormous amounts of money expended on the *Mezzogiorno* through special public schemes and policies have had a very significant effect upon the Italian economy without achieving significant economic development or an end to dualism. Furthermore, the case of public policy for the South reveals, perhaps more than any other example, how the institutions and processes of party-government and the activities of mafia-type organizations are linked in Italy. The 'Southern Question' may thus, in this perspective, be seen as centrally important in the 'disaster' of the Italian political system in the early 1990s. Though the term 'crisis' has often, incorrectly, been used to describe Italian politics at various times since the war, the 1990s have seen a genuine turning point as the dominant patterns of postwar political hegemony collapsed (Ginsborg 1996). The *questione meridionale* has been posed again not least by the autonomist politicians of the northern 'leagues', and the future of a unified Italian state is under discussion once more (Gundle and Parker 1996; Mershon and Pasquino 1994). Attempts by the government to develop a new constitution for Italy continue to be dogged by the problems of securing cross-party support which have characterized postwar Italian politics. At the same time, successive governments struggle to reduce the national debt and to meet the criteria for Economic and Monetary Union within the European Union, to counter the influence of the mafia, to deal with *tangentopoli*, and to restore public confidence in local and national politics. Public policy intervention in the South is implicated in all these areas and may thus be seen to have been a major contributor to the 'political disaster' underlying the current crisis in Italian politics.

Conclusion

In conclusion, three points may be made to link this case study with the more general study of policy disasters. First, this case gives clear evidence of the contested nature of policy disasters. Whilst many would point to the absence of economic development and continuing dualism after some forty years as a failure worthy of the description 'disastrous', from the perspective of the DC-led government, the mafia and many people living in the South, public policy for the

Mezzogiorno was a success. Second, in the absence of significant political change and the 'arrogance of power' of dominant governing elites, the apparent lack of response, by both public and government, to policy failures may conceal a growing political crisis for the system as a whole. Third, as this study has shown, the study of 'policy disasters' requires a concern not only with political institutions and processes, but also with the economic and social context within which policies are made. Thus, if we wish really to understand how 'policy disasters' are constructed, an interdisciplinary approach is likely to be the most fruitful.

Notes

1   This chapter focuses upon the special public policy interventions by the Italian government from 1957 to their cessation in 1993. It does not consider the role of other public policy interventions by, in particular, the EU via its Structural Funds.
2   The 'South', or *Mezzogiorno*, is usually deemed to comprise the following administrative regions: Abruzzi, Molise, Campania, Puglia, Basilicata, Calabria, Sicilia and Sardegna. These regions comprise 40 per cent of Italy's land mass and some 35 per cent of its population.
3   Italy's GDP rose by 50 per cent at an average annual rate of 2.8 per cent between 1976 and 1990. This was 6 percentage points above the EC average for this same period.
4   In 1991 the debt stood at 103 per cent of GDP and rose to more than 120 per cent in early 1996, more than twice the EU average.
5   In contrast, Lombardia (131 per cent), Valle d'Aosta (130 per cent) and Trentino-Alto Adige (124 per cent) in the North, and Emilia-Romagna (126 per cent), Liguria (120 per cent) and Lazio (120 per cent) in the centre are amongst the regions with the highest per capita GDP in the whole of the EU relative to the average.
6   Sample Centre-North rates were 5.7 per cent in Valle d'Aosta, 6 per cent in Lombardia, 4.1 per cent in Trentino-Alto Adige, 6.5 per cent in Emilia-Romagna and 8.0 per cent in Toscana, all better than the EU average of 10.5 per cent.
7   The term 'mafia' in lower case is used to signify all mafia-type organizations, including the Sicilian Mafia, the Neapolitan *Camorra*, the Calabrian *'ndrangheta* and the *sacra corona* of Puglia.
8   Cesoni's article indicates both the main themes of a wide range of studies on the mafia, and the disputes in analysis and interpretation between them. Our summary considers only the major points of consensus and her assessment.

References

Allum, P. (1981) 'Thirty years of southern policy in Italy', *Political Quarterly* 52(3): 314–323.
Apicella, V. (1996) 'Southern Italy and the underdeveloped regions of Europe', *Review of Economic Conditions in Italy* 1996(1): 119–127.
Arlacchi, P. (1980) *Mafia, contadini e latifondo nella Calabria tradizionale*, Bologna: Il Mulino.
—— (1983) *La mafia imprenditrice*, Bologna: Il Mulino.
Ascoli, U. (1987) 'The Italian welfare state: between incrementalism and rationalism', in R. Friedman, N. Gilbert and M. Sherer (eds) *Modern Welfare States*, Brighton: Wheatsheaf.
Bagnasco, A. (1977) *Tre Italie: la problematica territoriale dello sviluppo italiano*, Bologna: Il Mulino.
Banfield, E. (1958) *The Moral Basis of a Backward Society*, New York: Free Press.

Bevilacqua, P. (1993) *Breve Storia dell'Italia meridionale dall'Ottocento a oggi*, Rome: Donzelli Editore.

Bovens, M. and 't Hart, P. (1996) *Understanding Policy Fiascoes*, New Brunswick and London: Transaction.

Cesoni, M. L. (1995) 'L'Économie mafieuse en Italie: à la recherche d'un paradigme', *Déviance et Société* 19(1): 51–83.

D'Antonio, M. (1991) 'Economic policy for southern Italy: continuity, conservation, innovation', *Review of Economic Conditions in Italy* 1991(3): 401–426.

Dalla Chiesa, N. (1976) *Il Potere mafioso*, Milan: Mazzotta.

Del Monte, A. and Giannola, A. (1978) *Il Mezzogiorno nell'economia italiana*, Bologna: Il Mulino.

Del Monte, A. and de Luzenberger, R. (1989) 'The effect of regional policy on new firm foundation in southern Italy', *Regional Studies* 23(3): 219–230.

Donolo, C. (1980) 'Social change and transformation of the state of Italy', in R. Scase (ed) (1980) *The State in Western Europe*, London: Croom Helm.

EUROSTAT (1996a) 'Per capita GDP in the European Union's regions', *Statistics in Focus: Regions* 1996(1).

—— (1996b) 'Unemployment in the regions of the European Union in 1995', *Statistics in Focus: Regions* 1996(2).

Ferrera, M. (1996) 'The "southern model" of welfare', *Journal of European Social Policy* 6(1): 17–37.

—— (1984) *Il Welfare state in Italia: sviluppo e crisi in prospettiva comparata*, Bologna: Il Mulino.

Findaca, G. and Constantino, S. (eds) (1994) *La Mafia. Le mafie*, Bari: Laterza.

Furlong, P. (1994) *Modern Italy. Representation and Reform*, London: Routledge.

Ginsborg, P. (1990) *A History of Contemporary Italy*, London: Penguin.

—— (ed.) (1994) *Stato dell'Italia*, Milano: Il Saggiatore/Bruno Mondadori.

—— (1996) 'Explaining Italy's crisis', in S. Gundle and S. Parker (eds) (1996) *The New Italian Republic*, London: Routledge.

Giunta, A. and Martinelli, F. (1995) 'The impact of post-Fordist corporate restructuring in a peripheral region: the *Mezzogiorno* of Italy', in A. Amin and J. Tomaney (eds) *Behind the Myth of the European Union*, London: Routledge.

Graziani, A. (ed.) (1972) *L'Economia italiana dal 1945 a oggi*, Bologna: Il Mulino.

Gundle, S. and Parker, S. (eds) (1996) *The New Italian Republic*, London: Routledge.

Hine, D. (1993) *Governing Italy. The Politics of Bargained Pluralism*, Oxford: Clarendon.

Leonardi, R. (1995) 'Regional development in Italy: social capital and the *Mezzogiorno*', *Oxford Review of Economic Policy* 11 (2): 165–179.

Leonardi, R. and Wertman, D. (1989) *Italian Christian Democracy. The Politics of Dominance*, London: Macmillan.

Martinelli, F. (1985) 'Public policy and industrial development in southern Italy: anatomy of a dependent industry', *International Journal of Urban and Regional Research* 9(1): 47–81.

Mershon, C. and Pasquino, G. (eds) (1994) *Italian Politics. Ending the First Republic*, Boulder, CO: Westview Press.

Mingione, E. and Morlicchio, E. (1993) 'New forms of urban poverty in Italy: risk path models in the North and South', *International Journal of Urban and Regional Research* 17(3): 413–427.

Organization for Economic Cooperation and Development (1996) *Economic Survey: Italy 1995–1996*, Paris: OECD.

Padoa-Schioppa Kostoris, F. (1993) *Italy: The Sheltered Economy*, Oxford: Clarendon.

Pasquino, G. (1989) 'Unregulated regulators: parties and party government', in P. Lange and M. Regini, M. (eds) (1989) *State, Market and Social Regulation*, Cambridge: Cambridge University Press.

—— (1996) 'Italy: a democratic regime under reform', in J. P. Colomer (ed.) *Political Institutions in Europe*, London: Routledge.

Putnam, R., Leonardi, A. and Nanetti, R. (1992) *Making Democracy Work. Civic Traditions in Modern Italy*, Princeton, NJ: Princeton University Press.

Ranci, C. (1994) 'The role of the third sector in welfare policies in Italy', in Perri 6 and I. Vidal (eds) *Delivering Welfare*, Barcelona: CIES.

Saraceno, C. and Negri, N. (1994) 'The changing Italian welfare state', *Journal of European Social Policy* 4(1): 19–34.

Sassoon, D. (1986) *Contemporary Italy. Politics, Economy and Society Since 1945*, London: Longman.

6

AN UNAVOIDABLE DISASTER?

The German currency union of 1990

Wolfgang Seibel

Introduction

The currency union between the two Germanies of 1 July 1990 was the corner-stone of the dramatic process of the country's reunification after forty-five years of division between the democratic West and the Soviet bloc. The currency union itself, however, was a disaster according to all conventional economic criteria, as well as relative to the expectations that had been raised by the West German federal government. Technically, the disaster had been caused by the conversion rate of the East and West German currencies, which was set at 1:1 for private savings up to 6,000 DM per person and at 1:2 (one West German Deutschmark to two East German Marks) for any amount beyond that, as well as for the state budget and for stocks or industrial assets. Given the productivity gap between East and West German labour, this meant a revaluation of the East German currency of some 300 per cent. Consequently, commodities produced by the East German economy – based on outmoded technology – were not saleable at prices which covered their costs. Industrial output fell dramatically (to 46 per cent of its 1989 level by December 1990), causing mass unemployment at an official rate of 13 per cent in 1991 and, according to the federal labour authority itself, an underlying rate of 32 per cent in 1991/92 (cf. Siebert 1992). In 1993 gross domestic product (GDP) accounted for just 57 per cent of total domestic demand in East Germany. The remaining 43 per cent was made up by transfers to households. According to the Organization for Economic Cooperation and Development (OECD), 'almost two thirds of internal demand for domestic goods and services (i.e. total domestic demand minus imports) is generated by public consumption and investment spending. The remaining one third is largely accounted for by that part of private domestic demand which cannot be satisfied abroad, i.e. purchases of services' (OECD 1994: 24). In 1997 self-sustaining growth was still not in sight in East Germany (cf. DIW/IfW/IWK 1997).

However, the puzzle is not to explain the disastrous consequences of currency union. These consequences had been predicted by all the economic advisers of the

West German federal government. The major question is how decisions came about which produced the currency union despite its anticipated disastrous consequences. Another puzzle is why the West German federal government, once the disaster became obvious, adopted coping devices that ultimately aggravated rather than mitigated the negative effects of the currency union.

A policy disaster?

If a genuine 'shock-therapy' approach to economic transformation in the central/eastern European countries existed, it was applied to post-1989 East Germany. On 1 July 1990 the East German economy was thrown on to the world market literally overnight. East German firms tried to cope with that shock by means of short-term adjustment strategies. Variable costs and producer prices were reduced in a desperate attempt to stay competitive until long-term strategies such as investment in new technologies, new product lines, marketing and human resources began to pay dividends. Under such circumstances, the crucial question is always to what extent the owner of a firm can afford downward price adjustments and for how long he or she can afford to keep unprofitable firms while investing in long-term assets. What characterized the situation in East Germany after 1 July 1990 was that a substantial reduction in variable costs was subject to heavy institutional and political constraints and that the federal government, as owner, was not willing to keep its unprofitable firms until investment in long-term assets such as technological innovation, new markets and human capital could turn the tide.

The institutional and political constraints for short-term economic adjustment affected wages first and foremost. Whereas East German producer prices sank dramatically after 1 July 1990 – down to 50 per cent of their May 1990 level (cf. Akerlof *et al.* 1991: 8) – wages not only did not sink but started to increase steadily. The federal government – which from 3 October 1990, owned the majority of East German firms – endorsed a high wage policy since wage increases were an important indicator of whether or not the promises connected to the currency union were being kept. With labour productivity far behind West German levels (ranging from 31 per cent lower in 1991 to 49 per cent lower in 1994), unit labour costs nonetheless reached 158 per cent of the West German standard in 1991, 135 per cent in 1994 (DIW 1994) and 129 per cent in 1997 (DIW 1997). Thus, the average East German firm at the end of the 1990s remains uncompetitive.

The currency union also affected the structure of economic governance. Prior to 1 July 1990, the governance structure of the centrally planned economy of the German Democratic Republic (GDR) was supposed to be replaced by four huge joint-stock companies, so-called *Treuhand-Aktiengesellschaften*. These were designed to provide for a decentralized and flexible governance structure, which was perceived as the logical alternative to the centralized and rigid governance system of the GDR economy. However, given the economic chaos triggered by the currency union, the decentralization of governance represented by the

Treuhand-Aktiengesellschaften was perceived as counterproductive in terms of control and accountability. Consequently, the decision to create them was reversed in August 1990. Instead, regional branches of the *Treuhandanstalt* were installed as decentralized but hierarchically controlled units.

These organizational measures had serious, if partly hidden, institutional consequences. In an ironic twist of history, the centralized governance structure of the GDR economy persisted in its classic form as a result of decisions made by West German politicians and managers. The headquarters of the *Treuhandanstalt* was nothing less than a replica of the old GDR branch ministries (in March 1991 the *Treuhandanstalt* even moved into the giant building where most of the branch ministries of the GDR had been located – which was a historic coincidence, but nicely fitted this pattern). The local offices of the *Treuhandanstalt* in the provinces were nothing less than the immediate successors to the economic administration of the GDR at the district level.

In line with the defensive logic of protecting the government against the uncontrolled effects of the currency union, the *Treuhandanstalt* became the administrative tool of a decisively accelerated mass privatization. With the East German economy in deep depression, the federal government was determined to get rid of its unprofitable industrial assets as soon as possible. One year after its creation, by March 1991, the *Treuhandanstalt* had privatized just 15 per cent of its initial assets, but the percentage reached 40 at the end of the same year. At the end of 1994 the *Treuhandanstalt* had privatized, reprivatized or liquidated more than 95 per cent of its assets based on the status quo in 1990. The strict enforcement of accelerated privatization, however, caused an oversupply of firms in the marketplace. Oversupply of firms increased the pressure to reduce prices, which in turn shattered hopes that privatization would yield any revenues. On the contrary, mass privatization in East Germany created a public debt of 256 billion DM by December 1994 (BVS 1995).

The immediate economic effect was a severe depression. There were also indirect effects in terms of coping with this depression. However, the coping techniques – such as the high wage policy, the rigid governance structure for privatization and its massive acceleration – aggravated the negative outcomes of the currency union, both in terms of economic and fiscal disaster and in terms of a persisting centralism in the governance of the economy.

Explaining the failure of the currency union

A reconstruction of how the disaster came about has to answer the following questions:

Why, despite the explicit warnings of the government's own think tanks, did the West German federal government opt, in early 1990, for a quick currency union between the two German states at conversion rates which made East German firms uncompetitive?

Why, despite the commitment to achieve a competitive East German economy as soon as possible, did the federal government endorse a high wage policy which necessarily further undermined the competitiveness of East German firms?

Why, despite a promise to establish the West German constitutional order as well as the western pattern of economic governance, did the federal government endorse the persistence of what used to be the central administration of the state-controlled economy in East Germany?

Why, despite a commitment to the principles of a 'social market economy' (*soziale Marktwirtschaft*), did the federal government finally opt for a rigid shock-therapy approach to privatization, causing oversupply of firms and thus destroying the chance to obtain fiscal revenues from asset sales?

The German archives containing the definitive answers to these questions will remain closed until the year 2020. Accordingly, we are currently forced to resort to more or less intelligent speculation. Combining the facts we know with general hypotheses on political decision-making, we may nonetheless arrive at more or less plausible interpretations.

Why did the West German federal government opt for a quick currency union between the two German states?

The idea of a currency union between the two Germanies had dominated public discourse since February 1990. The currency union, however, was an economic issue only at first glance. Fundamentally, it was a political issue or, to be precise, an issue of political legitimacy and stability. The most striking phenomenon connected to that currency union – which was eventually scheduled to take effect on 1 July 1990 – was that it was pushed through despite grave objections from literally all relevant economic experts. Moreover, when the West German federal government made its first offer to the still communist-led government of the GDR to negotiate on a future currency union between the two Germanies, there was anything but a consensus, even within the West German government, on the appropriateness of such a fundamental step towards a tight linkage between the two economies.

The idea of a currency union was initially promulgated by the social-democratic politician Ingrid Mathäus-Maier, a prominent member of the Bundestag, and an expert for budget and fiscal policy. The initiative was immediately rejected by the federal minister of finance, Theo Waigel, who called it a 'breakneck' idea and a 'dangerous and completely aberrant message' (*Münchner Merkur*, 26 January 1990). The federal minister for the economy, Helmut Haussmann, pleaded for a long-term programme according to which currency union would be reached by 1993.

The most profound warnings came from the government's own think tanks and advisory bodies. The president of the Bundesbank, Karl Otto Pöhl – during a visit to East Berlin on 6 February 1990 – publicly warned the West German government against the premature introduction of the Deutschmark in what was then the GDR, especially at conversion rates which would not reflect the real relative purchasing power of the two currencies (Deutsche Bundesbank 1990). On 9 February 1990 the *Sachverständigenrat*, an advisory council of five top-ranking economists, appealed in the same terms to the chancellor – by the highly unusual means of an open letter (*Sachverständigenrat* 1990: 306–308).

Both Pöhl and the *Sachverständigenrat* emphasized the risks of a currency union for the East German economy. They stated, in particular, that an immediate introduction of the Deutschmark in the GDR would artificially boost the purchasing power of the East German money stock to a degree which, in the short run, could be matched neither by labour productivity nor by the quality and the unit costs of production of the GDR economy. Accordingly, the GDR would be thrown by currency union onto a world market in which it would not be competitive. The experts also emphasized that this would inevitably give rise to a claim for West German subsidies, which could only be paid by increased taxes. Moreover, the *Sachverständigenrat* pointed out that currency union was likely to cause an illusion among the East Germans that the mere introduction of the Deutschmark would also bring the West German standard of living to East Germany (*Sachverständigenrat* 1990: 306). This illusion would inevitably have to be disappointed. The financial compensation needed in this case would not only be extremely costly but also would need to be spent for consumption rather than for investment purposes. Therefore, it would undermine, rather than strengthen, the basis for a self-sustaining recovery of the GDR economy.

The opposition SPD never endorsed the suggestion of Mathäus-Maier. On the contrary, the de facto leader of the party at that time and its candidate for the chancellery, Oskar Lafontaine, picked up the arguments of the *Sachverständigenrat* and predicted mass unemployment in East Germany as the immediate consequence of the currency union. Lafontaine also predicted what he termed 'unification costs', which would have to be borne by the West German taxpayer at a crazy-sounding level of more than 100 billion DM per annum.

All these predictions turned out to be remarkably accurate. There are good reasons to acknowledge, however, that the economic risks of an immediate currency union were not simply ignored by those in charge in the two German governments, but that, in their perception, the currency union was the politically less risky option. Presumably, the West German politicians and the chancellor himself perceived a currency union not primarily as an economic but as a political issue. Helmut Kohl's judgement about the appropriateness of the currency union was closely linked to the strategic goal of national unity.

The main challenge to political stability since 9 November 1989 was East–West migration from the East. Leaving the country had been a deeply internalized pattern of dissent in the GDR (cf. Hirschman 1992). It had also triggered the fatal crisis of the communist government in the autumn of 1989, when thousands of GDR citizens had entered the embassies of the Federal Republic of Germany in

Budapest and Prague. With the inner-German border open but legally still intact, a massive wave of migration (*Übersiedlerwelle*) was triggered and the daily 'score' recorded by intensive media coverage.

The migration challenge materialized in West German public discourse as an issue of how to contain the *Übersiedlerwelle*. The feasible options for this kind of containment were subject to ideological constraints. The core principle was the idea of the reunified nation-state. National unity had become the subject of the federal government's operational policy in the chancellor's speech in the Bundestag on 28 November 1989, roughly three weeks after the Berlin wall had tumbled. What Helmut Kohl outlined on that occasion became known as the 'Ten-Point Plan'. In this plan, which, significantly enough, was not coordinated with the western allies, reunification was conceived as an objective for the mid-term. The Ten-Point Plan was primarily addressed to the government of the GDR, urging it to consider 'federative structures', to be built up between the two German states as a step-by-step approach to national unity.

In significant contrast to Kohl's mild but determined nationalism, opposition leader Oskar Lafontaine – in what he himself may have interpreted as a sober response to Kohl's plan – declared at the national party convention of the SPD in December 1989 that he did not care about the citizenship of the people in Dresden or Potsdam, but cared instead about their actual well-being (*Frankfurter Allgemeine Zeitung*, 20 December 1989). Apparently, Lafontaine wanted to separate the national issue from the economic one. In the following months, however, even the step-by-step approach of the Ten-Point Plan was abandoned in favour of dramatically accelerated progress towards immediate reunification. The currency union played a crucial role in this process as both a determined and a determining factor.

Since East–West travelling as such was no longer legally impeded after 9 November 1989, scarcity of hard currency became the main obstacle to any kind of mobility towards the West. At that time, the exchange rate between the Deutschmark and the East German Mark started to drop steadily. The all-German national impetus of the federal government and its outspoken commitment to the goal of reunification had made it vulnerable to the threat of uncontrolled migration. After all, it would have been unthinkable to reinstall any kind of legal or administrative impediment. In early 1990 the linkage between the national question and the currency problem was reflected by placards at rallies in East Germany reading 'Wenn die DMark nicht zu uns kommt, dann kommen wir zur DMark!' ('If the Deutschmark doesn't come to us we will come to the Deutschmark'). The West German currency had become a highly loaded symbol, linked both to the issue of trustworthiness as far as the promise of national unity was concerned and to the prospects of immediate well-being through the availability of the world-famous Deutschmark in one's own hand (cf. Zatlin 1994).

Thus, the illusions which the *Sachverständigenrat* had warned should not be provoked through premature currency union were already deeply rooted in the East German collective mind. Under these circumstances, the official announcement of currency union negotiations was the message of hope designed to prevent the East Germans from heading west. In addition, the currency union would enable the Federal Republic to control the GDR's monetary system, including the state budget, for which the West Germans, according to all probability, would be finally liable anyway. That was made unmistakably clear to the GDR's prime minister, Hans Modrow, when he visited Bonn in mid-February 1990. While Modrow tried to obtain an accord on substantial West German subsidies to the GDR, he was told that it would be unacceptable for the West Germans to subsidize the East German economy without having control over its basic institutions, including the monetary system.

However, the East Germans' demand for currency union as a promise of individual prosperity was a tragic illusion, since for most of them it meant substantial economic uncertainty and, for many, the destruction of their careers through unemployment. As a matter of fact, however, the East Germans were not the victims, but the proactive force behind the currency union. Rather than blaming the federal government and its presumed misperceptions, it makes sense to speculate about the misperceptions of the East Germans and their institutional and ideological roots.

People in the eastern parts of Germany had not been exposed to a market economy since the 1930s. Their money and wages had been subject to constant manipulation by state agencies. Any understanding of money as an indicator of real supply and demand ratios or of wages as being related to labour productivity had faded from their collective memory a long time before (cf. Kolarska-Bobinska 1988). Moreover, we may assume – following Jonathan Zatlin (1994) – a mental legacy of the socialist ideology according to which the state indeed was held responsible for the organization of labour and the redistribution of national income and, accordingly, also for the degree of individual economic well-being. It is therefore not surprising that the West German Deutschmark was primarily, if not exclusively, perceived as the means by which the West German government could bless the East Germans with those consumer goods which were known to them from West German television commercials or from the hard-currency shops (the so-called '*Intershops*').

However, even if the West German government and the chancellor himself were not responsible for these misperceptions of East Germans they certainly did not do much to correct them, to put it mildly. Both Free Democrats and Christian Democrats deliberately used the West German *Wirtschaftswunder* (economic miracle) of the 1950s as the historic parallel for what would happen in East Germany as soon as market forces were unleashed. As early as February and March 1990 the West German government's message to the public was clear enough: the government accepted not only national unity but also economic growth and the individual prosperity of East Germans as strategic objectives. Accordingly, not only the currency union as such, but the very core of it, the conversion rate of the two German currencies, was subject to political rather than economic considerations. This explains the economically disastrous gap between the conversion rate of the currency union and what, for instance, trade with West Berlin retailers indicated as the real ratio of purchase power between the West and the East German currencies. The former was 1:1 for wages and individual assets and earnings (up to 6,000 Marks), while the latter ranged from 1:6 to 1:10.

All this amounted to a dramatic dilemma. On the one hand, the West German government had to act quickly and decisively in order to convince the East Germans that reunification and economic prosperity were imminent. It also had to convince the West Germans that their prosperity would not be affected by reunification and that West German money would not be thrown into a bottomless pit because the federal government would soon take control over the East German monetary system. On the other hand, public debate focused on the currency union as the only means to meet the short-range needs of political legitimacy. The currency union, however, was foreseen by the government's think tanks as likely to destroy the basis for both short-range economic prosperity and self-sustaining growth.

Why did the federal government endorse a high wage policy in post-1990 East Germany?

High wages became the crucial constraint on the competitiveness of East German firms after 1990. The most important reason for high wages regardless of any labour productivity and capital profitability was, again, the need for political support and legitimacy. For the East Germans, the level of wages was the most visible indicator of whether or not the political promises of speedy prosperity were being kept. This visibility was supported by direct comparison with West German wages in the same currency. Rather than labour productivity, West German wages became the yardstick for East German earnings.

This particular logic of wage policy and the inherent vulnerability of the federal government became obvious in early 1991. At that time, the first massive layoffs had made hundreds of thousands of East Germans redundant. There were clear signs of unrest, including wildcat strikes, uncontrolled takeovers of plants and even the siege of a state parliament by outraged shipyard workers in the city of Schwerin (17 February 1991). The unions, and especially the most powerful one, the metal worker's union IG Metall, initially encouraged the spontaneous protests. However, the unions had no strong influence at the plant level. The wave of unrest gave them the opportunity to demonstrate their indispensability as the main voice for labour in the perception of both their clientele and the government. The relative weakness of the government and the relative strength of the unions, especially IG Metall, helped produce, in March 1991, an agreement whereby wages were scheduled to attain parity with West German wage levels by 1994 (the agreement was watered down, though not suspended, in 1993).

The wage agreement of March 1991 was a consequence of the illusions of 1990. In a way, the unions made East German firms pay the price for the governing parties' promises of 1990. Moreover, with the government still in charge of the vast majority of East German firms, a consensus with the unions was indispensable. Certainly it was desirable to avert imminent social unrest. The strategic issue, however, was to prevent the unions from general resistance to the government's privatization policy. It could easily be anticipated that privatization would continue to cause massive layoffs. In this perspective, the wage agreement of March 1991 was an implicit agreement that the unions would not choose a confrontational strategy in their fight against the social costs of privatization, in terms of unemployment.

Thus, the high wage policy, as it emerged in early 1991, was double-edged. On the one hand, it responded to the expectations of the East Germans raised by the promises and illusions of 1990, and disappointed by the economic depression resulting from currency union. In this respect, the wage policy was a coping mechanism. The government tried to deal with the unintended economic consequences of its own initial actions by spending money and by establishing the West German style of consensus-oriented or neo-corporatist cooperation between employers and unions. On the other hand, the high wage policy necessarily aggravated the economic depression whose social and political costs it was supposed to mitigate. With labour unit costs well above West German levels, East German firms became less competitive than ever.

Why did the federal government endorse the persistence of central administration of the economy of East Germany?

The institutional governance of privatization played a crucial, if not a decisive, role in the reunification process. The core of that governance structure became a central federal agency in Berlin, known as the *Treuhandanstalt*. Indeed, the *Treuhandanstalt* became both the backbone of the enforcement of a rigid privatization policy and the main institutional buffer against its potential political costs. The emergence of the *Treuhandanstalt*, however, is one of the most counterintuitive events in the course of the transformation of what used to be the communist regime in East Germany.

Famous (or notorious) as the *Treuhandanstalt* became later on as the federal government's privatization agency, one has to remember that this institution was founded by the last communist-led government of the GDR under Prime Minister Hans Modrow in early March 1990, and that its task at that time was not privatization, but merely changing the legal status of the state-owned enterprises according to the standards of West German corporate law (what was termed 'commercialization' elsewhere in central and eastern Europe). The central office of the *Treuhandanstalt* was located on the Unter den Linden in East Berlin. It was staffed at that time by ninety-one people and, reportedly, ten typewriters (Fischer and Schroter 1996: 29–30). It was not designed to be the administrative centre of a holding company for state-owned enterprises, but to act as a kind of notary office for corporate law. The old structure of corporate and industrial governance itself remained intact.

When the new democratic GDR government of the Christian Democrat Lothar de Maizière took office in April 1990 it redesigned both the policy and the organizational structure of the *Treuhandanstalt*. In terms of policy, there was no longer any doubt that the prime task of the agency would be the privatization of its assets. This was nonetheless described rather vaguely in the new *Treuhand* law, which mentioned the liquidation of public debts and the 'creation of competitive economic structures' as equally legitimate objectives of the agency (*Gesetzblatt der DDR I*, no. 33: 300). The new law stipulated that the *Treuhand*'s aims had to be financed through revenues from sales. Additional revenues were supposed to be transformed into shares, with GDR citizens as the sole shareholders. The legislators of the GDR parliament obviously took for granted that there would be such additional money.

As in almost every other communist country, the nucleus of the old system had been formed by more than a dozen ministries, each in charge of a particular branch of the economy. This structure was supposed to be replaced by the four huge joint-stock companies of the *Treuhand-Aktiengesellschaften*, as market-driven alternatives to central planning. The new regime of the *Treuhandanstalt* became effective on 1 July 1990, the day of the currency union. The president of this new *Treuhandanstalt* was Dr Reiner Maria Gohlke, formerly chief executive officer of the German Federal Railway.

On 1 July 1990, however, the circumstances under which the *Treuhandanstalt* was operating changed dramatically. Since the main framework of the new governance structure, the *Treuhand-Aktiengesellschaften*, did not yet exist, the *Treuhand* central office became the de facto headquarters of an industrial complex spanning 8,000 firms and roughly 4 million employees. The *Treuhandanstalt* was supposed not only to manage the system, but also to start privatization (cf. Seibel 1997). The immediate and most urgent task, however, was to mobilize the immense amount of liquidity in Deutschmarks, which the state-owned firms needed literally overnight. The entire economy of the GDR was virtually dependent on one small agency in Berlin.

There was a dramatic discrepancy between these tremendous tasks and the smallness and weakness of the agency in charge of them. What was desperately needed was a minimum of experienced staff, formal organization and standard operating procedures. All this had to be arranged as quickly and efficiently as possible. Meanwhile, the public and the federal government were waiting for the first signs of the miracles of privatization. However, a growing perception of the *Treuhandstalt* organization as chaotic (cf. Seibel 1996: 122–123) appeared to play a crucial role in shaping its institutional design. This perception was further nourished by spectacular cases of what in other central and eastern European countries has been termed 'spontaneous' or 'nomenclatura privatization', in which top executives of *Treuhand*-owned firms made dubious deals with West German investors. The new *Treuhand* elite, composed of top West German managers, had no commitment to what the majority of the democratically elected Volkskammer (East German Parliament) had intended as decentralization and democratization of the country's economic governance structures. The decentralized nature of the new structures was perceived as inappropriate, given the desperate need for a reliable organization. Reliability was supposed to be provided by a rigidly controlled organization, which would rule out 'nomenclatura privatization' as well as the ubiquitous risk of corruption (cf. Seibel 1996: 122–128, with further references). Accordingly, the *Treuhandanstalt* was reorganized to be a central authority in direct control of its more than 8,000 enterprises.

By means of what was literally an illegal coup which went unpunished in the agony of the GDR, the creation of the *Treuhand-Aktiengesellschaften* was cancelled in late August 1990. Instead, the regional branches of the *Treuhandanstalt*, the so-called *Niederlassungen*, were reinstalled as decentralized but hierarchically controlled units. This was the first decision of Dr Detlev Karsten Rohwedder as the new President of the *Treuhandanstalt*. He replaced Gohlke, who had held office for just six weeks and had been blamed for the organizational chaos of the early days of the post-1 July *Treuhand*. Rohwedder also reorganized the headquarters of the *Treuhandanstalt*. At that time, to reflect its legal objectives, the *Treuhandanstalt* had two main divisions, one for 'Privatization' and another for 'Reconstruction' (*Sanierung*). With the agency itself in direct control of its enterprises, this structure was perceived as a cause of undesirable organizational slack and coordination problems, since a clear-cut distinction between firms in the process of privatization and firms in the process of reconstruction was more or less impossible. Instead, the headquarters was reorganized according to the main branches of industry, which meant a divisional instead of a functional pattern.

The institutional emergence of the *Treuhandanstalt* took place while there was still a major difference between the GDR government's political rationality and the *Treuhand*'s administrative rationality. Due to the weakness of the GDR parliament and the entire East German political class, the administrative rationality of the new *Treuhand* elite became dominant during the three months from 1 July, the day of the currency union, to 3 October 1990, the official reunification date. The dominance of administrative rationality resulted in the persistence of the centralized governance structure of the GDR economy. The headquarters of the *Treuhandanstalt*, with its branch-oriented divisions, revitalized the organization and structures that had characterized the branch ministries of the communist regime. Essentially, everything the GDR parliament had intended to dissolve as a legacy of the communist regime had resurfaced through the decisions of those who were supposed to be its strongest opponents, namely the West German managers at the top of the *Treuhandanstalt*. Certainly, the old elites were replaced, but the organizational structure itself was reanimated. The *Treuhand* Bill of the GDR parliament was transformed into federal law through regulation of the unification treaty of August 1990. The *Treuhandanstalt* became a public agency according to West German public law, and, as such, the only major GDR institution to survive reunification.

Why did the federal government opt for a rigid shock-therapy approach to privatization?

Those in the executive elite of the *Treuhandanstalt* were the first to become aware of the real scale of the economic depression in East Germany. Moreover, *Treuhand* officials were also the first targets of the unrest which accompanied a wave of layoffs in *Treuhand* firms in February 1991. Finally, the new East German *Länder* slowly but surely became self-conscious actors on the political stage, and they too addressed their concerns about their regional economies to the *Treuhandanstalt* as the owner, at that time, of as much as 85 per cent of its initial assets.

The fading prospects for profits from the sale of heavy loss-making state-owned firms, and the political vulnerability of the federal government – as a result of owning a large share of a regional economy in depression – led both the government and the *Treuhand* elite to the conclusion that a substantially accelerated pace of privatization would not necessarily enhance economic risks, while it would at least reduce political ones. The basis for this presumed calculation was that – unlike the situation in any other former communist country – the Germans could afford, at least financially, to decouple the protection of people from the protection of firms (cf. Siebert 1992: 13). While all the other former communist economies were forced to sustain social and political stability primarily through employment by non-profitable firms, East Germans were enabled not only to keep but to improve their standard of living even if their firms were going out of business. The social costs of unemployment were being substantially reduced by an enhanced version of the West German welfare state, with special payments for short-time workers and a state-funded second labour market. Moreover, the *Treuhandanstalt* was committed to a case-by-case policy of sales contracts, with investment pledges and job guarantees as obligatory elements. Every liquidation of firms and plants was accompanied by so-called 'social plans', with generous compensations for the layoffs.

This consolidated strategy was only viable because the political and the administrative arena were now being coordinated for the first time, in a series of agreements. On 12 March 1991 a general agreement between the federal government, the East German *Länder* and the *Treuhandanstalt* was reached, establishing several mechanisms of coordination and information-sharing among these partners. In mid-April a master plan for social benefits in case of layoffs was agreed upon between the *Treuhandanstalt* and the trade unions. In July 1991 another agreement between the unions and the *Treuhandanstalt* was reached over employment and training companies (*ABS Gesellschaften*), most of whom were training and employing dismissed *Treuhand* employees.

The ingredients of disaster: power asymmetries, ideology and coping resources

Why did the federal government not follow the explicit advice of its own think tanks? Why did it choose coping devices which ultimately aggravated the disaster? Does the case of the inner-German currency union provide evidence of what might be factors increasing the probability of policy disasters in general? The general answer is that the West German federal government – to quote Karl W. Deutsch's famous definition of power – could 'afford not to learn' (Deutsch 1963: 111). This may be illustrated by referring to three dimensions: power relations, ideology and coping resources.

The West German federal government, under the chancellorship of Helmut Kohl, was the dominant actor in the reunification process of 1990, since power relations between the two German states were highly asymmetric. The West German federal government and the West Germans in general could afford to ignore what the experts said, since it was not they who were primarily affected by the disastrous effects of the currency union, but the East Germans. This holds true not only for the economic depression, but also for the high wage policy as an economically counterproductive means to reduce the social and political costs of the depression. After all, neither West German employers nor West German labour unions had an incentive to foster inner-German low-wage competition. In general, one may hypothesize that *policy disasters are likely to be facilitated by asymmetric power relations as soon as causal decisions are being made by the relatively powerful while the disastrous effects have to be borne by the relatively powerless.*

However, neither the decisions immediately connected with the currency union nor the decisions leading to the high wage policy can be exclusively explained by referring to interest-driven rational actors. However asymmetric both the power relations and the distribution of the disastrous effects of the currency union and the high wage policy may have been, this does not alter the fact that both the currency union and high wages were desired primarily by East Germans. Moreover, the disastrous effects of the currency were ultimately not confined to the East Germans. The fiscal disaster resulting from precipitate mass privatization primarily affected the prosperous West German taxpayer. In short, we can hardly assume victims decide rationally to be victimized.

What we can assume, though, is non-rational behaviour of potential victims. The public discourse on the inner-German currency union did not follow the sober logic of the economic experts. Reunification of the country was indisputably a goal in itself. Once the public discourse had linked this national goal to an economic means – the currency union – any alternative to a quick currency union at unrealistic conversion rates was transformed into a political taboo. Advocacy of postponement of the currency union or a link between conversion rates and labour productivity became stigmatized as quasi-unpatriotic. In short, the idea of a unified nation-state was what – in the related literature – is conceived of as a 'principled belief' (cf. Goldstein and Keohane 1993: 8–11). Thinking in terms of cause and effect was replaced by thinking in terms of 'good' and 'bad'.

A similar, though slightly different, pattern characterized the public discourse on money as such. Money is a particular myth to Germans. The hyperinflation after World War I and World War II represents an historical trauma. The Deutschmark, in turn, is the symbol of the 'economic miracle' (*Wirtschaftswunder*) of the 1950s. In the collective mind of East Germans, however, money was decoupled from basic economic facts. East Germans believed that availability of West German currency equalled availability of western consumer goods, ignoring the link between purchasing power and labour productivity. Moreover, the combination of the Deutschmark and the concept of a 'social market economy' (*soziale Marktwirtschaft*) symbolized the combination of economic growth, individual prosperity, and social and political stability.

Stimulated by two decisive elections – the first free elections in the GDR of 18 March 1990 and the all-German elections of 2 December 1990 – all these ideological components were mobilized by the West German federal government in preparing for currency union. The introduction of the Deutschmark in the GDR in 1990 was likened to the introduction of the Deutschmark in the western occupation zones in 1948. Leading politicians of the governing coalition hastened to promise a second 'economic miracle' as an immediate effect of the currency union. The core message 'Currency, Economic and Social Union' (*Wahrungs-, Wirtschafts- und Sozialunion*) was the promise of rapid reunification, rapid economic growth and individual prosperity.

In short, the role of money in public discourse and perception was subject to causal beliefs (Goldstein and Keohane 1993: 8 –11) in the sense of generalized assumptions about cause–effect relationships regardless of actual circumstances. In Germany's public discourse in 1990 'principled beliefs' and 'causal beliefs' constituted a dominance of belief-systems over causal analysis. The idea of reunification as an undisputed goal in itself and the role of the Deutschmark as a symbol of imminent economic growth and prosperity regardless of basic economic cause–effect relationships were the main ideological components preventing the public from acknowledging the sober warnings of the government's own experts as far as the currency union was concerned. Thus, one may further hypothesize that *policy disasters are likely to be facilitated by the dominance of belief-systems that prevent key actors from acknowledging the results of causal analysis connected to the decisions they have to make.*

However, neither power asymmetry nor the dominance of belief-systems over causal analysis sufficiently explains the way the West German federal government aggravated the disastrous effects of the currency union by choosing counterproductive methods of coping. Ironically, one reason why the governing coalition could 'afford not to learn' was the availability of a particular kind of coping resource designed to mitigate undesirable effects of the politically opportune currency union. Sober risk analysis may have been avoided due to affluence and due to trust in political and administrative capability. With the benefit of hindsight we know that the economic affluence of West Germany made affordable the economic depression in East Germany. Even if the leading West German politicians may have believed their own promises of imminent prosperity resulting from the currency union, the strong economic and fiscal basis of the West German state has facilitated the risky operation of burdening the East German economy with a currency revaluation of roughly 300 per cent, as well as with massive wage increases unconnected with improvements in labour productivity. Even if – as in 1993, three years after the currency union – East German GDP covered just 57 per cent of the total domestic demand, the remaining 43 per cent was easily covered by public transfers, which in 1997 totalled 1,000 billion DM. Even if all this was either neglected or just vaguely suspected in 1990, it was nonetheless clear that the West German economy was able to finance the expanded version of the West German welfare state necessary to mitigate almost any social costs that might result from the currency union, especially mass unemployment. This conforms to the finding in organization theory according to which 'slack' impedes rather than facilitates learning (Cyert and March 1963).

Moreover, the risky operation of a currency union may have been facilitated by trust in the neo-corporatist style of policy-making that had emerged in West Germany since 1945. The consensus-oriented cooperation between government, unions and employer associations turned out to be an indispensable resource for securing the loyalty of organized labour despite the high social costs of privatization in terms of unemployment. This resource was mobilized through a whole series of agreements between the federal government, the *Treuhandanstalt*, the employers' associations and the unions.

Finally, administrative tools were a crucial coping resource. If the *Treuhandanstalt* had not existed it would have had to be invented in order to mitigate the political costs of the economic depression that followed the currency union. Organizationally, the *Treuhandanstalt* was decisively shaped by the disastrous effects of the currency union. Located in East Berlin, it not only deflected public attention from the government located in Bonn (as an institutional scapegoat *par excellence* it literally absorbed all criticism of the privatization policy), but also combined organizational rigidity with flexibility. Rigidity was provided by the economic governance structure of the late GDR, while flexibility was provided by an adaptation to the West German pattern of federalism and neo-corporatism. By virtue of this hybridization, the *Treuhandanstalt* was the fundamental resource enabling the federal government to enforce the rigid privatization strategy and to control its political costs at the same time. A final hypothesis that may be deduced from the German case is that *policy disasters are likely to be facilitated when key actors may anticipate the availability of coping resources designed to mitigate undesirable effects of risky decisions they have to make.*

References

Akerlof, G. A., Rose, A. K., Yellen, J. L. and Hessenius, H. (1991) 'East Germany in from the cold: the economic aftermath of currency union', *Brookings Papers for Economic Activity* I: 1–101.

BVS (1995) *Abschlußstatistik der Treuhandanstalt per 31.12.1994*, Bundesanstalt für Vereinigungsbedingte Sonderaufgaben.

Cyert, R. M. and March, J. G. (1963) *A Behavioral Theory of the Firm*, Englewood Cliffs, NJ: Prentice Hall.

Deutsch, K. W. (1963) *The Nerves of Government. Models of Political Communication and Control*, New York: Free Press.

Deutsche Bundesbank (1990) *Auszüge aus Presseartikeln* 12, 12 February.

DIW (1994) 'Die wirtschaftliche Lage in Deutschland', Deutsches Institut für Wirtschaftsforschung, *Wochenbericht* 43/94: 724–733.

—— (1997) 'Die wirtschaftliche Lage in Deutschland', Deutsches Institut für Wirtschaftsforschung, *Wochenbericht* 17/97: 293–305.

DIW/IfW/IWK (1997) *Gesamtwirtschaftliche und unternehmerische Anpassungsfortschritte in Ostdeutschland*, fünfzehnter Bericht, Deutsches Institut für Wirtschaftsforschung/Institut für Wirtschaftsforschung Halle/Institut für Weltwirtschaft Kiel.

Fischer, W. and Schroter, H. (1996) 'The origins of the Treuhandanstalt', in W. Fischer, H. Hax and H. Schneider (eds) *Treuhandanstalt: The Impossible Challenge*, Berlin: Akademie Verlag.

Goldstein, J. and Keohane, R. O. (1993) 'Ideas and foreign policy: an analytical framework', in J. Goldstein and R. O. Keohane (eds) *Ideas and Foreign Policy. Beliefs, Institutions and Political Change*, Ithaca, NY: Cornell University Press.

Hirschman, A. O. (1992) 'Abwanderung, Widerspruch und das Schicksal der Deutschen Demokratischen Republik', *Leviathan* 20: 330–358.

Kolarska-Bobinska, L. (1988) 'Social interests, egalitarian attitudes, and the change of economic order', *Social Research* 55: 111–138.

OECD (1994) 'Country report', *OECD Survey*, part 3, Paris: Organization for Economic Cooperation and Development.

Sachverständigenrat (1990) *Sachverständigenrat zur Begutachtung der gesamtwirtschaftlichen Entwicklung: auf dem Wege zur wirtschaftlichen Einheit Deutschlands*, Jahresgutachten 1990/1991, Stuttgart: Metzler-Poeschel.

Seibel, W. (1996) 'The organizational development of the Treuhandanstalt', in W. Fischer, H. Hax and H. Schneider (eds) *Treuhandanstalt: The Impossible Challenge*, Berlin: Akademie Verlag.

—— (1997) 'Privatization by means of state bureaucracy? The Treuhand phenomenon in Eastern Germany', in G. Grabher and D. Stark (eds) *Restructuring Networks in Post-Socialism. Legacies, Linkages and Localities*, Oxford: Oxford University Press.

Siebert, H. (1996) 'Real adjustment in the transformation process: risk factors in East Germany', *Kiel Working Papers No. 507*.

Zatlin, J. R. (1994) 'Hard Marks and soft revolutionaries: the economics of entitlement and the debate on German monetary union, November 9, 1989–March 18, 1990', *German Politics and Society* 33: 57–84.

Part IV

THE STATE IN ITS INTERNATIONAL CONTEXT

7

'ERRORS OF AN ADMINISTRATIVE NATURE'?

Explaining the 'Arms to Iraq' affair

Pat Gray

Introduction

The 'Arms to Iraq' affair – which British ministers depicted as a series of minor errors 'largely of an administrative nature' (House of Commons Debates, 15 February 1996: 1152) – threatened to bring down the government of John Major in late February 1996. That crisis occurred after one of the longest running and most highly politicized public inquiries in British history (Tomkins 1996: 109; Barker 1997a). The affair centred around allegations that a government minister had encouraged companies to break the government's rules forbidding arms exports to Iraq and that the rules on exports had been secretly relaxed. Ministers had also lied to parliament, and risked sending innocent men to jail in an attempt to cover this up. These allegations not only served to sap the government's legitimacy over an extended period, but also may have represented a shift in the 'British' way of handling such crises, towards a more openly competitive 'politics of scandal' (Levi and Nelken 1996: 1–17) more common elsewhere (Markovits and Silverstein 1988). Although the affair produced few immediate reforms, it certainly contributed to the subsequent landslide election defeat of the Conservative government in May 1997, after eighteen years in power.

After a brief assessment of the outcomes of the various policies at the heart of the affair, the first part of this chapter will describe the political context in which the first major reports of illicit exports to Iraq appeared in 1990, events following the collapse of the Matrix Churchill trial, the public inquiry, and the debates and reform attempts which followed it. By taking an holistic view of the affair, rather than concentrating on specific aspects, a number of more general features of British government in the early 1990s will be explored.

The early part of the analysis will consider the predominant explanations currently offered of the affair, by the report of the public inquiry and by UK academic observers. These analyses, it will be argued, depart from broadly 'optimistic' opening assumptions about the feasibility of good government. Sir Richard Scott's inquiry into the affair, for example, tended to emphasize the importance of decision in explaining policy outcomes, and of clear rules, adequate information and competent staff in achieving objectives. Such a perspective had deep roots in the ideals of classical public administration and in conceptions of the state as a 'rational actor' (Allison 1971: 32–38).

The report of the inquiry was, however, tempered by liberal constitutionalism. Such an approach takes a more realistic view of human nature, arguing that significant institutional checks and balances are needed to guarantee that decisions are taken in a way which is representative of the interests of the wider society and which defends important rights. Such an approach was also important in the construction of explanations for the affair by academic commentators.

Existing accounts are therefore a blend of normative prescription and description; what is described is dependent on prior judgements about what is of value, or what is important. Such accounts serve to disguise a number of features of the affair by exaggerating others. This chapter will therefore aim to redress this balance by providing a brief outline of two alternative perspectives on the affair, which start from less optimistic assumptions about governability and a different view of what is important. Given the space available, this will inevitably be more of an exercise in agenda-setting than a detailed 'multi-theoretical' account.

The first alternative way of analysing the affair is as an example of 'bureaucratic politics'. Such an approach focuses not on key decisions, but on the social and institutional context within which actions are undertaken. Its object of study is the formal and informal rules of bureaucracies and wider networks, and the processes which generate policy amongst these networks. Such a focus on 'bureaucratic politics' tends to see policy-making as primarily determined by an iterative process of bargaining between more or less independent actors. The underlying assumption of such a model is that government is both highly dispersed and inherently fragile (Allison 1971: 162–181).

The second alternative perspective is that offered by instrumental Marxist accounts. Such perspectives see policy as the product of the inevitable influence of economically dominant classes on the policy process of the modern capitalist state (Miliband 1969: 23). The crisis of the state is thus explained by the existence of deep power structures, and policy failure is seen as largely inevitable.

A policy disaster?

Important groups in society undoubtedly saw 'Arms to Iraq' as a negative event, and one that was caused by avoidable and blameworthy failures by makers of public policy (Bovens and 't Hart 1996: 15). Yet the outcomes of the affair are not easy to evaluate, as disputes exist about the values involved, most notably about the desirability of Britain's participation in the arms trade. Evaluation is also made difficult by the fact that the affair involved separate policies on industrial competitiveness, foreign affairs, intelligence and freedom of information, each of which could be evaluated differently. Nonetheless, when evaluated in isolation against the objectives set by the government, most of these policies might be seen as successful.

Government policy on the arms trade had combined a vigorous export drive with a range of conventional arms control and technology transfer measures, derived from international obligations and ad hoc responses to specific threats. That policy was broadly successful in commercial terms. Britain's share of the world arms market remains the fourth largest in the world (Trust for Education and Research on the Arms Trade 1992). Indeed, since the mid-1980s the UK arms industry has taken a growing share of global exports, at a time when the total global value of such exports has declined. However, profitability and levels of employment in the UK industry have fallen over the same period (Cooper *et al.* 1996). There are strong military reasons, however, why such success in the export market might be self-defeating, including the obvious problems of global instability and the risk of facing one's own weapons in future wars (Keller 1995: 3–5).

Industrial policy was similarly directed towards maintaining Britain's competitiveness in manufacturing. Here policy seems to have been markedly less successful. Total numbers employed in manufacturing industry in the UK have continued to fall, from 7,301,000 in 1978 to 4,021,000 in 1995 (Office for National Statistics 1997).

In foreign policy Britain has consistently pursued the twin goals of preserving a world role while simultaneously disguising her industrial and political decline (Buller 1996). Despite the disruptions caused by the affair in domestic politics, and the trauma of the gulf war, Britain's international status may well have been stronger after the affair than before. The gulf war cemented Britain's important relationships with America, Saudi Arabia and Kuwait, while weakening enemies such as Iraq.

Intelligence strategy was also remarkably successful. In producing accurate information about Iraqi procurement, the UK system of intelligence gathering provided government with excellent evidence upon which to base decision. It was poor circulation and use of such information, rather than the information itself, which were to prove a problem.

It is the strategy on freedom of information, however, that proved unsuccessful. Given a background of low trust in government arising from 'sleaze', failings in economic policy and the changed circumstances caused by the gulf war (see below), high levels of secrecy deployed by ministers served to trigger a major crisis in confidence which could only be resolved by an independent public inquiry. This, in turn, deepened the legitimacy problems the government already faced. Taken as a whole, 'Arms to Iraq' was a political failure, rather than a failure of a particular programme or policy. Its main damage was not a failure to achieve the objectives of particular policies, but a more diffuse damage to the legitimacy of the Conservative government as a whole.[1]

In its form, the affair resembled the classic political scandal, following a distinct (if transient) cycle of discovery, allegations of cover-up, and inquiry followed by reform (Markovits and Silverstein 1988). Yet it is dwarfed by worse scandals in other countries – the affair is not comparable to *tangetopoli* in Italy, Watergate, nor even to the 'Iran Contra' affair. However, scandals are only labelled as such in terms of the values of the particular society in which they take place (Heidenheimer *et al.* 1989: 151–155). In terms of the distinctively British political culture, the affair appeared to transgress a number of critical procedural norms: those of fairness and justice (in the potential withholding by government of evidence from the Matrix Churchill trial), honesty (in the misleading of parliament) and responsibility (in ministers' refusal to accept blame for error). It thus had very high potential to damage the government.

Identifying who was involved in the affair and those responsible is less easy. The accountability process was strongly influenced by the structuring of the public inquiry and by the politics of its aftermath. It was also strongly influenced by prior value judgements about the nature, scope and limits of government. Moreover, as Bovens and 't Hart argue (1996: 55–62), it is difficult to identify individual involvement and responsibility in such cases, where long-time frames and complex institutional arrangements coexist.

'Arms to Iraq': an overview

Background

The decade of the 1990s started with the spectacular collapse of the Poll Tax, which had combined with deep divisions within the ruling Conservative party over Europe to trigger – in November 1990 – a successful challenge to Margaret Thatcher's premiership from within her own party. Her replacement, John Major, became prime minister with the UK in the grip of recession, persistent mass unemployment and a spate of corporate scandals which were slowly accustoming the British public to a less sanguine view of the benefits of the market (Dunleavy and Weir 1995: 57). Despite these inauspicious circumstances, John Major unexpectedly won the 1992 general election by a small margin, ushering in a fourth term of office for the Conservative Party. However, within months of taking office the Major government was to be humiliated by the events of 'Black Wednesday', in which the pound dropped out of the European Exchange Rate Mechanism (ERM) following extensive speculation, which heavy bank purchasing and interest rate rises had failed to stem.

Alongside this crisis, and amidst persistent divisions in the Conservative Party over Europe, the theme of corruption began to emerge more strongly in British politics, under the general heading of 'sleaze'. There is debate about the origins, nature and extent of this phenomenon (Doig and Ridley 1995; Doig 1995), but its most persistent consequence (or symptom) was to be widespread and deepening distrust of the political elite, fuelled by a succession of tales of sexual and financial impropriety which government action had failed to stop (Oliver 1995).[2] However, the 'Arms to Iraq' affair was not a case of sleaze. Rather, it threw an almost entirely different, wider set of allegations into play, which complemented the image of dishonesty and 'private government' that 'sleaze' had created. These allegations were of incompetence, corruption of the due process of law and systematic lying by ministers to parliament.

Exports to Iraq

The immediate trigger for the affair were export licence applications submitted to the government by a small Midlands engineering firm (Matrix Churchill Ltd) in March 1989, for the export of advanced lathes to munitions plants in Iraq. Given the Iraqi use of poison gas against Kurdish minorities at Halabja a year earlier, and the risk that sales of military equipment might enable the Iraqis to relaunch war in the region, trade with Iraq was highly sensitive. Government policy specifically forbade the export of 'equipment which would significantly enhance the capability' (Scott 1996: D3.60) of Saddam Hussein to breach the existing ceasefire in the region. Despite clear warnings that the lathes would be used to make shells and frequent claims in parliament that government guidelines forbade such exports, ministers nonetheless approved the licences for the lathes on 1 November 1989.[3]

The following year saw developments which were to harden opinion against *any* exports to Iraq and which significantly raised the stakes for any politician found to have enabled them. In February 1990 Iraq added to its reputation as a pariah state by executing a journalist from the liberal *Observer* newspaper. On 10 April 1990 British Customs & Excise officials made a sensational seizure of a quantity of metal pipes being exported to form part of an Iraqi 'Supergun' which was to be used to shell Israel (Trade and Industry Select Committee 1992). This provoked the first significant media attention paid to arms control issues (Negrine 1997) and sensitized the public to many of the issues which were subsequently to arise (see Figure 7.1). In August 1990 Iraq invaded Kuwait, threatening the West's oil supplies and complete destabilization in the Middle East.

These events served to galvanize Customs activity and, after a German tip-off, resulted in the arrest, on 16 October 1990, of three directors of Matrix Churchill Ltd on the grounds that they had exported to Iraq lathes 'specially designed' for arms manufacture and had failed to declare this on their applications to export. However, unknown to Customs, or the prosecuting counsel, two of the directors had been acting as agents for MI5, the British intelligence service, and had themselves been the source of some of the warnings the government had received. Following the arrest of the directors, a number of stories began to appear in the press. On 2 December 1990 an article in *The Sunday Times* alleged that the trade minister, Alan Clark, had been 'quietly helping British firms to arm Saddam [Hussein's] soldiers' (*The Sunday Times*, 2 December 1990). The article described in considerable detail a meeting between the minister and the Machine Tool Trade Association at which 'Clark told them that careful description of their exports should prevent them being caught by the embargo' (*ibid.*). The article, quoting a Foreign Office civil servant, said that 'everyone knew the equipment could be used

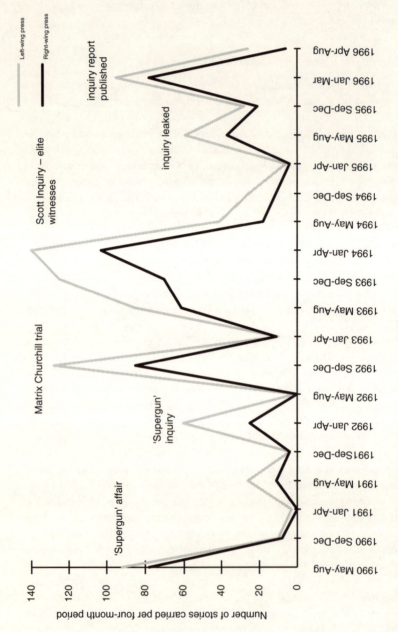

Figure 7.1 Media interest in the 'Arms to Iraq' affair by the right- and left-wing quality press in the UK,* 1990–96
Source: Clover Newspaper Index, Biggleswade: Clover Publications.
Note:
* right wing = *The Daily Telegraph, The Times, The Sunday Times*; left wing = the *Guardian*, the *Independent, The Observer*

for making shells' (*ibid.*). The paper followed with a further story in January, and on 14 April revealed that British intelligence services 'knew of British arms trade with Iraq' (*The Sunday Times*, 14 April 1990) because two of the three men charged with export offences were British spies providing intelligence about Iraqi procurement to M15. The formal charging of the three men, however, stifled further stories – under British law the matter became sub judice (meaning no further press coverage could take place until their trial began).

The defence lawyers for the three men subsequently requisitioned large numbers of government documents normally classified as secret, which they hoped would prove the government had connived at the exports and that their clients were spying for Britain. The government was reluctant to release the documents as they contained both advice given in confidence to ministers and information on espionage activities. Ministers had therefore signed Public Interest Immunity Certificates, which required the trial judge to assess whether the public interest in justice required release of the documents in open court. Against the background of public disquiet, such action smacked clearly of an attempted cover-up, particularly when the judge showed no hesitation in releasing most of the information the government had sought to keep secret. The defence lawyers were later to describe reading the secret papers as being like 'treading in a field of diamonds' (*The Daily Telegraph*, 11 November 1994).

But a debacle was to follow, on 9 November 1992 when the former trade minister took the witness stand. Under cross-examination he appeared to confirm the defence's case that he had encouraged manufacturers to be economical with the truth when applying for export licences. Given this new evidence of government encouragement for firms to evade export controls, counsel for the government advised that the case against the Matrix Churchill directors could not be proven, and the government withdrew. The trial collapsed in a blaze of pent-up media attention, with many papers across the political spectrum dubbing the affair 'Iraqgate', triggering sinister echoes. The media thus played an important role in concentrating public attention on the affair. At the same time, as Figure 7.1 shows, there was a marked divergence between the number of stories carried about the issue in the pro- and anti-government press, a divergence which was to be maintained throughout the affair.

Documents from the trial were by now circulating in parliament, seeming to confirm widespread allegations that there was a secret, more relaxed policy in existence for arms exports, other than that which had been announced to parliament. The opposition tabled a censure motion, and the government responded immediately by establishing a public inquiry under the auspices of Sir Richard Scott, QC. In doing so, their expectation was that an inquiry would take the matter off the political agenda and exonerate them (Bogdanor 1996; Norton-Taylor 1995).

The public inquiry

The establishment of the inquiry gave the government three important advantages: the rights to set the terms of reference of the inquiry, to appoint the chair and to agree the publicity arrangements for its report (Woodhouse 1995a). The terms of reference for the Scott inquiry, for example, precluded any examination of how the risk posed by Saddam Hussein had been so seriously underestimated or of whether the government's export control and arms sales policies were sensible or defensible, and concentrated instead on procedural issues.

Although the government approached the inquiry with some confidence, this confidence was to prove misplaced. This was partly due to the impossibility of explaining a policy on arms exports designed for the 1980s in the changed circumstances of the 1990s and partly due to serious weaknesses in the presentation of the government's case, weaknesses exacerbated by the procedures of the inquiry and the approach taken by its chair and counsel. By the mid 1990s there were good reasons to expect that inquiries chaired by judges might be more critical than in the past. 'Thatcherism' had found itself increasingly at loggerheads with the judiciary throughout the 1980s in its attempts to enhance executive power (Woodhouse 1995b). Sir Richard Scott had himself been involved in supporting challenges to the government in the earlier 'Spycatcher' case and hence had a reputation for independence.[4] The judge was to prove implacable in his pursuit of evidence of constitutional impropriety, at a time when the Conservative regime was particularly vulnerable to such an attack.

To expedite matters, the judge had truncated the procedures for the inquiry, but he had removed processes such as full legal representation and the right to cross-examination or to make verbal statements, which might have provided witnesses with the opportunity to present their cases more effectively. Ministers, including the prime minister and former prime minister, were obliged to submit to undignified grilling, stripped of the many advantages of parliamentary procedures and denied the strict time limits of the television studio or news conference. Civil servants, too, faced having to justify private advice or to explain detailed working practices. In the context of a largely secretive political system (Hennessy 1990: 344; Birkinshaw, 1997: 167) and a political elite which had held power more or less untrammelled for fourteen years, the experience was as unnerving for the participants as it was fascinating for the media (see Figure 7.1).[5]

Finally, in January 1994, the government launched the first of a series of overt attacks on the inquiry, with Sir Geoffrey Howe, a senior member of the government, denouncing it as an 'inquisition' (cf. Scott 1996: B2.41–2.46; Barker 1997b: 9). This was followed in the summer of 1994 by a number of leaks of critical passages of the draft inquiry report, just as press interest was beginning to wane. The government used this opportunity to redouble its attacks on the inquiry, which had the effect of refocusing press attention and further inflaming public curiosity as to the likely contents of the forthcoming inquiry report. Indeed, far from delay having defused the 'Arms to Iraq' affair, the prolonged wait for the inquiry report inspired public speculation that another cover-up was being planned, as the autumn of 1995 drew to a close in a climate of rumour, recrimination and counter-rumour, enhanced by the increased proximity of a general election.

The inquiry report and after

By January 1996 the argument had shifted to when and how publication of the inquiry report would take place. In the event, it was not until 15 February 1996 that the report was made public. Its main conclusions were that:

1   Ministers' 'failure to inform parliament [of changes in policy] was deliberate . . . the overriding and determinative reason was a fear of strong public opposition' (Scott 1996: D4.42). Indeed, Scott rejected as 'not even remotely tenable' (*ibid*.: D3.90) and as 'sophistry' (*ibid*.: D3.125) the government's defence that the guidelines for export control had merely been 'interpreted' rather than secretly changed.

2   'Lethal equipment and ammunition was not licensed for export to Iraq' during the Iran–Iraq war (Scott 1996: D2.361), but 'dual-use' equipment such as machine tools had been licensed, despite clear warnings that it would be used for military purposes.[6] Warnings were ignored for various reasons, including civil service errors, but Scott concludes that overall there was 'a lack of conviction shared by many sections of Government in the value of or need for this policy in so far as standard machine tools, and other goods freely obtainable from other western countries were concerned' (*ibid*.: D8.15).

3   The trial of the directors of Matrix Churchill was allowed to go ahead because the decision to prosecute was the responsibility of the independent Customs Agency, and because of errors by prosecuting counsel and a lack of supervision by the attorney-general.

4   The law on public interest immunity had been misunderstood by the attorney-general and, as a result, the government had risked denying the defence access to important documents. The attorney-general had also failed to pass on important reservations from the president of the Board of Trade to the trial judge about the use of the public interest immunity procedure in the case.

5   The legal basis of export controls was unsound, relying too heavily on ministers exercising delegated powers which were too broad and sanctioned only by outdated wartime legislation. Accountability for the enforcement of the law was unclear.

The report thus exonerated the government of those charges in the original censure motion which were of greatest concern to the ruling Conservative Party. As no 'arms' had apparently been approved for export and no deliberate strategy to send innocent men to jail or pervert the course of justice had been proven, they had less motivation to question the procedural background of decisions. However, the report had also clearly found against the government in other aspects, particularly on the dangerous issue of misleading parliament, and had revealed the practice to be much more widespread and systematic than the original allegations had supposed. It had also added other charges which had not been apparent at the time the inquiry was instituted, particularly those against the attorney-general and around the legal basis of export controls. More than this, the report was a damning indictment of a widespread culture of secrecy and of the weaknesses in accountability which followed from this. It is partly for these reasons that the government could claim to be exonerated of the main charges while the opposition claimed the opposite.

Debate on the inquiry report took place in parliament on 15 and 26 February 1996, with further exchanges at Prime Minister's Question Time. In the first day's debate the government had granted ordinary Members of Parliament (MPs) just ten minutes to read the 1806-page report, and hence were able to claim, inaccurately, that the inquiry report cleared ministers of intentionally misleading parliament, a claim echoed by the Conservative press. The government's defence also rested on showing that there were good reasons why parliament had not been given full information and on repeated assertions that their ministers had acted 'honourably'. Geoffrey Howe, for example, argued that there were 'powerful foreign policy reasons why any reformulation of policy could not be announced' (Scott 1996: D4.9). Ian Lang, in his opening defence, declared that 'Ministers believed they were avoiding a formal change to the guidelines, and in holding that belief they had, to quote his words [Sir Richard's], "no duplicitous intent"' (House of Commons Debates, 15 February 1996: 1143).[7] They were also inadvertently assisted by Sir Richard Scott himself, who refused to guide press coverage in any way, either by producing press summaries of what the report said or by answering detailed questions about it at the press conferences following publication (Negrine 1997: 38).

Professional opinion from some lawyers also backed the government's interpretation of the law on public interest immunity. More importantly, the fact that control of exports was shared between many departments, and hence that responsibility ultimately could not fall to any one minister, enabled the government to disperse opposition attempts to assign blame. Alan Clark, who had played a key role throughout, had announced his decision to retire from politics well before the publication of the report. (Although he did retire, he has since returned to the House of Commons as an MP.)

The result of the crucial vote on the censure motion was not a foregone conclusion, however. Although the executive has normally been able to rely on the support of parliament in key votes, assisted by the existence of stable and disciplined parliamentary majorities and the dependence of MPs on prime ministerial patronage for promotion, this support could no longer be relied upon. Indeed, since 1992 there had been a gradual erosion of the government's parliamentary majority and Conservative Party discipline. Combined, these turned the vote on the inquiry report into a crisis, by reducing the government's potential majority and making defeat on the issue seem possible. The approach of a general election had also added an extra incentive for the opposition Labour Party, already galvanized by new leadership under Tony Blair. However, paradoxically, this very weakness in the government's parliamentary position may have concentrated Conservative MPs' minds on the need for discipline, regardless of their personal feelings. When the censure motion was voted on, the government thus had a majority of one, and no resignations took place (Gray 1996: 104).

During the parliamentary debate the government had accepted recommendations that would clarify the accountability of those preparing future Customs prosecutions, and had commenced a review of public interest immunity and questions in parliament on defence-related matters. It also ordered better circulation of intelligence reports, and proposed that further discussion of ministerial accountability would take place in the Public Service Committee. After the debate the issue sank from view. When the committee reported, the government accepted its proposals in some areas, but rejected the most important suggestions for reform (Public Service Committee 1995–96; Cabinet Office 1996).[8]

There were thus some limited, but significant, procedural changes following the 'Arms to Iraq' affair, but these were accomplished largely invisibly, away from the glare of media attention.[9] One year after the publication of the inquiry report the *Guardian* was able to point out not only that the main ministers implicated in the affair were still in office, but that many of the civil servants involved had been promoted. Answers to parliamentary questions continued to restrict information on defence exports, and stories about arms exports to regimes and groups with pariah status continued to trickle out in the national press.[10] Ultimately, the Conservative government was defeated in the landslide election of May 1997. The incoming Labour government immediately announced its intention to 'moralize' the arms trade and to examine the options for new legislation on 'freedom of information'.

Understanding 'Arms to Iraq': competing explanations

The Scott account: flawed decisions and constitutional weakness

Within a 'rational-actor' framework the decisions of government are often seen as calculated responses to new threats, which are assessed by their 'benefits and costs in terms of strategic goals and objectives' (Allison 1971: 33). Thus, Sir Richard Scott ultimately traces export-control outcomes back to the government's competitive industrial strategy and its 'lack of conviction . . . in the value of . . . or need for policy in so far as standard machine tools freely available from other western countries were concerned' (Scott 1996: D 8.15). Secrecy about government policy is traced back to reasonable fears about the effect of publicity on the government's other objectives (*ibid.*: D 4.60). Throughout, the inquiry assumes that government is, and ought to be, a calculating and ultimately cohesive actor responding to threats as they arise.

Failures in government are then explained by 'errors' in decision-making, which tend to be thought of as exceptional, or at least controllable through sound management techniques. Sir Richard Scott's inquiry into the 'Arms to Iraq' affair largely shared this assumption. His method, relying on the pursuit of key decisions, through trails of internal memoranda, and the evidence of individual officials and ministers, had a predominant 'decisionist' focus. This focus dispersed responsibility amongst many actors, and offered a highly restricted view of the wider framework of commercial interests within which the UK arms trade was carried out (Pythian 1997). Instead it tended to highlight a number of classic weaknesses in information distribution, management supervision, and personal capacity. The intelligence system was 'unsatisfactorily haphazard' (Scott, 1996: D 2.287). 'Muddle' was accompanied by poor record keeping (Scott, 1996: F4.80), and poor communication (Scott, 1996: F3.88). Rules were either unclear (Scott, 1996: D 2.22), or applied with too great discretion (Scott, 1996: C 3.5). Alternatively, rules were so complex that officials had difficulty keeping up with the workload (Scott,1996: C2.19) and 'unacceptable negligence' occurred through long delays (Scott, 1996: D.6.70). These errors formed a complex, cumulative pattern, which enabled ministers to approve the disputed exports of machine tools to Iraq.

However, Sir Richard Scott also condemns a widespread culture of secrecy in his inquiry, and thus broadens his argument to include the absence of explicitly liberal, constitutional checks upon limited failures in rationality. He suggests that had policy been made more openly, with more accountability, such errors might have been corrected (Scott 1996: D4.52–4.63, K8.1–K 8.16). This 'constitutional weakness' explanation forms a second strand to Scott's arguments about the roots of failure in 'Arms to Iraq'. Indeed, such general weaknesses in the UK constitution and of the wider 'Thatcherite' institutional inheritance are frequently invoked by political scientists as an explanation for British policy disasters (Adonis *et al.* 1994; Dunleavy 1995; Rhodes 1988; Marsh and Rhodes 1994).

Evidence of an absence of checks on executive conduct may be widespread: in the system of ministerial responsibility which allows ministers and civil servants to escape sanction (Gray 1996; Dowding 1996); in the overriding and downgrading of impartial policy advice (Bogdanor 1997; Foster 1996; Wass 1996); in the conspicuous lack of collective working by cabinet, or other mechanisms for the oversight of the work of junior ministers; and in the use of party discipline to ensure that Conservative MPs supported the government at the close of the affair (Oliver 1996). Whether absence of these checks amounts to the weakness or strength of the policy process is, however, open to debate.[11]

Many features of such executive dominance have been in existence for a long time, yet have not repeatedly produced policy disasters on this scale. The system of executive decision described above was well established when the fatal licences to export lathes were issued, and the policy had, until then, seemed fairly successful in terms of the objectives of those who supported it. Although many observers are critical of the performance of the UK political system, few would seriously claim that the 1980s were a decade of disasters in all the major areas of public policy. Moreover, had the secret policy at the heart of the affair been made as critics suggest – with independent-minded civil servants, having access to all the warnings that were given, advising in sufficient number; by ministers who feared for their careers should things go wrong, and whose decisions were routinely checked by cabinet colleagues and subject to parliamentary scrutiny from independent minded MPs – there is every chance that an identical arms control policy would still have been pursued, given Conservative views about foreign and defence policy, and their parliamentary majority at the time.

Alternative explanation 1: bureaucratic politics

An alternative explanation for the affair sees it not as the result of errors in decision, but rather as the product of a largely irrational, indeterminate and fluid process of bureaucratic bargaining, in which the intentions of government are less important than the institutional advantages held by actors at specific stages of the game, and the specific interests they sought to advance (Allison 1971: 162–181; Gray and Jenkins 1985).[12]

'Arms to Iraq' was a long running affair involving many players inside and outside the government. 'Government' was not a unified actor, and the game, players and the problems they tackled changed as the affair unravelled. Policy emerged from 'compromise, conflict and confusion of officials with diverse interests and unequal influence' and from 'intricate and subtle, simultaneous, overlapping games among players located in positions in a government' (Allison 1971: 162). In its pursuit of key decisions and the intentions that underlay them, the Scott inquiry inadvertently produced evidence of a system that was quite different from that which would be expected from a rational-actor perspective.

Evidence for this view of the policy process is extremely widespread in the report of the inquiry – several sections summarize the various divergent positions adopted by key players and departments (Scott 1996: D.8.4–8.7, D 2.24). Specific policy episodes within the main story clearly show an iterative approach to policy, including the decision to relax the guidelines on exports (*ibid*.: D.3.1–3.65), later attempts at relaxation (*ibid*.: D3.152–D3.165) and discussion of the 'Hawk' aircraft project (*ibid*.: D6.1–D6.28). Deliberate, strategic decisions as such were extremely rare, in the sense that clear outcomes rarely emerged from the interactions among senior politicians and within the executive branch. The points at which policies changed were extremely hard to pinpoint. Policy had a number of distinct conflicting meanings to the participants, and emerged as an aggregation of many individual acts, rather than as a collective rational choice between clearly defined objectives.

However, the advantages enjoyed by participants varied greatly. Different players had very different views of the game they were playing. In the early stages of the affair, before it became public, powerful institutional legacies dominated decisions about export control and foreign policy issues. Within this overall context, decisions about export-control issues were taken low down in the bureaucratic hierarchy (Scott 1996: D1.118) or through processes of secret bargaining between interests in the Department of Trade and Industry, the Ministry of Defence and the Foreign Office (*ibid*.: D2.24, D8.4–8.7). Although informed by intelligence reports and by technical and diplomatic assessments, disputes ultimately would be adjudicated in an ad hoc manner by junior ministers, away from the glare of publicity and in a way which clearly reflected their interests. The inquiry's evidence on Alan Clark shows how a 'determined participant' was often able to swing these arguments in favour of exports. When Clark's role was altered through a ministerial reshuffle to one more closely connected to the main 'action channels', his power increased. However, even such powerful players faced limits on their actions; for example, on the occasions when Clark attempted to get approval for further relaxations of the rules or to clear particularly controversial exports, his bureaucratic opponents would organize to ensure he was overruled. 'On the occasions when . . . [an] agreement was referred to senior ministers or to the PM [prime minister], Mr Clark invariably lost' (*ibid*.: D3.134).

The Scott report summarizes the main stands taken by bureaucratic actors as follows: 'the core of the argument between the DTI [Department of Trade and Industry] and the FCO [Foreign and Commonwealth Office] . . . was throughout the question of whether the vital interests of trade, of exports and of employment in the UK should be set aside in deference to the various political, diplomatic and presentational concerns relied upon from time to time by the FCO' (Scott 1996: D2.24). Although the Department of Trade and Industry was responsible for export licensing, actual decisions about the granting of licences relied on extensive advice from the Ministry of Defence and the Foreign and Commonwealth office, where final decisions tended to be made.

Even within ministries, however, there was scope for disagreement. The Defence Export Sales Organization (DESO) in the Ministry of Defence had the role of both supporting arms sales abroad and assisting with advice on the approval of licence applications, which were handled by the Defence Export Services Secretariat (DESS). A separate Defence Intelligence Staff (DIS) provided intelligence which informed decision-making. In the Foreign and Commonwealth Office, the Middle East Desk (MED) dealt with Iran, Iraq and Saudi Arabia. The Foreign Office also maintained units dealing with arms control and disarmament (ACDD), science, energy and nuclear issues (SEND) and its own defence department, with links to the intelligence services (SIS). These formal departmental structures also included a number of important ad hoc interdepartmental committees, of which the Ministry of Defence Working Group (MODWG) and the Interdepartmental Committee (IDC) were probably the most important, as they considered most of the more problematic decisions about individual export licences before they were passed on to ministers. Other working groups included the Restricted Enforcement Unit (REU) and the Working Group on Iraqi Procurement (WGIP). The actual enforcement of export controls was the responsibility of the quasi-autonomous Commissioners of Customs & Excise. Here the investigation division (ID) carried out investigations, while the Solicitor's Office prepared prosecutions once instructed to do so by the Customs' Policy Division.

These complex relationships were therefore always vulnerable to problems of coordination, and decisions almost inevitably involved processes of bargaining and discussion between shifting groups of actors, depending on the particular issues being considered for decision. These problems of coordination were fully exposed as a result of the collapse of the Matrix Churchill trial.

'Arms to Iraq' was clearly not just a domestic affair, however. Nor was political bargaining restricted to the bureau-political networks of the state alone. The inquiry report shows some of the very complex, multiple interconnections between the main UK ministries and private industries involved, on the one hand, and, on the other, military, trade and diplomatic systems abroad. Complex deals were sometimes made which involved a combination of diplomatic, military and commercial objectives. There was a very real threat that some purchasing nations would withdraw from non-military contracts if military ones were not fulfilled. Moreover, those excluded from the arms trade could find innumerable ways to reorganize and evade controls by purchasing via third nations and acquiring ownership of firms specializing in advanced technologies, and by establishing their own production facilities for weapons (Krause 1992: 206–208).

This complexity was also reflected in the ease with which issues in one country were rapidly transferred to the domestic agenda in the UK – for example, decisions by Saddam Hussein to use gas against the Kurds at Halabja placed new pressures on the way in which arms controls were enforced. The state and its agencies therefore existed in an increasingly complex and rapidly changing web of dependency relationships which stretched well beyond its immediate boundaries.

The 'bureaucratic politics' explanation suffers from a number of weaknesses. First, it is unable to explain why and under what circumstances networks of relationships change, other than by referring to 'external' factors or to the resources and interests of participants, which themselves require explanation. Second, the focus of analysis of the bureaucratic politics model tends to disguise the distributional impact of policy outcomes in the wider society, and focuses instead on the outcomes for actors within the bureaucracy. Accounts from within a Marxist framework attempt to redress these weaknesses, by concentrating on wider structural relationships which inhibit or dominate the processes of decision, and on their outcomes.

Alternative explanation 2: dominant interests

Explanations in terms of institutional complexity, bargaining and mutual dependence serve to disguise the extent to which the outcomes of those decisions served to benefit the defence industry and their networks of industrial suppliers, despite a public face of government which declared its opposition to arms and arms-related exports to Iraq. According to neo-Marxist models of the state and the policy process, such an outcome can be explained by the existence of a class which 'owns and controls the means of production, and which is able by virtue of the economic power conferred upon it to use the state as its instrument for the domination of society' (Miliband 1969: 23). Support for this interpretation can easily be found in the case evidence. The defence sector in the UK employs 400,000 people, or 10 per cent of all manufacturing employment, and currently earns around £12 billion per year from arms sales, 40 per cent of which are from exports. Engineering firms such as Matrix Churchill are tied into this network through subcontracting and direct work on military contracts. The Ministry of Defence has close contacts with the defence industry, with around 400 applications per year received from ministry personnel to join the industry, and one company alone receiving 2,000 government contracts in one year (Cooper 1996).

Military production in the UK is still heavily subsidized, the subsidies in the form of export guarantees. The industry is powerfully organized and is dominated by a small number of large firms, many of whom are donors to Conservative Party funds. Despite cuts in defence spending, an increasingly 'efficiency conscious' approach to procurement by government and a decline in demand for weapons as a result of the end of the Cold War, direct influence in government remains high (Dunleavy 1990: 42–43). Indeed the 1980s saw the increasing involvement of high-level state actors in the establishment of 'mega-deals' with foreign governments whose primary aim was to maintain the UK's defence capacity through an aggressive approach to exports. Such deals included the Al Yamanah contract with Saudi Arabia and the Pergau Dam contract with Malaysia.

Evidence from the Scott inquiry clearly showed the intermingling of staff concerned with the regulation of arms exports and those concerned with promoting arms sales, sometimes on the same committees. Indeed, some observers have suggested that the main motivation throughout discussion of arms controls was to preserve the UK's arms industry from the effects of adverse publicity, rather than to restrict its sales (Cooper 1996; Norton-Taylor 1995). The failures of regulation examined by the Scott inquiry therefore seem less a matter of individual error, lack of checks on government or inherently complex, fragile systems than the result of an interpenetration of the state by military and commercial interests which renders its attempts at arms control ineffective.

There are, nevertheless, important limits to this type of analysis. The state did successfully accomplish some regulatory functions vis-à-vis the arms industry (Scott 1996: D2.194–D2.435). For one, it succeeded in bankrupting Matrix Churchill. Moreover, the core institutions of the state were not merely the playthings of economic interests, but played a vital role in re-establishing legitimacy. The prime minister, as we have seen, was portrayed by important elements of the media as being 'above' the affair; there were heated debates in parliament, and an inquiry which showed a marked degree of independence.

Conclusions

The objectives of many of the policies which underlay 'Arms to Iraq' may largely have been achieved. The affair was therefore not so much a programme failure as a complex political disaster, with many interrelated dimensions. The brief summary of the case details will inevitably have obscured or ignored some features of the disaster while exaggerating others. To reduce the possibility of biased explanation, initial analysis of the affair has been taken from three contrasting perspectives, each of which is representative of a major tradition in disaster analysis. We have therefore attempted to give, if not the full picture, one which is rounded by the possibility of alternative viewpoints. Although space has prevented a fuller exposition of each of these, and although such an approach can be criticized from a number of positions (Bovens and 't Hart 1996: 116), it has nonetheless served to illustrate some of the initial effects upon analysis of using different approaches, and some specific features of this case.

It is clear that neither interpretations of the affair in terms of the government's flawed decision-making and constitutional weakness nor interpretations of 'bureaucractic politics' alone provide a complete explanation. Such predominantly state-centred theories, as we have seen, have a limited focus. Marxist theory, by contrast, attempts to integrate explanations at a number of different levels, but, in so doing, itself suffers from a number of well-known weaknesses.

Each perspective, however, illustrates that government is seriously constrained by circumstances such as those surrounding the 'Arms to Iraq' affair. It is therefore open to question whether at any time better alternative policies were available. In any event the inquiry into the affair was not asked to seek an answer to this potentially more important question, and chose not to do so.

Notes

1 Polls in the *Guardian* showed that 74 per cent of those who had followed the inquiry thought ministers should resign, while 55 per cent believed the government had attempted to pervert the course of justice by engaging in a cover-up (ICM polls). A similar poll in the *The Sunday Times* on 18 February 1996 showed that amongst former supporters of the Conservative Party a ten-to-one majority wanted key ministers to resign.

2 In Britain, poll evidence showed a major long-term decline in confidence in governing institutions, with 48 per cent of the population in 1973 believing 'the sytem works well', 33 per cent in 1991 and only 22 per cent in 1995 (Dunleavy and Weir 1995: 67); and a similar decline in respect for Members of Parliament (Mortimore 1995: 39).

3 In all, thirty-one separate warnings about different aspects of Iraqi weapons procurement were available to the government in the period November 1988 to July 1990 (Scott 1996: D5.25). The immediate reasons for allowing the Matrix Churchill exports to proceed were: to protect the Matrix Churchill directors, who were supplying intelligence to the government; for contractual reasons; and to protect employment in the firms affected. The briefings ministers were given also did not make sufficiently clear the fact that the machine tools were destined for military uses (*ibid.*: D6.107–D6.193).

4 In the 'Spycatcher' case the government had sought to prevent the publication of the memoirs of Peter Wright, a former MI5 agent.

5 In the period May 1993 to May 1994, when key elite witnesses appeared before the inquiry, some 677 stories were carried by the 'quality' national press, including 60 on the front page, more than one-quarter of all such stories about 'Arms to Iraq' (*Clover Newspaper Index*).

6   However, using material from the inquiry report itself, Pythian illustrates a different conclusion: that many arms are likely to have reached Iraq from Britain via diversionary routes (Pythian 1997: 42).

7 The phrase 'no duplicitous intent' used in the inquiry report in fact refers to ministers' evidence to the inquiry, not their approach to parliament (Scott 1996: D3.124).

8 The government agreed that the number of refusals by ministers to answer parliamentary questions should be monitored annually, with a right of appeal for MPs refused answers. It rejected calls for new powers for Parliamentary Select Committees and for changes to the existing conventions of ministerial responsibility.

9 The government later admitted that they had been wrong to risk keeping evidence back from open court solely because the evidence fell into a category of information normally labelled secret.

10 See the *Guardian*, 21 January 1997, 11 March 1997, 13 March 1997.

11 The counter-argument to this view is the so-called 'Whitehall' model, which suggests that effective government requires a degree of executive dominance. The foreign secretary, for example, argued that 'A minister might in theory act as Sir Richard [Scott] appears to wish him to act. . . . In practice a minister who acted this way would not last long' (Hurd 1997: 11).

12 Allison's 'bureaucratic politics' paradigm analyses government action as 'resultant of political bargaining among a number of independent players' (Allison 1971: 162). Players tackle 'complex problems in which differences about goals, alternatives and consequences are inevitable', and hence solutions 'result from compromise, conflict and confusion of officials with diverse interests and unequal influence' (*ibid.*). Business proceeds 'neither at random nor at leisure', and decisions are often 'really agglomerations of relatively independent decisions and action by individuals and groups of players' (*ibid.*: 164). Players use their bargaining advantages, skill and will in the game. Influence, however, is also related to position, and the best positions are those attached to 'action channels', which are defined as a 'regularized means of taking governmental action on a specified issue' (*ibid.*: 169). Government action is thus 'rarely intended by any individual or group', though certain groups may 'win' particular games (*ibid.*: 175). Some features of Allison's 'organizational process' model may also apply, particularly the conception of government as a 'conglomerate of semi-feudal, loosely allied organizations, each with a substantial life of its own' (*ibid.*: 67), and the use of some 'standard operating procedures' by departments to handle uncertainty.

References

Adonis, A., Butler, D. and Travers, T. (1994) *Failure in British Government: The Politics of the Poll Tax*, Oxford: Oxford University Press.

Allison, G. T. (1971) *Explaining the Cuban Missile Crisis*, Boston, MA: Little Brown.

Barker, A. (1997a) 'Practising to deceive: Whitehall, arms exports and the Scott inquiry', *Political Quarterly* 68(1): 41–50.

—— (1997b) 'The inquiry's procedures', *Parliamentary Affairs* 50(1): 9–26.

Birkinshaw, P. (1997) 'Freedom of information', *Parliamentary Affairs* 50(1): 166–189.

Bogdanor, V. (1996) 'The Scott report', *Public Administration* 74(4): 593–612.

—— (1997) 'Ministerial accountability', *Parliamentary Affairs* 50(1): 71–83.

Bovens, M. and 't Hart, P. (1996) *Understanding Policy Fiascoes*, New Brunswick: Transaction.

Buller, J. (1996) 'Foreign and defence policy under Thatcher and Major', in S. Ludlam and M. J. Smith *Contemporary British Conservatism*, Basingstoke: Macmillan.

Cabinet Office (1996) *Government Response to the Second Report from the Committee on Ministerial Accountability and Responsibility* (HC67), 5 November, London: HMSO.

Clover Newspaper Index (1990–96) vols 8–18, Biggleswade: Clover Publications.

Cooper, N. (1996) 'Understanding Arms to Iraq', paper presented to the Conference on Policy Disasters, University of Luton, 1 May.

Cooper, N., Dunne, P. and Smith, R. (1996) *Killing Jobs: Arms Trade, Economy and Unemployment*, London: Campaign Against the Arms Trade.

Doig, A. (1995) 'From Lynskey to Nolan: the corruption of British politics and public service?', *Journal of Law and Society* 23(1): 36–56.

Doig, A. and Ridley, F. (eds) (1995) *Sleaze: Politicians, Private Interests and Public Reaction*, Oxford: Oxford University Press.

Dowding, K. (1996) *The Civil Service*, London and New York: Routledge.

Dunleavy, P. (1990) 'Reinterpreting the Westland affair: theories of the state and core executive decision making', *Public Administration* 68: 29–60.

—— (1995) 'Policy disasters: explaining the UK's record', *Public Policy and Administration* 10(2): 52–70.

Dunleavy, P. and Weir, S. (1995) 'Media, opinion and the constitution', in A. Doig and F. Ridley (eds) *Sleaze: Politicians, Private Interests and Public Reaction*, Oxford: Oxford University Press.

Foster, C. (1996) 'Reflections on the true significance of the Scott report for government accountability', *Public Administration* 74(4): 567–592.

Gray, P. (1996) 'When the minister won't resign', *Talking Politics* 9(2): 100–106.

Gray, A. and Jenkins, W. (1985) *Administrative Politics in British Government*, Brighton: Wheatsheaf Books.

Heidenheimer, A. J., Johnston, M. and Levine, V. T. (eds) (1989) *Political Corruption: A Handbook*, New Brunswick and Oxford: Transaction.

Hennessy, P. (1990) *Whitehall*, London: Fontana.

Hurd, D. (1997) 'The whig illusion', *Prospect* 16: 10–12.

Keller, W. W. (1995) *Arm in Arm: The Political Economy of the Arms Trade*, New York: Basic Books.

Krause, K. (1992) *Arms and the State: Patterns of Military Production and Trade*, Cambridge: Cambridge University Press.

Levi, M. and Nelken, D. (1996) 'The corruption of politics and the politics of corruption: an overview', *Journal of Law and Society* 23(1): 1–17.

Markovits, A. S. and Silverstein, M. (1988) *The Politics of Scandal: Power and Process in Liberal Democracies*, New York and London: Holmes & Meier.

Marsh, D. and Rhodes, R. A. W. (eds) (1994) *Implementing Thatcherite Policies*, Milton Keynes: Open University Press.

Miliband, R. (1969) *The State in Capitalist Society*, New York: Basic Books.

Mortimore, R. (1995) 'Politics and public perceptions', in A. Doig and F. Ridley (eds) *Sleaze: Politicians, Private Interests and Public Reaction*, Oxford: Oxford University Press.

Negrine, R. (1997) 'The inquiry's media coverage', *Parliamentary Affairs* 50(1): 27–40.

Norton-Taylor, R. (1995) *Truth is a Difficult Concept: Inside the Scott Inquiry*, London: Fourth Estate.

Office for National Statistics (1997) *Annual Abstract of Statistics*, London: HMSO.

Oliver, D. (1995) 'The Nolan Committee', in A. Doig and F. Ridley (eds) *Sleaze: Politicians, Private Interests and Public Reaction*, Oxford: Oxford University Press.

—— (1996) 'The Scott report', *Public Law*, autumn: 357–368.

Public Service Committee (1995–96) *Ministerial Accountability and Responsibility: Second Report of the Select Committee on Public Services* (HC313), London: HMSO.

Pythian, M. (1997) 'The arms trade', *Parliamentary Affairs* 50(1): 40–54.

Rhodes, R. A. W. (1988) *Beyond Westminster and Whitehall*, London: Unwin Hyman.

Scott, Sir Richard (1996) *Inquiry into Exports of Defence Equipment and Dual-use Goods to Iraq and Related Prosecutions* (HC 115), London: HMSO.

Seymour-Ure, C. (1996) *The British Press and Broadcasting Since 1945*, 2nd edition, Oxford: Blackwell.

Tomkins, A. (1996) 'The Scott report: the hope and failure of Parliament', *Political Quarterly* 67(4): 349–353.

Trade and Industry Select Committee (1992) *Export to Iraq: Project Babylon and Long Range Guns* (HC86), London: HMSO.

Trust for Education and Research on the Arms Trade (1992) *Count the Cost: The Economic Effects of the Arms Trade*, London.

Wass, D. (1996) 'Scott and Whitehall', *Public Law*, autumn: 461–471.

Woodhouse, D. (1995a) 'Matrix Churchill: a case study in judicial inquiries', *Parliamentary Affairs* 8(1): 24–39.

—— (1995b) 'Politicians and the judiciary: a changing relationship', *Parliamentary Affairs* 48(3): 423–440.

8

IN DEFENCE OF THE SWEDISH CROWN

From triumph to tragedy and back?

Eric Stern and Bengt Sundelius

Introduction

Late August and September of 1992 was a period of great turbulence for the major European currencies, many of which fell like dominoes under intense waves of speculation. Heavy pressure provoked the devaluation of the British pound, the Finnish mark, the Spanish peseta and the Italian lira in quick succession. The National Bank of Sweden, in partnership with the government and the Social Democratic opposition, withstood the onslaught of the international money managers. The most memorable moment of that episode was the afternoon of Wednesday, 16 September, when the National Bank signalled its firm intention to defend the fixed value of the Swedish krona (crown) by raising the overnight marginal intervention rate to the astounding level of 500 per cent, where it remained until Monday, 21 September. The guardians of Swedish financial credibility weathered that storm and maintained their aspirations for the krona's classification as one of the few remaining 'hard' currencies of world finance. Sweden had earned its place in the 'financial A-team of Europe' as a result of this major achievement, claimed the triumphant prime minister, Carl Bildt (cited in Hempel 1993: 168).

Yet, just two months later, the krona was once again under assault. Some 160 billion Swedish krona (around US$29 billion) in foreign currency had fled the country. The foreign currency reserves of the small nation, estimated at 177 billion krona, were rapidly being depleted by defensive measures. At 2.15 p.m. on 19 November the head of the National Bank, Bengt Dennis, phoned the conservative prime minister to inform him of the independent bank board's painful decision. At 2.28 p.m. the National Bank announced a discontinuation of the Swedish krona's tie to the Ecu, leaving the krona floating freely for the first time since 1933. The Swedish currency market closed thirty minutes later. By then, the currency had dropped by 10 per cent, and over the next few days it fell a total of some 20 per cent.

In an afternoon news conference, the prime minister and the finance minister, Anne Wibble, expressed their deep regrets about the outcome of this crisis of financial confidence. Their non-socialist, four-party, minority government had been firmly committed to the fixed-rate policy for a variety of political and macroeconomic reasons, which will be discussed below. Bildt did not mince words, referring to the free float as 'a failure . . . that . . . should be called a failure' (press conference, 19 November 1992).[1] Scapegoating began the very same afternoon, with an exchange of press releases between the major parties. The following Sunday Bildt gave his version in an article in the influential daily *Svenska Dagbladet* (22 November 1992). He pointed to 'overpowering' international pressures and the irresponsibility of his erstwhile collaborators, and to the Social Democratic opposition as the main culprits. They were described as having 'thrown in the towel' (*ibid.*). In a simultaneous salvo in the competing morning newspaper, *Dagens Nyheter* (22 November 1992), the Social Democratic shadow finance minister, Allan Larsson, pointed an accusing finger at the alleged shortcomings of the incumbent government's policies. He explained his party's participation in the September austerity measures by pointing to the necessity of building international confidence in Swedish financial stability. He then went on to argue that 'this time there were no such international factors. The currency crisis of the past week was caused by internal conditions for which the conservative-led cabinet is responsible' (*Dagens Nyheter*, 22 November 1992).

Two competing explanations of the 19 November shock were thus presented. One focused on the constraints placed upon the government by global financial market pressures. The other targeted domestic factors; for example, the economic policies of the sitting government causing business to lose faith in the capacity of the Bildt government to manage the large Swedish public debt, control rising interest rates and bring down unemployment. In this chapter both these interpretations will be discussed. We shall argue that each provides insights into the defence and ultimate fall of the krona but fails to explain fully the different choices made by key actors in September and in November, despite the fact that the structural features of the international market and domestic political arena were largely similar. Therefore, a third and complementary line of explanatory logic will be added here: cognitive and policy processes contributed significantly to facilitating the multi-partisan defence of the fixed currency in September and the lack of such a multi-partisan consensus in November. Our analysis suggests that differential perception, deliberation and learning processes among the key actors over the course of this policy crisis provide important clues in understanding the differences between these successive episodes (cf. Stern and Sundelius 1997).

A policy disaster?

Before moving into the details of this case, we should pose the question of whether the float of the krona qualifies as a policy disaster. There are definite grounds for reflection here. Although the post hoc public debate focused heavily on the failure to achieve the official policy goal of keeping the currency value fixed, in retrospect one may ask if the most disastrous element of the September–November ordeal was the free float and de facto devaluation of 19 November or the massive and ultimately futile investment, at the public's expense, to maintain a fixed currency level at any cost. The defence of the krona, particularly the last stand on 18–19 November, proved especially costly to a government already heavily in debt. Figures released four years later by the National Bank indicate that the three-month defence effort involved purchases of Swedish currency to a value of 250 billion krona. In the final two days of the ordeal 81 billion krona were purchased (*Dagens Nyheter*, 5 November 1992). This investment in financial credibility cost the government between 25 and 95 billion krona in direct depreciation losses after the event. This staggering amount can be compared to the annual defence appropriation of that time of around 39 billion krona. Thus, the vigilant defence of the krona may have cost the Swedish taxpayers almost three times their annual investment in more traditional forms of national defence. From a public-expenditure perspective, it could be argued that this was disproportionate.

The question of whether a given dramatic and seemingly largely negative policy episode should be termed a fiasco or a disaster is deceptively complicated. Recent contributions to the literature suggest that the term must be used in a rigorous and yet relatively broad-based fashion if biases are to be minimized. Otherwise the concept is of limited utility as a basis for sound empirical research and theorizing (Bovens and 't Hart 1996; Shiels 1991). In this vein Gray (1996: 77) has identified a number of elements which together constitute a preliminary set of criteria for identifying policy disasters, partly drawn from Bovens and 't Hart's criteria discussed elsewhere in this volume. The Swedish currency crisis (September–November 1992) will now be assessed in the light of these seven criteria.

1   *Failure against implicit and explicit objectives*: it is very clear that the float on 19 November was contrary to the explicitly stated objectives of the relevant set of political and administrative actors. Not only the coalition partners in the Bildt-led government, but also the leaders of the Social Democratic opposition explicitly favoured maintenance of the fixed value. The same was true of the Swedish National Bank, and no sustained objections to this policy line had been articulated by local economists. The actors in the crisis demonstrated their commitment to the fixed currency by their resort to, and political support of, drastic interventions and austerity measures in defence of the krona during the September episode and its aftermath.

2   *Perception as 'disastrous' by a wide range of opinion*: prior to the float, the consensus among political elites and leading economists (with only a few notable exceptions) was that another Swedish devaluation would be disastrous in the light of its track record in that respect. Afterwards, the float was portrayed as a very serious failure by both government and opposition, who blamed each other for the inability to stay the course. Ironically, but not atypically – as a number of studies have shown – perceptions of such dramatic episodes may change

radically over time (e.g. Bovens and 't Hart 1996; Stern 1997). In the aftermath of this crisis, the dominant frame did indeed shift. The consensus five years later seems to be that the float of the krona has had a largely positive impact on the Swedish economy, proving conducive to export-driven growth and economic recovery. Nor has it been possible to find tangible evidence of credibility 'dividends' for Sweden, such as lower commercial interest rates compared to those offered to Finland, which capitulated to market pressures earlier, on 9 September (Lundgren and Söderström 1995). From this line of thinking it was not the fall in the value of the currency that was disastrous, but rather the lengths to which the cabinet, the opposition leaders, and the National Bank were prepared to go to defend the policy.

3   *Falling short of what is achievable, even from a pessimistic viewpoint*: here one might argue that Sweden could have saved the fixed value of the krona in November if only the Social Democrats had stood shoulder to shoulder with the cabinet, as they had done in the intimate all-night sessions of September. However, this view would entail a certain amount of optimism regarding Sweden's prospects of convincing a very sceptical financial market of its determination and, even more importantly, its capacity to withstand speculative attacks. This is reminiscent of counterfactual debates (see Tetlock and Belkin 1996) in the USA over whether the Vietnam War could have been won, if only the military had been given a free hand. From a more pessimistic viewpoint, it seems that by November the prospects were not good for Sweden, given the weak fiscal and financial situation of the government. From this point of view, too, it is the last stand in defence of the krona at exorbitant cost which becomes a candidate for the label 'disastrous'.

4   *Intensive or extensive disruption to social and political processes*: the currency turbulence during the autumn of 1992 created dramatic political, economic and social disruption. Dealing with this crisis and justifying various sacrifices and compromises to key constituencies became a tense endeavour, which crowded out other potentially important issues to be dealt with by central policymakers. For citizens at large, the impact of the crisis was widely felt due to painful hikes in variable-rate mortgages and through government austerity packages, including cuts in various benefits. For major banks and industries, high stakes were involved, as financial holdings had to be moved as turbulent events unfolded. In fact, as part of the September crisis it was deemed necessary to issue a government bank guarantee to save Swedish banks from bankruptcy due to severe losses from poor investments (Renius 1996).

5   *Significant loss of control*: participant accounts of the crisis-management efforts emphasize the sense of helplessness experienced by many insiders. The financial leverage of the small state was overwhelmed by the waves of speculation in the global currency marketplace. There was a dramatic asymmetry between the financial resources available to the relatively short-changed government and National Bank, and the massive sums moved by independent currency traders. The removal of national financial controls during the wave

of deregulations in the late 1980s greatly affected the government's ability to withstand the whims of the market. The Swedish finance minister at the time, Anne Wibble, later testified to her sense of acute vulnerability and impotence as she experienced how market forces could take control of the small nation's financial destiny (Wibble 1994: 39).

6   *Meets criteria of foreseeability/avoidability*: a plausible case can be made that the fall in the value of the krona was inevitable in the light of developments in the international financial system, the obvious weaknesses in the Swedish economy and, not least, the fates of peer countries with relatively sounder finances, which had already succumbed. Aside from the currencies mentioned above which fell prior to the krona, even Norway with its enormous financial reserves and oil holdings bowed to the international pressure and floated its currency shortly after the Swedish fall. From this sobering perspective, the de facto devaluation was foreseeable but not avoidable. The question for the policy-makers remained whether to go down fighting, to build international financial credibility for the future or, instead, to capitulate in the face of over-whelming pressures and instead minimize losses at home.

7   *Events must appear to be substantially traceable to the actions or inaction of policy-makers*: the dramatic defence effort in September, involving interest rates of 500 per cent (derided by many foreign observers as foolhardy), was clearly the result of determined joint action by policy-makers. If more determined political action in November would have made the difference, one could argue – as did some of the participants after the event – that the fall stemmed from lack of will or solidarity on the part of political rivals. Alternatively, one could argue that while the float may have been inevitable, the dramatic costs incurred by Swedish taxpayers during the 'last stand' in November stemmed largely from the actions and inaction of policy-makers (Shiels 1991: 2). Thus, the timing and the costs of the defence of the krona at least – if not the ultimate result of the ordeal – can certainly be traced to the behaviour of Swedish policy-makers. Thus there are grounds for labelling the episode a policy disaster in this respect as well.

The 'external constraints' interpretation

In the field of security policy, national postures are commonly explained by refer-ence to the enduring structures of the international system (Waltz 1979). According to Andrews this logic can be extended also to the sphere of national monetary policy: 'Capital mobility is fully consistent with Waltz's underlying conception of a structural feature of international politics: a constraining condi-tion which rewards certain behaviors and punishes others' (Andrews 1994: 202). We will now explore how the international economic context severely limited the autonomy of Swedish actors and institutions.[2]

In the autumn of 1992 the guardians of Swedish financial stability and actors across the political spectrum were united in their desire to maintain and even improve Swedish economic credibility abroad. Instead of a potentially hostile neighbouring country, the adversary in this crisis was perceived to be the diffuse and increasingly globalized 'market', which became a key target of signalling efforts and interventions. As in military confrontations, secrecy and strategic precision were deemed to be of the utmost importance so as not to undermine the defence effort with a misstep, miscommunication or an intelligence leakage (Angel 1991: 269).

The Swedish confrontation with the international money traders can be understood in the context of the parallel currency crises in progress at that time in several other European countries. A primary focus for the National Bank of Sweden over this three-month period was the aim of convincing the market of its determination to hold the fixed currency against private speculation on a forthcoming depreciation. This confidence-building strategy was also pursued by France, in collaboration with the German Bundesbank. While the British pound and most other European currencies suffered depreciations in September, the franc maintained its pegged value as a result of this assertive strategy. During this period the National Bank and the Swedish cabinet engaged in various carefully synchronized confidence-building measures.

In a sense Swedish policy-makers played a game of 'chicken' with the international money dealers, and in September they appeared to have won.[3] At that time they raised the costly marginal overnight interbank rate inducement all the way to the dramatic 500 per cent level. They also secured an international loan guarantee of 16 billion Ecu on 9 September, with a possibility of doubling that amount. In November Swedish actors once again intervened heavily in trading, covering up the heavy outflow through short-term credit manipulations. They even unsuccessfully attempted to link the krona formally to the Exchange Rate Mechanism (ERM) in order to gain access to the bilateral currency support facilities of the European Monetary System (EMS) (Cameron 1993: 33; *Dagens Nyheter*, 5 November 1996). Two-thirds of the direct cost of the entire effort was incurred during the final days of the November ordeal (Lundgren and Söderström 1995: 200; *Dagens Nyheter*, 5 November 1996).

The delicate relationship with the international market was managed alongside another important political arena. The coalition cabinet was involved in secret negotiations with the leadership of the Social Democratic opposition party. Efforts were launched to build a multi-partisan consensus in favour of austerity packages demonstrating a broad parliamentary base for dealing with the minority government's growing budget deficit, reducing the domestic cost level and improving the international competitiveness of Swedish industry.

This domestic political process was seen as part of the confidence-building effort directed at the international money markets. The head of the National Bank, Bengt Dennis, was active in both spheres, positioned in a vital linchpin role in the policy network. At crucial junctures Dennis was asked to diagnose the situation and assess the market's response to particular austerity measures, providing him with agenda-setting and virtual veto power during the crisis negotiations.

Like its French counterpart, the Swedish political leadership was acutely aware of the symbolic importance of maintaining the fixed value of the national currency (cf 't Hart 1993). Demonstrating Sweden's resolve was seen as a way of proving the country a worthy partner in European economic and political cooperation. This concern was all the more acute for the leaders of the coalition government, given Sweden's record as a notorious devaluer. Several major devaluations of the krona had taken place during previous periods of non-socialist government (1976–82). The Social Democrats initiated an even larger and more surprising devaluation immediately upon regaining power in October 1982 (Jonung 1991; KU 1996–97). All the principal actors were very conscious of Sweden's image problem with peer countries and the market, a credibility problem which could be greatly exacerbated by another weak performance in 1992.

The then finance minister, Anne Wibble, later noted that 'the market has a long memory and does not forget those nations which devaluate themselves out of problems' (Wibble 1994: 34). This had been pointed out by her Belgian colleagues, who still felt they were paying for earlier mistakes. The key to success in the long term was to build international credibility the hard way, i.e. through a steadfast deterrence strategy aimed at punishing those that gambled on another Swedish devaluation. Carl Bildt's triumphant press statement on 30 September – 'Those who have speculated [on a devaluation] can consider themselves badly burned' (quoted in Hempel 1993: 166) – should be understood in these terms. His public declaration of a policy fiasco on 19 November, following a failed attempt at a repeat performance, must be understand in the context of the previous 'triumph'.

The 'domestic politics' interpretation

The 'international imperative' in defence of the krona was buttressed by domestic and party-political interests as well. David Cameron (1993) has focused on these latter dimensions in his analysis of the British and French responses to the turbulence of 1992–93 (see also Thompson 1996). In Sweden, as well, the relationships between the various political parties must be included if one is to understand the different outcomes of September and November. Particularly interesting are the apparent links between the actions at the domestic level and the outwardly directed behaviour analysed above. The Swedes were engaged in a form of double-edged diplomacy, playing in several critical arenas simultaneously (Evans *et al.* 1993).

The Swedish cabinet, particularly the Conservative Party and some factions of the Liberal Party, were intent upon cutting back the overextended Swedish state. The 'European argument' – that the approach to the European Community demanded public-spending retrenchments – became a powerful weapon in this domestic endeavour.[4] The austerity measures which, in tandem with the National Bank's manipulation of marginal interest rates, became a prime weapon in defending the currency were actually quite palatable to several (though not all) of the factions within the coalition government. The pro-austerity factions were thus able to exploit the crisis to pursue their domestic political agenda. The political stress generated by the crisis tended to soften resistance from factions opposed to the cuts, allowing them to blame 'the market' for these sacrifices in the name of national solidarity. Thus, in addition to posing serious threats to the international credibility of the state, the crisis should be seen as presenting an opportunity for many of the actors to advance preferred policies (Morse 1973; Kingdon 1984).

For the leading figures in the cabinet, for the most part, announcing and explaining the expenditure-reducing side of the multi-partisan austerity packages to the party grass roots was not an unpleasant task. For the Social Democratic leadership, on the other hand, selling the results of their collaboration to the rest of the party was a formidable, and at times painful, task, since in Wibble's subsequent observations 'the Social Democrats [had] signed up to a rather bourgeois policy' (Wibble 1994: 33).

In particular, the second September crisis package (which included, among other measures, the removal of two holidays for blue-collar employees) was difficult to swallow for large parts of the Social Democratic Party. For example, an influential Social Democratic union leader, Leif Blomberg, made use of a soccer metaphor to describe the package, suggesting that his party leader, Ingvar Carlsson, had kicked an unstoppable ball right into the corner of his own team's goal (Hempel 1993: 169). Aware of the painful effects on his constituents of high interest rates, which he regarded as being more harmful even than the cut in holidays, Carlsson defended the policy in the following terms: 'We are doing this to save jobs. I wouldn't have been able to look the voters in the eye if I didn't know that I had done all I could, and instead stood on the sidelines' (quoted in *ibid.*: 169).

If this 'domestic window of opportunity' interpretation helps to account for the Conservative-led government's response, the question remains why the Social Democratic opposition supported the policy. A partial answer is that the Social Democratic Party leadership was able to exploit the crisis in a similar fashion. Prior to his election defeat in September 1991, the then prime minister, Ingvar Carlsson, had initiated several domestic reforms aimed at liberalizing the Swedish economy. For example, national controls on international money flows, such as investments or capital transfers, had been dismantled (Svensson 1996). In May 1991, the krona was pegged to the Ecu and was widely seen as being an informal party to the EMS (KU 1996/97).[5]

The Social Democrat's fixed-krona policy was buttressed also by the party's newfound commitment to European integration. The intent to apply for EC membership was first announced on 26 October 1990, as part of a reform package sparked by an acute domestic economic crisis. This politically and economically highly significant redirection towards becoming a committed, rather than reluctant, European partner had been initiated by the previous Carlsson government (Sundelius 1994). The new foreign policy orientation was aggressively pursued by the centre-right government, led by Carl Bildt, which took office in October 1991 (Miles 1996). Thus a shared appreciation of the importance of European integration was in place across the Swedish government–opposition divide in 1992.

Within the Social Democratic Party this recent development was not unrctroversial, however. Throughout the 1980s a 'war of the roses', largely over fiscal and monetary policy, had been fought between the left and the right wings of that party. [6] The party establishment by and large represented the right, while the rank and file and parts of the trade unions represented the left. At its height, this rift led to the dramatic resignation of the Carlsson cabinet in February 1990, only for them to be reappointed following the resignation of a frustrated minister of finance, Kjell Olof Feldt.[7] He was replaced by Allan Larsson, who as shadow finance minister became a key actor in the 1992 dealings.

Larsson revealed his own inclinations in a public appeal on 24 August 1992 in which he called for 'national unity' across party lines in order to deal with the government's ballooning budget deficit, record unemployment and severe problems in the banking sector. At a closed meeting of the party's Executive Committee on 4 September Larsson argued in favour of working together with the minority coalition government in order to avoid being seen as a party without economic competence and as refusing to take responsibility for the economic well-being of the nation (Assarson 1996: 110). This posture of active participation, responsibility and influence, as opposed to a more passive and critical opposition role, was by then the preferred party strategy of Carlsson and the party secretary, Mona Sahlin, as well. Thus, the top leadership of the Social Democratic Party had articulated a clear disposition in favour of working with the cabinet to restore the economy well before the currency crisis hit them with full force on 16 September. The mounting crisis atmosphere served to provide additional political cover for this potentially controversial posture. Given this background, the spectacle of the leaders of the centre-right coalition and the Social Democratic opposition working long nights together in a desperate search for budget cuts which could be used in a bid to placate an awkward market becomes more understandable. The elite consensus behind the existing fixed-rate policy was thus reinforced, rather than shaken, by the mounting threat to the krona caused by the September waves of speculation.[8]

The political determination to defend the krona was articulated by the prime minister in a memo to his party officials after the September phase. At that time Bildt argued that he was prepared to make decisions which were painful in the short run, if they were important to Sweden´s well-being in the long run. He wrote: 'better to ensure the Swedish currency value and the economic policy's long-term credibility through a compromise [with the opposition] than to be blind to reality and face a domestic conflict' (quoted in Assarson 1996: 84–85). At a meeting with his party executive on 18 September Bildt declared that the 'cabinet wants to avoid a devaluation *at any cost* and therefore has chosen to find an agreement with the opposition' (quoted in *ibid.*; emphasis added). In a very similar tone, opposition leader Ingvar Carlsson argued during a party meeting on 17 September that 'we must be able to look people in the eye and say that we *did everything possible* to defend the fixed currency rate' (quoted in *ibid.*: 120; emphasis added). The head of the National Bank and former Social Democratic state secretary of commerce, Bengt Dennis, echoed this sentiment, indicating that the sky was the limit as far as defence of the krona was concerned.

The Social Democratic grass roots and backbenchers were never included and, it would turn out, did not readily support the 'concessions' made by the party leadership in the name of monetary stability. The secretive and rapid decision-making processes during the September crises were questioned by several constituencies within the Social Democratic Party. The highly centralized and restricted procedures used in concluding the austerity packages became a target for criticism from the party's left wing. A leading Social Democratic newspaper, *Dala-Demokraten*, stated in an editorial that the lesson from the crisis packages

> ought to be that quick, acute developments require reasonable efforts to build support from below. Had twenty-five individuals – instead of, as was the case, four or five – been allowed to twist and turn the Social Democratic options in the austerity packages, the self-inflicted goals would possibly have been avoided. In short: the more cooks, the better the soup. Especially when dealing with fast food.
>
> (quoted in Assarson 1996: 139)

The evidence suggests that the Social Democratic leadership was led to reflect critically upon both the content of the decisions taken in late September and upon the process by which they were generated. The angry reactions of the left wing of the party set in motion a process of re-evaluation which would ultimately lead to a questioning of the two key premises behind the fixed-rate policy: the necessity (in light of the approach to Europe) and the feasibility of retaining the Ecu-pegged krona at high domestic cost.

Informal contacts with sceptical Swedish industrialists also fuelled this concern among the Social Democrats, with the costly domestic consequences of the fixed-currency policy line. Confidential hearings in late October with the leaders of a number of professional associations and unions added to the emerging doubts. According to Allan Larsson, the sceptical views of private industry on the question of feasibility were instrumental in leading him to change his mind about the viability of the fixed-currency policy (Assarson 1996: 141). According to individual critics of the official line, in November it was no longer a question of if, but rather when, the currency would fall.

In September the major Swedish banks had large portions of their liquid assets in local currency and would have suffered serious losses from a depreciation at that time. Subsequent reports indicate that funds were quietly moved into foreign holdings during the autumn months. Several leading banks even made slight profits from the November devaluation, since by then they held more of their assets abroad than in the krona (*Dagens Nyheter*, 5 November 1996). The European Union (EU) Monetary Committee's rejection, on 16 November 1992, of the Swedish request for financial support was symptomatic of the lack of confidence in the fixed-value strategy. Critics abroad argued in the specialized media that further investment in this policy would be futile and foolhardy.

The Social Democratic leadership (Carlsson, Larsson and Sahlin) chose in November to abandon the multi-partisan austerity and high interest rate 'script' established in the previous episodes. The Social Democratic realignment did apparently take place, at least in part, during the interim between the late September and mid-November phases of the crisis, in which the currency situation was relatively quiet. During this period parliament came into session, and the two September crisis austerity packages were subjected to the scrutiny of the relevant legislative committees. At this point, the Social Democratic leadership was coping with an acute intra-party legitimacy crisis, triggered by the close collaboration with the centre-right government during this period.

After its reassessment of the situation the opposition chose to sit on the sidelines in November, rather than to stand shoulder to shoulder with the government as before. The prime minister and the finance ministers thus had to present a unilateral austerity package in a morning press conference on 19 November. The flight from the currency proved unrelenting. Ultimately, in the absence of a sufficiently dramatic demonstration of political will across party lines, and with the national reserves being rapidly depleted, the Board of Governors made its decision to allow the krona to float just after lunch.

The 'cognition and policy process' interpretation

Less than a dozen key actors shaped the Swedish responses to the attack by the heavyweights of the international money market upon the national currency. Crucial decisions were taken in a series of highly confidential and insulated interactions across multiple interlocking groups and networks. Obviously, these face-to-face processes were embedded in the larger domestic political setting and international market structures, as discussed above. This section gives a complementary analytical cut to the two previous perspectives by placing in the spotlight the cognitive frames and motivational biases behind the decisions of Swedish policy-makers.

Policy-makers relied upon initially shared and unchallenged problem framings linked to common perceptions of the external threat, the need for domestic austerity and aspirations toward EU membership. Through differential learning from the September to the November phase of the crisis, one faction of this multi-partisan policy-making group defected from what had been the common mindset. What had been axiomatic in September, in November became subject to interpretation, judgement and interest-based rivalry.

The September crisis decision-making was highly centralized. A limited number of actors among the top echelons of the political parties and at the National Bank made the key decisions. The second crisis package in late September was concluded in a hectic night-time session which went on until after 4.00 a.m. At key junctures, only Ingvar Carlsson and his party secretary, Mona Sahlin, were in the room, while the two specialist assistants were requested to wait outside. Sahlin confessed later in an interview:

In all honesty, the negotiations took place in a very small group. They were so extremely sensitive, one had constantly to consider the so-called market. Thus, we had to be somewhat vague on the details in the [larger] meetings. We requested a mandate, which we received.

(quoted in Assarson 1996: 130)

In September all of the actors adhered rigidly to the policy of a fixed currency value despite mounting pressures from the market, which led the National Bank to respond with heavy purchases (38 billion krona on 16 September) and astronomically high (and costly) marginal interest rates. The policy-makers were locked into a cognitive frame within which the value to the nation of the fixed-rate policy was assumed to be pivotal. The crisis response was heavily affected by ambitions to retain an established policy line despite countervailing pressures from the international environment. In this shared defence against external forces it was possible to develop a consensus across party lines in favour of substantial austerity measures thought likely to reassure the market in the short term and to strengthen the Swedish finances in the long term. This was accomplished within a closed circle of party leaders, in spite of personal animosities among several of these key participants.

As with the 500 per cent remedy, the public reform packages had a symbolic significance which went far beyond their actual contributions towards resolving the serious financial problems besetting the Swedish government. The confidence-building rate changes vis-à-vis the market made by Bengt Dennis were thus synchronized with the multi-partisan deal-making within the four-party coalition and between the cabinet and the opposition leaders. Concrete deadlines were imposed on the politicians by the politically experienced and assertive head of the National Bank, who acted as a policy entrepreneur, expert and decision-maker in his own right. In the aftermath of the first phase of the crisis it was widely argued in the media and among lower-level politicians excluded from these deliberations that effective political leadership had been exercised.

What lessons were drawn from the September experiences by the various actors? The record suggests that the centre-right government declared the September crisis management a triumph with respect to both domestic and foreign constituencies, and reaffirmed its commitment to defending the pegged value. This confident mindset and positive reading of the crisis experience served to desensitize the government to the progressive unravelling of the ERM regime which was under way. There is no evidence that the experience triggered any rigorous and critical self-evaluation on the part of the cabinet leaders. On the contrary, it seems that they may have 'overlearned' the apparently successful response to the September incidents.[9] The concrete feedback of reduced market pressures and a return to business as usual at home by mid-October reaffirmed the earlier established script. It thus became difficult to question or challenge this apparently tried and tested strategy for coping with pressures on the krona.

In the November crisis the cabinet followed rigidly the script developed in the previous episodes. In response to warnings from the National Bank, the government once again contacted the Social Democrats to attempt to put together yet another austerity package. This time, after some preliminary flirtation, the Social Democrats refused to collaborate with the government and stood on the sidelines in precisely the manner which Carlsson had rejected in the September episodes.

One interpretation of the events of the final twelve hours of the monetary crisis argues that the Social Democratic leadership deliberately stalled the announcement of whether or not it was prepared to work with the cabinet again in order to avoid the risk of being caught with its rivals in a joint fiasco. In the pivotal morning session of the party executive on 19 November, Carlsson and Larsson argued against another package deal on several grounds, including that it was not feasible in light of the massive currency flows and that internal opposition from the party left would be severe. According to one inside source, there was no sense of urgency in informing the cabinet about this negative position. On the contrary, the meeting was allowed to drag out in the expectation that market events would run their course independently of any actions by the party executive (Assarson 1996: 142).

Particularly interesting is the more flexible response of the Social Democrats to the threat posed by the flight from the krona in November. The Social Democratic leaders did not follow the script established in the previous incidents and did not respond rigidly. The accountability of the Social Democratic leadership to the left wing and large portions of the rank and file membership of the party apparently motivated a more vigilant decision-making process and helped to sensitize Ingvar Carlsson, his shadow finance minister, Allan Larson, and other intimates to the changing political context, leading to reassessments at three levels.

First, the evidence suggests that their assessment of the domestic (particularly the intra-party) political context changed. They were intensely aware that further concessions in the name of austerity would lead to even more serious rifts in the party and to vocal opposition from the already aroused and indignant left flank. Second, the magnitude of the outflows and the experience of peer countries called into question the feasibility of stemming the market tide and mounting another defence of the currency, as did assessments garnered through consultations with union and industry leaders. Third, their judgement of the potential costs of revising the fixed-rate policy appears to have changed. In the context of the virtual collapse of the ERM system and a rash of devaluations from states with formal and informal links to the system, it was reasonable to assume that the 'European core' would be relatively forgiving. In this context, Sweden's 'crime' in devaluing appears more of a misdemeanour than a felony.

The Social Democratic policy change on this issue from late September to mid-November seems to indicate learning from one phase of the crisis to the other. In contrast, the reluctance of the leading cabinet members to abandon their cherished fixed-rate policy suggests cognitive rigidity. The key ministers spent the final night in the Cabinet Office waiting and hoping for a positive signal from the Social Democratic opposition. Even without such political backing, an austerity package was announced in the morning. The cabinet leaders also endorsed a financially very costly and massive market-intervention policy by the National Bank through the last day of the crisis.

The cohesiveness of the multi-partisan policy-making group was undermined in November to the extent that the key Social Democratic players did not fully partici-pate. The abortive joint decision process in this phase looked radically different from the intimate September negotiations described by Sahlin (1996) and Wibble (1994). Ingvar Carlsson and Mona Sahlin subsequently argued that the perceived urgency and need for secrecy mandated a concentration of authority in 'a very small circle' (Assarson 1996: 135–136). These consultations reportedly led to bonding and stress-induced cohesion across party lines, characterized by the finance minister as reminiscent of the famous 'Stockholm syndrome' that epitomizes a similar process occurring between hostages and their captors (Wibble 1994).

In November the leading Social Democrats stayed away during the most intense phase of crisis negotiations. Key communications were handled by messenger, phone and fax. This ensured that no undue bonding took place and minimized the risk that the Social Democratic negotiators might get carried away in the crisis atmosphere. Similarly, in November the need was emphasized for formal decisions to be made by the party's Executive Committee, and not directly by a handful of top officials. The final authority of the Executive Committee of the party and of the parliamentary group was asserted, in stark contrast to the carte blanche enjoyed by the top leaders in September.

The ability of government and opposition to reach a crisis accommodation in September and their inability to do so in November are in part a function of the different procedures used to manage the delicate, stressful and chronically conflictual relationship across the party political divide. Even more fundamentally, the divergence of cognitive frames and the corresponding differential sensitivity to changes in the domestic and international political contexts provide important clues as to why the outcomes diverged across these two seemingly parallel incidents.

In a counterfactual analysis one could speculate that if the same type of informal process had been used in November as in September, and if no cognitive shift had occurred between these two periods, the Swedes might have been able to weather the storm once again. Plans were in progress to explore the possibility of a formal link to the German Deutschmark as a stabilizing strategy to complement additional domestic austerity measures. In a speech on 2 December 1992, National Bank director Bengt Dennis articulated his view of who failed in the crisis: 'The National Bank did what it could do. Only the political system could have produced a turnaround'. Dennis's statement clearly implies that the defence of the fixed krona was a feasible undertaking in November as well, given sufficient political will. Let us therefore conclude by returning to the question of for whom this episode was a disaster.

Disaster for whom?

Although the free float was labelled a failure by all concerned in November 1992, the record appears more ambiguous in hindsight. Clearly it was a failure as measured against the official policy lines of the government and of the Social Democratic leadership at the time. In addition, Swedish failure to withstand the financial market pressures contributed to mounting turbulence in the EMS. Days later, the Spanish and the Portuguese currencies were depreciated by 6 per cent. Next, the Norwegian krone came under assault, only to fall on 10 December, after a costly defence.

When set against various other criteria, however – such as the potential for export-driven economic growth, an increased public-revenue base and the opportunity cost of defending the fixed rate through market interventions – the picture becomes far more complex. In late 1996 a Swedish debate developed briefly over the direct and indirect costs of this currency-defence effort (*Dagens Nyheter*, 5 November 1996; KU 1996/97). Critics argued that an underlying motive for the costly and futile interventions by the National Bank in November was actually to enable Swedish industry, banks and trade unions discreetly to transfer their liquid funds into some harder currency than the failing krona. Financial figures released by the National Bank in late 1996, under pressure of a court decision ordering their disclosure, fuelled the debate. According to this controversial view, the public rescue operation of the financial establishment was carried out at the direct expense of future wage earners and of small business operators not privy to inside information.

Except for a brief series of articles in late 1996, Swedish journalists have so far not picked up on the allegations by these critics about the handling of the crisis. Considering the huge amounts of public money spent in such a short period of time, the relative media and political silence is surprising. Given the subsequent unravelling of the narrow-band ERM-system in 1993, one can ask whether another heroic multi-partisan defence effort in November would have accomplished very much. Further assaults on the krona were to be expected. Even the larger and sounder economies of Europe, such as that of France, had great difficulty in coping with the market onslaughts. Sweden's macroeconomic position was far more precarious.

Should Sweden have accepted the inevitable sooner and avoided the costs of defending the krona in September? Should even more drastic efforts have been made in order to save this symbolically salient commitment? Ultimately, these are politically controversial and perhaps even unanswerable questions. It is clear, however, that the distributional implications of these various alternatives are dramatic, with different scenarios favouring very different stakeholders.

Notes

1 Quotes drawn from Swedish language sources have been translated by the authors.
2 For an overview of the Swedish monetary and financial system, see Henreksson (1992).

3 In his classic treatise on the impact of international structure, Waltz (1979) acknowledged in passing that weak states, through clever strategies and costly mobilization efforts, can for a time go against the tide of the international structure. He also recognized that the structural effects are generated in part through socialization of the actors into a mindset supportive of adaptive behaviour (*ibid.*: 74). Andrews picks up on that point in his claim that 'the belief or mindset of monetary authorities that international collaboration to limit capital mobility is unlikely to succeed becomes one element in a self-fulfilling prophecy' (Andrews 1994: 202). One interesting facet of the Swedish case was the ability of the national leadership to break out of this cognitively based limiting logic of structural constraint. The leaders were instead focused on the imperative of building national credibility for the future, as practised for decades by their peers in the sphere of Swedish security policy.

4 This strategy, which rested upon the assumption that the consensus in favour of 'joining Europe' was rock solid, proved to be a dangerous one. In fact, the consensus in favour of joining would gradually decline, to the extent that the November 1994 referendum on EU membership resulted in only a narrow victory for the pro-Europe side.

5 However, the German Bundesbank had insisted when establishing the European ERM that the 'intervention mechanism would be based on a bilateral parity grid rather than on ecu parities' (Goodman 1992: 217), as was the case with the Ecu-linked Swedish currency. Sweden did not conform to this German-induced and autonomy-reducing EMS norm. This deviation had important consequences when the National Bank in November requested, but was denied intervention support by the EMS Monetary Committee.

6 The red rose is the symbol and logo of the Swedish Social Democratic Party.

7 In 1994 Feldt became chairman of the Board of Governors of the National Bank, replacing the Conservative Staffan Burenstam Linder.

8 In the 1971 Japanese monetary crisis, goal displacement was evident as the defence of the exchange rate became an intrinsic objective instead of being regarded as a technical means toward a larger economic goal (Angel 1991: 273). The similarity to the Swedish case is striking on this point.

9 Our findings here parallel those of Rosenthal and 't Hart (1989) in their study of a sequence of crises provoked by hostage-takings by South Moluccan terrorists in the 1970s. The apparent success in the first case of 'the Dutch method' of using a psychologist to talk to the terrorists apparently led to a fixation with that approach which ultimately served to prolong and perhaps exacerbate the management of the second crisis.

10 In addition to the sources cited in the reference list, a large number of newspaper articles have been used to reconstruct the case events. Among the more important newspapers scanned are *Dagens Nyheter, Svenska Dagladet, Dagens Industri, Affärsvarlden, Veckans Affärer* and *The Financial Times*.

References[10]

Andrews, D. (1994) 'Capital mobility and state autonomy: towards a structural theory of international monetary relations', *International Studies Quarterly* 38: 192–218.

Angel, R. (1991) *Explaining Economic Policy Failure: Japan in the 1969–1971 International Monetary Crisis*, New York: Columbia University Press.

Assarson, J. (1996) *Krisuppgörelserna och den svenska kronans fall*, Department of Government, Uppsala University, mimeo, 177 pages.

Bovens, M. and 't Hart, P. (1996) *Understanding Policy Fiascoes*, New Brunswick: Transaction.

Cameron, D. (1993) 'British exit, German voice, French loyalty: defection, domination and co-operation in the 1992–93 ERM crisis', Yale University, unpublished paper.

Evans, P., Jakobson, H. and Putnam, R. (eds) (1993) *Double-edged Diplomacy: International Bargaining and Domestic Politics*, Berkeley: University of California Press.

Goodman, J. (1992) *Monetary Sovereignty: The Politics of Central Banking in Western Europe*, Ithaca, NY: Cornell University Press.

Gray, P. (1996) 'Disastrous explanations – or explanations of disaster? A reply to Patrick Dunleavy', *Public Policy and Administration* 1(1): 74–83.

't Hart, P. (1993) 'Symbols, rituals, and power: the lost dimensions of crisis management', *Journal of Contingencies and Crisis Management* 1: 36–50.

Hempel, T. (1993) 'Årets match: politikerna vs marknaden', in *Bra Böckers Årsbok*, Höganäs: Bra Böcker.

Henreksson, M. (1992) 'Sweden: monetary and financial system', in P. Newman, M. Pilgate and J. Eatwell (eds) *The New Palgrave Dictionary of Money and Finance*, London: Macmillan.

Jonung, L. (ed.) (1991) *Devalvering 1982 – rivstart eller snedtändning*, Stockholm: SNS Förlag.

Kingdon, J. (1984) *Agendas, Alternatives and Public Policies*, New York: HarperCollins.

[KU 1996–7] 'Regeringens eller enskilda statsråds hantering av kronförsvaret 1992', *Konstitutionsutskottets betänkande och yttranden*, KU25, Stockholm: Riksdagen 173–207.

Lundgren, N. and Söderström, H. T. (1995) 'Kronförsvaret hösten 1992 – var det värt sitt pris?', *Ekonomisk politik: en vänbok till Assar Lindbeck*, Stockholm: SNS Förlag.

Miles, L. (ed.) (1996) *The European Union and the Nordic Countries*, London: Routledge.

Morse, E. (1973) *Foreign Policy and Interdependence*, Princeton: Princeton University Press.

Renius, U. (1996) *Stålbadet: finanskrisen, penserkraschen och nordbankens rekonstruktion*, Stockholm: Ekerlids Förlag.

Rosenthal, U. and 't Hart, P. (1989) 'Managing terrorism: the South Moluccan hostage takings', in U. Rosenthal, P. 't Hart and M. Charles (eds) *Coping with Crises*, Springfield, IL: Charles C. Thomas.

Sahlin, M. (1996) *Med mina ord*, Stockholm: Tiden, Athena.

Shiels, F. (1991) *Preventable Disasters: Why Governments Fail*, Savage, MD: Rowman & Littlefield.

Stern, E. (1997) 'Crisis and learning: a conceptual balance sheet', *Journal of Contingencies and Crisis Management* 5(2): 69–86.

Stern, E. and Sundelius, B. (1997) 'Sweden's twin monetary crises of 1992: rigidity and learning in crisis decisionmaking', *Journal of Contingencies and Crisis Management* 5(1): 32–48.

Sundelius, B. (ed.) (1989) *The Committed Neutral: Sweden's Foreign Policy*, Boulder, CO: Westview Press.

—— (1994) 'Changing course: when neutral Sweden chose to join the European Community', in W. Carlsnaes and S. Smith (eds) *European Foreign Policy*, London: Sage.

Svensson, T. (1996) *Novemberrevolutionen* (Ds 1996: 37), Stockholm: Finansdepartementet.

Tetlock, P. and Belkin, A. (eds) (1996) *Counterfactual Thought Experiments in World Politics*, Princeton: Princeton University Press.

Thompson, H. (1996) *The British Conservative Government and the European Exchange Rate Mechanism, 1979–1994*, London: Pinter.

Waltz, K. (1979) *Theory of International Politics*, Reading, MA: Addison-Wesley.

Wibble, A. (1994) *Två cigg och en kopp kaffe*, Stockholm: Ekerlids Förlag.

Winnerstig, M. (1993) *Valutakriserna hösten 1992*, Stockholm: Stockholm University, mimeo.

Part V

THE EUROPEAN UNION LEVEL

9

THE COMMON FISHERIES
POLICY

A European disaster?

Ella Ritchie and Anthony Zito

Introduction

The politics of fishing is capable of generating intense debate and the European Union's (EU) Common Fisheries Policy (CFP) has received a range of criticism from a diverse array of actors. Questions about local communities falling into oblivion, as well as issues of sovereignty over maritime natural resources and sensitivity about state boundaries, have led this policy area to imitate the characteristics of pitched naval battles. Whatever the socio-economic and political costs of the alleged policy failures to local and national communities, the involvement of the European Union adds an important dimension. The key theme of this chapter is that the inherent tensions found in EU policy-making – particularly the difficulties in constructing a consensus for new policy solutions and the problems of implementing community policies – create political compromises which appear to be moving the EU towards a policy impasse.

It is only in the context of the evolution of the Common Fisheries Policy that one can understand the potential pitfalls in the construction of the policy and see the gradually unfolding socio-economic impact of the EU policy-making processes. The problems of the fishing regime are not the product of any one catastrophic incident; rather, they represent a gradual incremental march towards policy confusion and conflict. In exploring these problems, however, we emphasize the inherently difficult demands placed on actors in this sector. Any fisheries management regime has to strike a balance between demands for produce, the need for conservation and social/community interests. Given the global pressures on many fish stocks and the highly migratory nature of fish, any fisheries policy will have to operate within an uncertain and unpredictable environment. The EU's fisheries management regime exhibits the difficulties of trying to achieve conflicting objectives: operating in line with international agreements, ensuring continuing stocks of fish, protecting fishing communities and supporting restructuring – all within a 'common European pond' where fishing states compete vigorously. The policy area itself is a difficult one involving high levels of policy uncertainty and dispute about the nature of the fishing problem and the effectiveness of any given solutions. Furthermore, individual groups of fishermen, who question not only the benefit of the imposed guidelines but their very legitimacy as well, have violated many of the regulations. Nevertheless, our main argument rests on the structure of EU policy-making and its vulnerability to individual national and sectoral interests.

We contend that the policy disaster associated with the CFP is due more to the perception of policy reality than to the policy itself. In the countries where the CFP has received the harshest criticism, such as the UK, the CFP has been tied to questions of the legitimacy of the EU's general performance – at a time where politics and public governance are held in extremely low esteem by the general public. Both national governments and the general population are very willing to perceive failures in EU policy-making. The chapter stresses that the reality of the CFP is far more complex, involving, in particular, actions taken by national governments which are very willing to let the EU level carry blame for policies that might be accorded justifiably to them. In this chapter our argument concentrates heavily on the nature and structure of the EU policy process in explaining the outcomes of the CFP policy effort. Because of the difficulties of adequately assessing motivations for all fifteen member-state governments in a single case chapter, we focus our attention on Britain.

The CFP as a policy disaster

In presenting the CFP as a disaster case, we first need to emphasize the ambiguity and contested quality of the claim that the CFP is actually a policy disaster. Large segments of the European Union policy apparatus would vehemently contest the judgement that the CFP is a disaster. Nevertheless, we argue that many aspects of the CFP match elements of the policy disaster criteria outlined in the introduction to this volume (Chapter 1). Several aspects of this definition are stressed here: a significant group of people hold a negative opinion about the outcomes of the policy and the policy failures that did occur have been seen to be at least partly foreseeable and capable of being controlled.

There are a number of different stakeholders involved in the CFP, who perceive the policy to be failing for different reasons. The *European Commission* itself published a number of reports pointing to the CFP's lack of success. The 1992 Gullard report acknowledged that targets set by the Commission had failed to check overcapacity in fishing fleets, and that overfishing and diminishing stocks continued to be a problem. It has also been acknowledged that early policy instruments were crude. Holden (1994), head of the conservation unit in Directorate-General (DG) XIV from 1979 to 1990, argues that the policy may have been a political success, but that it was a practical failure.

Member states' governments also criticize the CFP. In particular, the British government has persistently argued that the policy disadvantages Britain by opening up its rich fishing waters to its European rivals. Similarly, Ireland, since joining the Community in 1973, has argued intensely for the protection of its inshore waters A further complaint is that uneven monitoring of policy across the EU creates a situation in some, especially southern, countries, where the catching of 'juveniles' is not restricted and quotas are not adhered to. Further, the infamous problem of 'quota hoppers', whereby 'foreign' (largely Spanish and Dutch) fleets buy up British boats and with them the licence to fish the British quota, is laid at the door of the Commission.

The most vigorous critics of the CFP are the *fishermen and their organizations*, who blame the CFP for destroying their industry. In France, fishermen's organizations, often deeply divided, have periodically demonstrated, rioted and gone on strike against both the policy inertia of their own governments and the EU solutions (Thom 1998). The most vociferous complaints again came from the UK, where critics range from the radical, populist Save Britain's Fish Campaign, which advocates the UK's immediate withdrawal from the CFP, to the more moderate Scottish Federation of Fishermen (SFF), which argues for a regionalized policy within the context of a newly negotiated fisheries policy. The thrust of the criticism from these groups is that the policy establishment (from which they feel excluded) is not in touch with the needs of the fishing communities and does not make use of their expertise. Fishing organizations not only criticize the bureaucratic nature of the CFP but argue that an ill-devised and poorly constructed policy has encouraged a 'race to fish'. The annually negotiated total allowable catches (TACs) and the quotas allocated to each fishing state for different species operating within a largely free-access system sets up, in their view, a fishing Olympics whereby fishermen catch as much as possible as quickly as possible. The gap between the 'fishing managers' – Commission officials and the fishing inspectors – and the 'hunter-gatherers' remains very large (Cann 1998). This poses severe problems because ultimately the fishing communities themselves are the regulators and implementers of the policy. Finally, *environmental groups* are now beginning to criticize the CFP for its inability to deal with the global depletion of fish stocks and with industrial fishing.

Depending on whether or not they believe there is a wider ecological problem in fishing stocks, critics see the CFP as either needlessly restricting the amount of fish caught or as a policy that is doing an inadequate job of protecting those stocks from overfishing. Therefore aspects of both the policy design and policy implementation are seen as being at fault. While the critics mentioned above tend to fall into the categories of experts and/or fishing communities, this negative attitude has tended to diffuse into the position of national governments and of the general public, who see the policy as violating local/national autonomy as well as being ineffective or misdirected.

While it may be demonstrable that a substantial portion of the EU political arena holds the CFP outcomes to be destructive and contrary to its aims, defenders of the CFP have some scope for arguing that the degree of stress to the fishing stocks was not fully understood prior to the 1990s, and therefore policy-makers did not fully understand the situation and could not control it. The impact of new technologies and net sizes entered the thinking of CFP players only gradually. Furthermore, the Commission argues that it is continually being thwarted in its efforts to devise and implement successful stock management policies by the vested interests, expressed in the Council of Ministers, of the key fishing states (Spain, Portugal, the UK, France, Ireland and Holland).

Nevertheless, the majority of specific interests relevant to fishing and the general public perceive the EU structure and the EU way of doing business as having a negative impact. Those fisherman who do not accept the scientific predictions of stock failure see the EU as creating an imagined problem with disastrous consequences for local fishing communities. Those actors who do accept the ecological predictions tend to assume that the CFP has, at the very least, created a process that works against the conservation of stock. From this perspective, the policy actors directing the CFP have committed sins of commission, using the means at hand to deleterious effect (Bovens and 't Hart 1996). Most experts calling for conservation do believe that the situation can be saved, from a scientific point of view, by the imposition of drastic cuts in the short term. This implies a belief that the situation is controllable.

Accordingly, the case does fit the criteria of being perceived as a policy disaster, regardless of the actual reality. At the same time, there do seem to be viable alternatives to the current EU course of action, but they are based on very different frames of reference. The scientists are fairly confident that conservation methods could work. UK and Spanish fishermen are equally confident that, if the EU intervened less, most of the problems would disappear. These differing points of view require either substantial authoritative intervention for a particular side or else sufficiently capable powers of persuasion. The EU system has so far proved incapable of providing either direction. The issue then becomes a matter of what is politically practicable, given that the EU structure is seen as one that does not work. According to this perspective, the lack of political will leads to a sin of omission, allowing the current ecological situation to deteriorate. This failure of the policy process is reflected in problems both in policy design and in policy implementation for the CFP.

The evolution of the CFP

Provision was made for a Common Fisheries Policy under Articles 38 and 39 of the Treaty of Rome, dealing with agricultural products. As with many EU policies, political circumstances triggered the development of the policy. In many ways the development of the CFP has been more gradual and more subject to political interference than most other policy areas of the EU. This has led to incrementalist policy-making vulnerable to further external political disruption. The tendency for some member states, most notably the UK and Spain, to turn fishing issues into 'high politics' has tended to mitigate against optimal policy outcomes.[1] Both internal pressures and the international fishing environment shaped the political conditions for the CFP.

Initially, the six founder member states showed little interest in developing a collective fishing policy. The Commission was relatively weak at this stage, with few resources of its own to drive a policy forward. However, by the mid-1960s the French and Italians were aware that their fleets were becoming increasingly uncompetitive, and they put pressure on the community to devise structural policies to assist the restructuring of their technically backward industries. However, even this modest policy initiative proved to be controversial and was resisted by the Germans. Here we see immediately the problem of joint decision-making where member states hold very different interests and can block settlements in order to force their preferences. The proposed enlargement of the European Economic Community (EEC) to include the 'fish rich' countries of Denmark, Ireland, Norway and the UK stimulated the six to hatch a common policy (completed six hours before the entry negotiations began), incorporating the principle of free access to community waters, before enlargement took place.

The applicant states wanted to ensure that their fishing territories were protected and opposed the equal access principle. In the end, Norway declined to join the European Community (EC), largely because it feared the effects of the equal access principle on its fisheries. Britain, Ireland and Denmark, however, negotiated as much temporary protection – in the form of 6- and 12-mile limits around their coastlines – as they could before joining. At the time of joining the EEC the UK and, to a lesser extent, the Irish government sacrificed fishing rights in return for wider political goals (Farnell and Elles 1984; Wise 1984).

In 1970 the Common Structural Policy was established. It affirmed the principle of non-discrimination among member states and laid down the right to 'equal conditions of access' to fishing grounds (with certain derogations). It also made some provisions for conservation measures to deal with overfishing, and laid down some rules for financial aid for restructuring the industry. The principle of equal access has continued to be a contested by many fishing communities.

The other pressure for the development of the CFP came from international forces. For much of the postwar period a 'high seas' regime had been in place whereby states controlled a narrow coastal strip of water outside which all fleets were free to fish where they chose. This regime operated reasonably well in times of buoyant fish stocks. However, as the problem of overfishing became more apparent, various international fisheries commissions, such as the North East Atlantic Fisheries Convention (NEAFC), began to try to regulate catches and manage resources. At the same time, in the mid-1970s a number of states bordering on the North Sea, Canada, the United States, Iceland and Norway introduced 200-mile fishing limits, or Exclusive Economic Zones (EEZs). This had major implications for distance fishing by EC fleets, and the EC responded by setting up its own 200-mile EEC zone under the 1976 Hague Convention.

During the period 1976–83 the CFP underwent a period of consolidation (Wise 1984; Commission background documents). The Commission was trying to devise a policy of resource allocation based on the principle of 'relative stability' (or fixed percentage shares) in quota allocation – based on historic fishing patterns – and a system of TACs for different species of fish. It was also moving towards instituting a more effective conservation policy to deal with the problem of overfishing (exacerbated by increased technology) and industrial fishing. The member states were locked in battle with the Commission. Countries such as the UK and Ireland, which between them historically had 60 per cent of the EU's fishing stocks, demanded preferential treatment for their fishermen. Other countries, such as France and Denmark, also argued that they had special rights which needed to be protected.

Again the deadlock over the details of the CFP was broken by political events. A change of minister in the UK brought a fresh approach to the problem, and the linking of fishing to the British budget settlement encouraged more flexibility from the British government. A change of government in France in 1981 also brought a fresh approach. Most importantly, the impending membership of Spain and Portugal – both of which had larger fleets than the UK – forced the ten to agree a common policy in order to negotiate with the new states from a position of strength. Consequently, in 1983, the EEC reached an agreement on the structure of the CFP. It centred around four pillars: markets, structural policy, conservation and external relations. The principle of equal access was established, with derogations for member states to have exclusive fishing rights in waters up to 12 miles from its coasts, subject to traditional fishing rights of other member states. The UK negotiated a special deal to set up a protective 'box' of 50 miles around the Orkney and Shetland Islands. The CFP gave the Community the right to prescribe in considerable detail the operation of fisheries within Community waters (discussed below, in the 'Policy contents' section) and to negotiate on behalf of its members with third parties. The policy laid down in 1983 was to last until 2002, with a mid-term review in 1991. In addition, the policy was subject to annual reviews for the setting of TACs and quotas, and to multi-annual reviews for structural policy from 1983 to 97.

There have been two interrelated challenges to the CFP – the enlargement of the EU to include Spain and Portugal, and the continuing problem of declining fish stocks. The issue of fishing reached monumental proportions during the entry negotiations with Spain and Portugal. Changes in the international fisheries regime, which led to the loss of deep sea waters for British and German fleets, increased sensitivity over the equal access principle. France, Ireland and the UK feared that if the equal access principle was applied they would be inundated with fleets from the Iberian peninsula. Pressure from these countries meant that Spain and Portugal were prevented from accessing EU waters fully until 2002. Although the Spanish government received considerable compensation from the CFP in the form of aid to restructure its fleet (thereby paradoxically increasing its fishing capacity), it felt the CFP deal to be severely disadvantageous. The impending enlargement to include Norway in 1994 gave Spain the opportunity to redress this grievance when it threatened to veto the accession of Austria, Finland, Norway and Sweden unless it was given greater access to EU waters. Consequently, Spain has secured some fishing rights in the Irish Sea (forty vessels) and the Western Waters since January 1996.

The European Union is faced with the increasingly difficult challenge of trying to devise a policy to satisfy a growing number of states fishing fewer stocks. The issue of fishing within the EU has now clearly become a policy which, through its more substantial structural features, is now more redistributive in character, setting North against South (Wallace 1996). Simultaneously, in the last few years fishing rights have assumed a symbolic importance for several countries, provoking intense support from sections of the public. In the case of the UK, the most obvious expression of this wider nationalist support is to be found within the Eurosceptic camp of the Conservative Party, which took up and dramatized the cause of fishing. The issue of Spanish and Dutch 'quota hoppers' was used by the Conservative Party to vent nationalistic fervour. In France, fishing and agricultural areas tended to vote 'no' in the 1992 Maastricht referendum on further European integration, reflecting disillusionment with the CFP and Common Agricultural Policy as well as alienation from the whole European venture.

Policy content

The CFP draws both on the EC treaties, which emphasize fundamental market freedoms, and on its own legal bases – with special derogations for some member states. There are two basic principles which underpin the policy:

1   Equal conditions of access to all member states, but with 6- and 12-mile limits around states, and special derogations (e.g. the North Sea Box) which control access to waters. These are likely to persist beyond 2002, according to Commission officials.
2   The principle of 'relative stability'. Each EU fishing state was allocated a fixed percentage of the total allowable catch on the basis of independent scientific advice and historic fishing patterns from the years 1973–78. The principle of relative stability is operationalized through the setting of TACs for different species and the subsequent allocation of national quotas. The UK and Ireland secured preferential treatment; the UK received, for example, additional cod quota allocations to compensate for exclusion from the Icelandic waters.

The free-market principle has meant that EU fishermen can buy up boats and their licences from neighbouring European countries. Because of the rich fish stocks around the UK this has generally meant that Spanish, Dutch and German operators have bought British ships. One reason why British boats were relatively easy prey to foreign purchasers was that the British government at the time did not match EU funding for decommissioning and restructuring. As stocks have declined and quotas have become tighter, the issue of 'quota hoppers', or 'flagships', has become highly controversial. Approximately 20 per cent of British tonnage (and between one-quarter and one-third of the quota) is now owned by foreign operators. British fishermen claim that even these figures underestimate the size of the Spanish catch, which, they argue, is grossly augmented by illegal catches.

The CFP is divided into four main policy areas: marketing, external relations, conservation and structural policy. These are reflected in four units in DG XIV. Although the DG is relatively small and personal relations are close, the units tend to work relatively independently of each other. Inevitably there is some degree of policy incoherence between the units, although the midterm review of the CFP has reinforced coordination.[2] Under the *marketing policy*, fishing is subject to similar principles that apply to agriculture. This includes common marketing standards, the institution of a price support system and the establishment of producers' organizations. The marketing policy is commonly viewed as a successful part of the CFP. In *external relations* the Commission has the sole power to negotiate and conclude fisheries agreements with non-member states. These include reciprocal arrangements over fishing rights, access to surplus stock, access to stock in return for financial compensation and, more recently, the development of joint enterprises. The EU participates as a contracting partner in the work of numerous international fishing organizations such as the North Atlantic Fishing Organization and the North Atlantic Salmon Conservation Organization. External relations is a relatively successful and uncontroversial aspect of the CFP, although it has recently come under criticism from environmentalists and the European Parliament, who argue that the EU is 'exporting' its fishing problem by exploiting third-world resources. British actors criticize the agreements with third-world countries (e.g. Morocco) as often favouring the southern states of the EU. The aim of the *conservation policy* is to provide for national and responsible exploitation of living marine resources on a sustainable basis, taking account of its implication for the marine eco-system and of its socio-economic implications for producers and consumers (Council Regulation (EEC) No. 3760/92). This means that the Commission aims to ensure a steady and thriving supply of fish, which will ensure a viable future for European fishermen. This is no easy task as many stocks are seriously overfished and fishing technology is improving constantly. The European Commission bases its policy recommendations on information received from the International Council for Exploration of the Sea (ICES). ICES collects information from national research centres, which is then fed into its Advisory Committee on Fisheries Management (ACFM), which gives advice on future fish stocks. Once the Commission receives advice from the ACFM it refers it to its own Scientific, Technical and Economic Committee on fisheries (STEC), which consists of national representatives, and draws up policy recommendations on TACs and quotas for the December meeting of the Council of Fisheries Ministers. The Commission generally tries to strike a balance between what ICES recommends and what will be politically acceptable.

There is much dispute about the scientific evidence for declining fish stocks. Assessment of stocks is highly technical and very complicated. In some cases it is difficult to quantify fish stocks and there is considerable controversy over the exact levels needed to keep the stocks replenished. It is particularly difficult for the scientists to 'predict that the stock will collapse at point X'.[3] In spite of this uncertainty, all the advice from ICES points to the fact that many stocks (e.g. North Sea cod) are seriously overfished (possibly beyond recovery) and most are moderately overfished. Another difficulty is the different timescales involved. ICES and, to some extent, the Commission, are concerned with both the long- and the short-term perspective. The annual cycle of negotiations and agreements, however, means that the policy tends to be driven by short-termism. TACs and quotas for all types of fish are set at the same time in the calendar year. This situation is not particularly satisfactory for fishermen because once they have fished their quota they may have to stay in port. This tends to be at a point in the year when prices are good. In response to this the Commission has come up with some proposals introducing flexibility across years (e.g. using some of next year's quota if fishing is good). However, the unpredictability of fish stocks and the general lack of confidence which the industry has in the management of them reduce the viability of these proposals.

In addition to recommending TACs and quotas the Commission makes numerous recommendations on minimum net sizes, minimum sizes for species landed, fishing period and fishing areas. The introduction of Community identity papers for boats in 1995 was designed to effect closer control over fleet activity. The policy recommendations are discussed by the Council of Fisheries Ministers and its advisory committees. Although, as in most other EU policy areas, some ground is cleared by the Committee of Permanent Representatives, many seemingly technical issues, as well as the TACs, find their way to the full Council. This is because, unlike in some other EU sectors, the key to the policy may lie in the technical details. As one of our interviewees observed, 'the political issue is not the principle, it is the size of net'. Prior to discussion in full Council, the fisheries ministers will typically have been lobbied by a large number of groups and may also have had to respond to national parliamentary pressure. The pressures to protect national interests force the decision into the EU arena most oriented to lowest common denominator negotiation.

Structural assistance for fishing was instituted in 1971 as a rather crude form of aid for fishing communities. Over time the policy has, like other EU structural policies, become more sophisticated, more flexible and more integrated with other policies. Since 1983 Multi-Annual Guidance Programmes (MAGPs) have laid down the broad policy guidelines for restructuring fleets. The last two MAGPs (MAGP III, 1992–6, and IV, 1997) have been much more radical in their attempt to reduce the Community fleet by 40 per cent. This marks a shift in EU policy towards controlling the fishing effort. The targets put forward by the Commission under the MAGP are vigorously debated – and invariably moderated upwards – by the fisheries ministers, who are keen to ensure that the burden of cutback is as small as possible and is fairly distributed among the member states. The actual detail of how to reduce fishing capacity – for example through decommissioning or 'days at sea' legislation – is left to the member state to decide.

Financial assistance for communities dependent on fishing is now integrated into a Single Financial Instrument for Fisheries Guidance, which forms part of the EU structural funds. EU aid for fishing now systematically requires some form of co-funding from the member states. Financial assistance cannot be obtained if states have failed to meet their decommissioning targets. In addition, a new Community Initiative was launched in 1994 to aid coastal regions in structural decline.

Policy implementation

Whilst the Commission issues detailed guidelines for some aspects of the CFP, the bulk of the implementation of the policy and, equally importantly, of its regulation is left to the member states' fishing inspectorates, to national fishing organizations and ultimately to the fishermen themselves. Herein lies one of the major problems of the CFP. Procedures and guidelines are misunderstood, ignored, circumvented, falsified or merely flouted (Cann 1998).

The uneven implementation of the CFP can to some extent be put down to differing organizational, structural and institutional capacities of fishing inspectorates amongst the member states. These discrepancies have been identified by the European Commission. It has praised the United Kingdom for its 'well developed national fishery control system, which is matched by the allocation of substantial resources' and it acknowledges 'the efficient and competent manner with which the United Kingdom has tackled the enforcement task at sea' (European Commission 1996). This efficiency is contrasted with the 'poorly coordinated set of national and regional departments with non-specialised personnel in another member state' (*ibid.*). One of the responses of the Commission to the unevenness of CFP regulation and its implementation has been to put forward additional controls. This has served to alienate the fishermen further.

Of course, however well resourced a country is in terms of fishing inspectors, ultimately it is the fishermen themselves who are responsible for 'obeying the rules'. In some cases, fishermen ignore the rules – or the paperwork – because it is too time consuming or perceived to be unnecessary. In others, rules are broken because they are not consented to, because they are deemed irrevocable or simply because fishermen are trying to make a living. Examples abound of fishing in illegal waters, fishing over quota through the illegal landing of 'black fish', and fishing juveniles. Perhaps one of the most wasteful consequences of the CFP is the case of discarding fish (those over quota, the wrong species in multi-species catches or juveniles). It is estimated that in the UK nearly 50 per cent of some species are thrown back dead into the sea (House of Lords Select Committee Report 1993). Not only is this wasteful but it also, arguably, causes environmental damage.

For fishermen and their organizations, the widespread breaking or ignoring of the CFP rules demonstrates that the policy faces a crisis of legitimacy. They argue that the centralized bureaucratic system of the CFP has created an unbridgeable gulf between the fisheries managers and the fishermen. This position gains considerable support from the public, whose natural sympathies lie with the last of the 'hunter-gatherers'. This public support is not undermined by ecological concers since apparently, fish cannot compete with dolphins or whales when it comes to mobilizing public opinion.

Understanding the failure of the CFP

Having rehearsed the basic story of the CFP's evolution, we now turn to some possible alternative explanations for why the resulting negative policy consequences have ensued. The perspectives analysed here all emphasize systemic factors, instead of placing blame on any particular national government, fishing fleet or CFP agency. In the end we come to the conclusion that the EU institutional process is the linchpin of the disaster.

Policy uncertainty and the problem of timing

The Common Fisheries Policy represented a difficult challenge for EU actors in large part due to the uncertainty of information. Difficulties in gaining reliable projections of future conditions of individual fishing stocks, as well as the impact of new fishing techniques and human activity, made it very difficult for the CFP actors to readjust both means and goals to the changing circumstances. Majone (1989: 17–18) notes that conditions of uncertainty undermine the premise of the traditional rational decision-making style. When the factual basis for making a decision is uncertain, decision-makers cannot look for the optimum decision point. Instead of being a rational actor maximizing utility, actors become more focused on procedural consistency, which may not produce the most appropriate decision. Typically actors will go with prior beliefs and established procedures in determining how they should respond to the new situation. Confronting aspects of the situation in which they cannot successfully use established ways, policy-makers often will incompletely perceive the problem, ignoring salient points (Haas 1992: 28–29; Haas: 1990).

This problem manifests itself in a number of ways within the case. In a number of the most controversial areas, the EU decision-making system has turned to rational scientific analysis to set policy. However, there is a fundamental dispute about whether most fishing stocks are at the point of disaster. It becomes extremely difficult for political actors to impose quite substantial costs on such concentrated economic communities in the face of such uncertainty. The problem of uncertainty also creates difficulties with the specific management of the CFP system. A particularly important and controversial example of this is the TACs mechanism. Here scientists are supposed to set the actual sustainable catch – a very rationalistic approach. The fishermen reject these purely scientific efforts at regulation. The fishermen, using their expertise and enhanced technology, are finding stocks which thus appear readily available, while scientists, surveying a number of locations over time, see a very different picture.

A key aspect of this problem is the fact that there are communication barriers among the actors. It is in times of uncertainty that rational options and processes, and traditional methods face problems, and where persuasion and new ideas can come to the fore (Majone 1989). However, the policy brokers and entrepreneurs who would have the influence and persuasiveness to come to the fore and define the problem in a way that leads to a convincing solution have not been found (Kingdon 1995). On the one hand, scientists and fisheries managers have some difficulty in communicating their analysis and evidence to fishermen and politicians. Many scientific studies of TACs, for example, will have a considerable margin of error, which fishermen will interpret as a safe risk. Furthermore, scientists are often specialists in subfields and, while expert in their specialization, find themselves unable to present an overall picture that would convince a policy audience. On the other hand, because the influence of the scientists is largely associated with their knowledge resource, it requires actors with true political resources to be willing to embrace these new scientific ideas and force the fishing economy to re-evaluate its interests and outlooks (especially since the knowledge does not involve certainty).

There are several disjunctures that prevent this from happening. On the issue of communication, many of the repeated difficulties found in the history of the CFP have been due to the fact that the different groups of actors have widely different senses of time (cf. Bovens and 't Hart 1996). The differences in policy time can severely hamper mutual understanding, let alone coordination. Uncertainty, fairly distinctive among other EU policy sectors, factors into these different perspectives. Thus, fishermen tend to think in very short-term stretches – they measure success in terms of recent catches. Scientists tend to work out problems in long research periods, where results and policy solutions depend on new findings which arrive at unpredictable speeds. In further contrast, the Commission officials have yearly meetings where they have to provide some measure of explanation for what is happening, as well as solutions to deal with it. National politicians are on their own political cycles, often responding to demands from fishing communities only at election times. Thus the ability of science to provide actors with the necessary explanations and solutions is operating under substantial constraints.

Raising the problem of uncertainty brings back the issue of whether the fishing problem was actually controllable and thus merited the label of a policy disaster. The CFP certainly had the technology and the means of limiting quotas if sufficient political will could be mustered. It is more open to debate how foreseeable the changes in environment were for the CFP actors. As is outlined in the case history, concerns about fishing levels were raised at specific points in time, so policy-makers were aware that this was a potential problem. More significant is the fact that the system was unable to adjust to changing circumstances and the need for radical learning and persuasion in the policy area; this suggests that something in the policy-making structure and process (and their inherent inflexibility) outweighed the problems of uncertainty in the current crisis situation.

The structure of key decision-making at the EU level, where national interests have to be defended, is more decisive in explaining CFP's problems. Policy uncertainty and EU structure both contribute to patterns of incremental CFP policy modification. The Council, because of uncertainty, has an added reason to be reactive, as it deals with issues that have very distinct, concrete costs to communities within a particular member state. Even if the policy uncertainty was removed, it is difficult to see how the EU decisional process would work any better – the distributional consequences of alternative options would still remain. Given the reality of policy uncertainty, complex scientific presentations of the problem and the solution face the challenge of overcoming a more basic, simpler discussion of distribution of costs which the public finds a lot easier to follow. In the attempt to create radical, systemic change, as opposed to incremental change, policy-makers must confront the reality that ultimate decision-making power rests with the Council. Given the fact that the institution represents particular territorial interests, it is not surprising that the Council would reduce, for example, the Commission's proposed targets for decommissioning ships within the Multi-Annual Guidance Programme.

The 'Tragedy of the commons' problem and the consequences of implementation

As the fishing question involves a domain that stretches within and beyond individual state territorial waters, the policy problem raises the major challenge of how individual European policy-makers and fishing communities take collective action. The nature of this policy domain suggests that there might be an inherent tendency toward decisional pathology. The most famous expression of the decision-making pathology is found in Garrett Hardin's 'Tragedy of the commons' analogy. Hardin uses the example of a common pasture to show that all individuals have the incentive to overutilize the common domain since the costs of over utilization are shared out among a number of people and are usually of a long-term nature (Hardin 1968: 1244). This analogy focuses on how the larger environmental context leads the range of individuals to act in a fashion which, rationally, is detrimental to their long-term common interests.[4]

Our analysis of CFP operations reveals that fishermen do ignore rules because they view them as wrong or unnecessary. Many do place fish on the black market to avoid quotas. The commons analogy implies that a set of workable rules are required to solve the dilemma. Such a resolution may be impossible in a general commons but it can be applied to EU fishing waters. Much of the failure of the current rules is attributed to their lack of fit with the operating environment in which the fishermen find themselves. The uncertainty about changes in quotas and the fear that the quotas have been reached for a particular community tend to make fishing crews aim to catch as much as they can to get through the current quota. This behaviour has the dysfunctional effect of increasing overfishing, even under harsh and dangerous physical conditions. Another example is the Multi-Annual Guidance Programmes, which provide aid in attempts to restructure and reduce the fishing fleet, while other moneys are being allocated to increase the capability of the boats in the national fleets. While this will probably increase fishing safety, it also ensures that boats are able to make larger catches. Equally important is the impact of the complexity of the rules. A region-wide system, dealing with both scientific uncertainty and political compromises, will find it very difficult to translate the elaborate policy into terms that can be readily digested by the regulated actors (Deas 1998). Frustrated, as well as often unconvinced, the fishing fleets accord little legitimacy to these rules. The incremental changes due to new scientific findings or the iterations in the political bargaining add to, rather than reduce, this complexity.

In addition, a most significant reason for qualifying the responsibility on the regulated is the fact that very different levels of implementation and different kinds of policy guidance have been undertaken by the individual member states. There are straightforward ways of altering fishing crews' behaviour, for example by reducing the number of boats. The question then arises of how well the states are willing to pursue such courses of action.

Vested interests and the nature of policy implementation

One of the recurring themes in the story of the CFP is the failure of national governments to implement the spirit as well as the letter of the law with regard to their own industry. National ministries are entrusted by the EU and the general public with the task of exercising control over the fisheries. Given the objective of national ministries to promote the interests of their respective fishing communities (in terms of enhancing national priorities as well as building stable partnerships with the groups being regulated), it is plausible to expect that different countries will work at cross-purposes. Public choice theorists note varieties of this phenomena, such as agency capture and rent-seeking (Lane 1993). The Commission has neither the informational resources nor the political power to effectively monitor and intervene in the national implementation of the CFP (Mazey and Richardson 1993). It is very dependent for information on the network of actors with an interest in the fishing industry, particularly national regulators and the relevant regulated fishing industries. Naturally this resource dependency is not all one way, but it does substantially limit EU-level intervention. Equally, national regulators must build informational relationships and trust with the regulated to carry out their own aims. These relationships are not set in stone, however. It is sometimes the case that close networks change as the result of outside group pressure. In the Netherlands, for example, the parliament and environmental groups have forced a change in the closed nature of fisheries policy-making (De Vries and Jorna 1996).

In the CFP policy realm there are distinct variations in national implementation. The European Commission (1996) has clearly identified that certain countries have placed substantial resources into implementation and monitoring of fisheries policy, while other countries have allowed poorly resourced institutions, lacking coordination with other elements of the government, to handle the situation. Although the Commission offers strong praise for British actors on this account, the case history reveals that in some areas the British government has taken independent decisions about implementing EU law that have strained stocks, as well as the credibility of the policy in the eyes of the UK and continental fishermen. Operating according to a free-market ideology, the Thatcher government did not fully take advantage of EU funding for the restructuring of fleets, and hence allowed 'foreign operators' to gain a substantial foothold in the British quota.

Blaming variations in national performance on agency capture or rent-seeking may be exaggerated. Countries with inadequate monitoring capability simply have not made the investment in developing effective, well-resourced agencies a top priority as the UK has done. The southern countries are starting at a much later date and with the countervailing pressure to emphasize national economic expansion. The monitoring of fishing catches remains a very expensive proposition. It is estimated that in the UK alone the annual cost of policing the CFP is approximately £25 million on an annual catch worth between £400m–500m (interviews), and the total annual value of catch is approximately £450 million.[5] Not surprisingly, there are substantial differences in implementation, and the differences lead to stresses on the stocks, as well as strains on the legitimacy of the policy, for both the fishing nations who adhere closely to the CFP provisions and those who do not.

At the same time, it is dangerous to become fixated on the implementation records of the individual countries. Regardless of the country, the EU could develop measures that would mitigate the potential impact of variable country implementation – flat cuts in fishing boat numbers are fairly easy to monitor, for example. However, even if we assume that all fishing communities would be forced to implement the EU regulations evenly and completely, such a change does not overcome the difficulties of creating a policy design that has politically difficult distributional consequences.

European Union structure and policy sectoralization

The dissatisfaction found in the fishing-issue area feeds into the general dissatisfaction that national policy elites and the general population feel about the EU. This section addresses two aspects of the EU structure that interact to help contribute to this situation: joint decision-making and policy sectoralization.

EU decisions are made in each of its constituent, territorial units – the member states – as well as in the common policy-making arena. In the EU arena, the Council of Ministers and the European Council (more infrequently) form a critical institutional structure that defines member-state behaviour. Because of its ultimate role in determining the direction of the CFP, the Council also constrains, to a large extent, the possible policy options and negotiating positions of the other institutions, including the Commission and the European Parliament. Given the importance of this intergovernmental link, the nature of the institutional structure becomes important; in the CFP policy area, unanimity voting still decides critical issues about the CFP direction, such as quota-setting. This voting structure gives the member-state governments the institutional resources to block solutions that do not conform to their calculation of individual national self-interest. Given the fact that all member-state governments are in the position to operate this blocking device on the diverse issues they hold to be salient, the negotiating process tends to move towards the lowest common denominator. These deficient outcomes cannot be explained by the goals of the actors, their resources or the behaviour of interest groups without acknowledging the overarching structure of the process (Caporaso and Keeler 1995: 6).

The kind of decision-making pathology that this generates has been highlighted by such scholars as Fritz Scharpf. Scharpf argues that the EU and similar political systems which determine policy jointly at two levels will fall prey to certain sub-optimal patterns of unanimity decision-making, which he terms the joint-decision-making trap (Scharpf 1988: 254–255). Scholars have since pointed to the increasing use of qualified majority voting in the Council and the fact that the EU institutional structure has the capacity to set the agenda in a way that may circumvent the decision-making trap (Peters 1994). Nevertheless, the model has some resonance with the situation found in the CFP. Perhaps the most important insight is the fact that non-agreement, which constitutes the protection of the status quo and the continuation of current policies, may end up being preferable even though it is a sub-optimal outcome. Because the decision requires an EU-level determination, member states are precluded from coming up with their own individual remedies.

The CFP has a long history of actors striving to seek consensus among the member states, which are following their particular interests. It is important to understand how these interests were generated. The costs of a substantial reduction in the fishing fleets are clearly felt, while the collapse of the stocks tends to be a long-term problem, noted by scientists, which will manifest itself in the uncertain future. Because of this and the fact that fishing communities tend to represent strong symbols of community culture, national publics and politicians are generally sympathetic to the very concrete and evident costs that these communities are likely to suffer. Moreover, the sustainability/ecological concerns seem to be less of a spur in countries with sizeable fishing fleets than in those without. Fishing stocks are treated as natural resources to be harvested and extracted.

Given this orientation, and the alleged problems of dwindling stock, national governments are locked in a situation where they have to bargain to get a minimum level of consensus. The outcomes are likely to be political compromises that do not fully take into account scientific, 'rational' policy solutions and approaches. This situation exists to the extent that the Commission bureau must anticipate what the politically feasible options are beforehand, thus heavily constraining their own decision-making process, as could be seen in the 1976–83 period, when the Commission attempted to develop a conservation policy to deal with rising concerns about fishing.

Equally important, the nature of decision-making leads to a process that is incremental. Because of the potential costs of adjustment, long negotiation periods occur for key issues. Thus Spain fought the issue of water access from the period of its own enlargement negotiations until the period when the Scandinavian countries and Austria applied and were accepted. Political intervention, such as the 1972 enlargement, did have the benefit of forcing consensus among the original six and inducing compromise among the three applicants. This is an example of policy linkage creating consensus.

One possible way of escaping Scharpf's (1988) joint-decision trap is the recognition that the EU constituent units must deal with each other across a number of issue areas, which may create possibilities for log-rolling to break the impasse created by unanimity voting in any given issue. However, scholars have pointed out that one of the distinctive institutional characteristics of EU policy-making is its extreme sectoralization/segmentation (see, for example, Mazey and Richardson 1993; Grant 1993). Not only the Commission DGs, but also the Council of Ministers and the European Parliament confront EU policy on a largely functional, sectoral basis. EU actors and interest groups are forced to concentrate their efforts on concerns on a very narrow front. Not only does this inhibit any potential direct log-rolling between issue areas, but it also helps to exclude other EU goals and interests from the insider core most directly involved in policy areas like the CFP. Other policy perspectives, such as those of actors emphasizing environmental issues, will find themselves in a different policy stream, and will have much less direct interaction with and impact on the CFP – even though fishing issues directly and indirectly impinge on their values and interests as consumers and environmentalists.

It is therefore not surprising that actors in the fishing sector tend to focus on the relative positions of individual national fishing communities. The external pressure to reform the CFP for reasons external to the sector do not exist to the degree found, for instance, in the Common Agricultural Policy, where pressure is mounting in General Agreement on Tariffs and Trade (GATT) negotiations and in fears about the budgetary impact of eastern European enlargement.

Another debilitating aspect of the decision-making process (from the standpoint of a common policy) is that it gives the member states strong opportunities to deflect blame for national situations on to EU institutions. The necessity of finding some compromise allows member governments a chance to take credit for the gains successfully achieved in the negotiations while blaming the EU processes and other coalitions of national interest for the failures. UK actors, for example, usually attribute the undermining of UK fishing prospects to the 1972 enlargement negotiations and the disadvantageous bargaining position of the UK (as an applicant state).

Conclusions

The previous sections have dwelt only on the perceived failures of the CFP. These are just a part of the entire picture. The CFP, for example, has areas of undisputed success. Most observers are willing to concede that the CFP has handled market management and external relations, two out of four key policy headings, rather well. A more fundamental challenge to the portrayal of the CFP as a policy disaster centres on a key policy question: have there been any better policy alternatives that the EU could feasibly have put into place and then implemented? This question links back to the issue of control and responsibility, necessary elements in categorizing a policy as a disaster. Problem uncertainty, and the policy complexity it has generated, has raised doubts about all the alternatives; political constraints raise severe practical doubts as well. The intellectually attractive solution of setting up local zones with exclusive rights, for example, would still have to contend with the political costs of limiting access for specific fleets from other member countries.

We cannot at present isolate a better alternative, taking into account all the important variables, but the case history does suggest some overarching conclusions. The CFP case history reveals the special problems raised by an issue area that involves high technical complexity and high policy uncertainty. In this context, where rational policy-making holds even less sway than in other hypothetical circumstances, policy-makers can be easily swayed by particular scientific information or national interests which cut across this uncertainty, and thus may be less open to compromise or alternative perspectives.

Integral to this issue of uncertainty, yet perhaps more important, was the communications gap between the various actors – fishing communities, technical experts, politicians, civil servants and the general public. Policy-makers, with their very different time frame and political objectives, find it very difficult to translate into an effective policy – a policy which the fishing communities must understand and accept – what the scientists, operating under uncertainty and experiencing different operational constraints, might consider to be the key considerations. The EU regulators also confront the difficulty of having different member-state governments, possessing both differing levels of public concern about the particular CFP issues and different levels of policy resources they can devote to the problems. This leads member states to implement CFP regulations in different ways, and the Commission is very dependent on the member states and their fishing industry cooperation.

However difficult these problems are, all possible compromise remedies face a central institutional hurdle: the EU structure works against the learning process that potentially might develop new, alternative ideas. Actors, including Commission officials, have had to struggle to build flexibility into the regulations, reflecting the difficulty of achieving joint decision-making consensus. As it stands now, the EU decision-making process emphasizes lowest common denominator bargaining where the focus on particular territorial interests runs deep. This structure tends to force the maintenance of the status quo, a situation that is reinforced

by the strong sectoralization of EU policy. While Commission and national regulators participate in extensive consultation with actors affected by the particular
functional policy area, the sectoral emphasis makes it difficult to incorporate the
other societal and economic interests that might create cross-cutting pressures for
change. In this context, specific policy solutions for the CFP problem may be less
decisive than creating new EU institutional dynamics enabling the EU 'to learn
how to learn'.

Notes

1   Interview, UK Rep. official, 1997.
2   For example, Article 11 of the midterm review establishes an explicit link between
    conservation of resources and the restructuring of the Community fishing fleet, i.e.
    between measures to limit fish mortality by managing the volume of catches and their
    composition, and those for limiting it by managing the means deployed.
3   View expressed by DG XIV officials.
4   Critics of Hardin, such as Ostrom (1990), argue that grassroots institutions can develop
    in local communities which manage common pools of resources very effectively. In the
    case of the fishing economy of the EU, however, such initiatives have never had the
    chance to develop.
5   Interview, Commission official (1997).

References

Bovens, M. and 't Hart, P. (1996) *Understanding Policy Fiascoes*, New Brunswick and London:
    Transaction.
Cann, C. (1998) 'Introduction: a fisheries management viewpoint', in T. Gray (ed.) *The Poli-
    tics of Fishing*, Basingstoke: Macmillan.
Caporaso, J. and Keeler, J. (1995) 'The European Union and regional integration theory', in
    C. Rhodes and S. Mazey (eds) *The State of the European Union*, vol. 3, Boulder, CO: Lynne
    Rienner.
CFP Review Group (1996) *A Review of the Common Fisheries Policy*, 2 vols, prepared for UK
    fisheries ministers by the CFP Review Group.
de Vries, J. and Jorna, F. B. A. (1996) *Neocorporatism, Iron Triangles and Issue Networks*, Working
    Paper no. 96–93, Enschede: Netherlands Institute of Government.
Deas, B. (1998) 'Coastal state management', in T. Gray (ed.) *The Politics of Fishing*,
    Basingstoke: Macmillan.
European Commission (1996) *Monitoring the Common Fisheries Policy*, COM (96) Final, Brus-
    sels: European Commission.
Farnell, J. and Elles, J. (1984) *In Search of a Common Fisheries Policy*, Aldershot: Gower.
Grant, W. (1993) 'Pressure groups and the European Community: an overview', in S.
    Mazey and J. Richardson (eds) *Lobbying in the European Community*, Oxford and New York:
    Oxford University Press.
Haas, P. (1990) *Saving the Mediterranean*, New York: Columbia University Press.
—— (1992) 'Introduction: epistemic communities and international policy coordination',
    International Organization 46: 1–35.
Hardin, G. (1968) 'The tragedy of the commons', *Science* 162: 1243–1248.

Holden, M. (1994) *The Common Fisheries Policy*, Oxford: Blackwell.

House of Lords Select Committee on the European Communities (1993) *Review of the Common Fisheries Policy*, 2nd report, London: HMSO.

Kingdon, J. (1995) *Agendas, Alternatives, and Public Policies*, New York: HarperCollins.

Lane, J. (1993) *The Public Sector: Concepts, Models and Approaches*, London: Sage.

Majone, G. (1989) *Evidence, Argument, & Persuasion in the Policy Process*, New Haven and London: Yale University Press.

Mazey, S. and Richardson, J. (1993) 'Introduction: transference of power, decision rules, and rules of the game', in S. Mazey and J. Richardson (eds) *Lobbying in the European Community*, Oxford and New York: Oxford University Press.

Ostrom, E. (1990) *Governing the Commons*, Cambridge and New York: Cambridge University Press.

Peters, B. G. (1994) 'Agenda-setting in the European Community', *Journal of European Public Policy* 1: 9–26.

Scharpf, F. (1988) 'The joint-decision trap: lessons from German federalism and European integration', *Public Administration* 66: 239–278.

Thom, M. (1998), 'The determinants of fishing policy: a comparison of British and French policies', in T. Gray (ed.) *The Politics of Fishing*, Basingstoke: Macmillan.

Wallace, H. (1996) 'Government without statehood', in H. Wallace and W. Wallace (eds) *Policy-making in the European Union*, Oxford: Oxford University Press.

Wise, M. (1984) *The Common Fisheries Policy of the European Community*, London: Methuen.

10

THE CHANCE OF A LIFETIME?

The European Community's foreign and refugee
policies towards the conflict in Yugoslavia,
1991–95

Joanne van Selm-Thorburn and Bertjan Verbeek

Introduction

In 1991 the member states of the European Community (EC) were deep in negotiations over a Treaty on European Union.[1] These negotiations were to pave the way for the development of a political Union, to go alongside the deepening economic integration of the west European states. The discussions were taking place in a new political climate. The Cold War was over; security and foreign policy concerns regarding the immediate eastern neighbours were changing; Germany was reunifying and the former East Germany was being tied into the new Union. Meanwhile, waves of refugees and migrants were expected to be on their way from former socialist states. Security, foreign policy, and asylum and immigration policies were therefore high on the agenda. The European Union (EU) states saw the need to stand together and draw closer on these issues.

In the summer of 1991 conflict erupted in the republics of Yugoslavia. It has often been claimed that this Yugoslav crisis provided a concrete and perversely 'ideal' opportunity to show both the necessity and the feasibility of a common European foreign policy. The crisis was also immediately catapulted to the top of the list of potential sources of refugee flows. The member states sought to meet the conflict with a common diplomatic and foreign policy. Yet the Community failed to formulate a genuine common approach to the migration and displacements produced by the Yugoslav crisis. A policy disaster was to ensue as a result of decision-making which failed to foresee the spillover consequences for other areas of EC interest.

This chapter seeks to explore the puzzling disunity in EC foreign and refugee policy in relation to the Yugoslav crisis. We perceive not only different patterns of disunity between the member states in the two policy fields, but also a disunity of policy-making, as the two areas were apparently treated as if they were entirely unrelated. EC member states gave their highest priority to the maintenance of

175

European unity. As we will show, however, attempts to present a united front to the outside world produced several partly unwanted, partly unforeseen consequences. Instead of developing a common European approach to the problems of displaced populations, EC member states acted in a non-unified fashion. While collectively supporting protection of those at risk of displacement *in situ*, EC member states developed inharmonious protection policies for those who reached the various EC borders. These diverging policy outcomes can be explained by the structure and dynamics of the policy-making process in separate policy areas, as well as by the national interests that were at stake.

This chapter contains the following sections. We initially discuss the contrasting evaluations possible in relation to this crisis. We then show how European foreign and security policy during the early phases of the crisis (1991–92) affected events in Yugoslavia, and reinforced and complicated the nature of the refugee problem. We examine the EU's policies towards refugees and conclude by offering an explanation of the difference in European approaches to foreign and refugee problems.

A policy disaster?

The start of our analysis is from the vantage point of the European Community. One definition of success in the Yugoslav case is the extent to which Europe managed to adopt a common security and refugee policy. At the same time, such a common policy can be seen as a response to the earlier failure to prevent the conflict from intensifying (cf. Haas 1983). We prefer to start with the high stakes set by Europe itself: the definition of the Yugoslav crisis as a test of common European policy capabilities. To assess the disastrous qualities of the EU's foreign, asylum and immigration policies vis-à-vis former Yugoslavia we shall employ Bovens and 't Hart's criteria of judgement (Bovens and 't Hart 1996).

How bad is bad?

We understand the EC's top priority to have been the maintenance of its own internal unity on foreign affairs. The initial policy towards the republics of Yugoslavia was that they should remain united and claims for independence would not be recognized. The specific form of continued Yugoslav unity was to be developed in an EC-organized conference chaired by Lord Carrington. With regard to displacements, there was such concern about movements from other former communist countries that the possibility of a mass movement from or within Yugoslavia was not a main consideration. Over time, the question of Yugoslav unity gave way to the priority of EC unity, and other states capitulated to the strong desire of Germany to accord recognition to Croatia and Slovenia.

If 'unity no matter what' is the yardstick to measure the European Community's performance in the area of foreign policy – and that was the measure the policy-makers of the EC were using at the time – then its policies can, on the whole, be called a moderate success. The twelve member states managed to keep a united front throughout most of the Yugoslav crisis. The glaring exception is the German unilateral recognition of Slovenia and Croatia in December 1991. However, even that move should be assessed in the context of a strong incentive to EC member states to develop and maintain a common policy. If chain-gang diplomacy (Jones 1996) was the only way to achieve the German goal of recognition for those states, then that was the means to be used.

However, if the EC's own publicly announced substantive policy goals are used as a criterion to judge its policies, evaluation will be more critical. The EC's objective from the outset had been to negotiate ceasefires and to cajole the warring parties into a solution that would satisfy demands for more autonomy within the framework of a Yugoslavian federation. The subsequent recognition of Slovenia and Croatia meant that that objective could no longer be met. Moreover, it endangered the conclusion of a lasting solution because Croatian independence, in particular, was bound to incite and inflame ethnic conflict in Bosnia–Hercegovina. The multicultural republic could envisage no alternative other than its own declaration of independence, fearful as it was of being swallowed up by the rump of Yugoslavia, dominated by Serbia. At the same time, Bosnian independence was bound to increase inter-ethnic tension within the republic because many Bosnian Serbs and Bosnian Croats wanted close links with their ethnic kin in Serbia and Croatia. In addition, Croatian independence, occurring before the question of Croatian Serbs (in Eastern Slavonia and the Kraijna) had been settled, was the spark which ignited war between Croatia and Serbia.

At a later stage, when the EC and the United Nations had made several attempts to solve the crisis in Bosnia–Hercegovina, the European Community re-established unity behind the Vance–Owen plan. This action implied recognition of the geographical concentration of the various ethnic groups, which the European Community had previously denounced. Furthermore, other member states' acceptance of Germany's unilateral recognition reduced to nothing Lord Carrington's attempts to come up with a definitive reconciliation of the republics' troubles within the framework of the Yugoslav federation.

From the vantage point of the various actors in Yugoslavia, the EC's policies were a mixed blessing. Slovenia and Croatia greatly benefited from the EU's recognition policies. Bosnia–Hercegovina, however, was faced with a tragic choice between domination by Serbia in rump Yugoslavia and ethnic conflict under newly won independence. Serbia was hindered in its attempt to create a Greater Serbia encompassing all territories dominated by ethnic Serbs. Macedonia suffered badly from the EC's recognition policies, despite the fact that it met all the criteria of democracy set by the Badinter Commission when judging applications for recognition. Macedonia was, on Greece's insistence, not recognized by the European Community. As a consequence, Macedonia was not eligible for foreign financial support and was submitted to an economic boycott by Greece, which deprived the country of essential goods. For several minorities in Yugoslavia, the EC's recognition policies implied the end of their hopes of legal incorporation in larger territorial units: this was the case, for example, for the Kraijna Serbs in Croatia, the Bosnian Croats and the Bosnian Serbs.

If we are going to ask how bad is bad, then the lack of safety and protection in Srebrenica is as bad as it can get from everyone's perspective. EU governments may have succeeded in keeping people in need of international protection out of their territory, but they clearly failed to protect lives. They failed in any attempt at intergovernmental cooperation to coordinate their protection policies beyond the attempted securing – under their UN and NATO guises – of the 'safe areas'. Whether their populations considered keeping needy people away a success or not is unknown and unquantifiable. From the point of view of the displaced persons, they clearly failed. Potentially the Bosnian Serbs would see the 'safe areas' and the closing of other protection options as a useful EU policy, as it left pockets of isolated, unprotected Bosnian Muslims to be massacred in order to prove to the world that a partition of territory and 'cleansing' of the resulting areas was the only way to achieve an initial settlement.

What sort of damage resulted from this seemingly overwhelming fiasco? To give a non-exhaustive inventory: there is the clear physical damage to cities and, above all, lives destroyed and lost; there is the psychological damage to the displaced persons – the relatively few lucky ones who escaped leaving friends and often family behind – and to the soldiers and aid workers who tried to carry out the task of protection and assistance on the ground; there is also psychological and political damage incurred if one acknowledges that by leaving those who wished to escape in the path of the enemy, Europe's citizens, represented by their democratic governments, had essentially not heeded the cry of 'never again' sounded by their forefathers in 1945; there is the political damage of the loss or denial of the first opportunity for EU states to act together on the protection of displaced persons and refugees under the third-pillar arrangements of intergovernmental cooperation in the fields of justice and home affairs; there is the economic, political and psychological damage to the newly independent states of Slovenia and Croatia, which took in such a disproportionate number of the displaced.

Who or what brought the disaster about?

At the start of the conflict in Yugoslavia in early 1991 the international community looked to the European Community to take the initiative. The United States considered the matter as principally a European crisis and called upon Europe to show some resolve. The United Nations was unlikely to take action unless it was backed by the United States. In addition, the European Community was not at all unwilling to take a lead. The new institutional framework that was being devised at the time, which would eventually result in the Maastricht treaty, was supposed to encompass foreign affairs. The Yugoslav crisis thus proved an opportunity to show the necessity for, and feasibility of, a common European policy. It can thus be safely concluded that at the early stages of the conflict the European Community was a central actor.

At that moment, however, the Community's foreign and security policy was still a strictly intergovernmental arrangement, labelled European Political Cooperation (EPC). Only a small intergovernmental body was in place in Brussels to deal with questions of foreign policy: the so-called EPC Secretariat, consisting of a number of temporary civil servants from the Foreign Offices of those countries that were members of the EC *troika* (the current, previous and forthcoming presidencies) at the time. This arrangement implied that the Council of Foreign Ministers and the European Council were a sort of watchdog, permanently guarding against a possible infringement of a member state's national interest. Although it is true that the European Community was the main mediator during the early stages of the Yugoslavian conflict, national interests and actors lay beneath the surface, and from time to time individual member states would take initiatives outside the EPC framework.

The European Community's involvement in (former) Yugoslav matters varied greatly through the different stages of the conflict (Lavdas 1996: 218–226). Until the spring of 1991 the European Community was hardly involved at all. It paid little attention to the process of disintegration that had been consuming Yugoslavia. When, in the spring of 1991, it became clear that Slovenia and Croatia were heading fast towards a declaration of independence, the European Community became actively involved. Its objective was to find a solution, based at first on keeping Yugoslavia together, then on recognition of independence provided the Yugoslav republics met certain conditions. It co-sponsored an international conference in The Hague in the autumn of 1991 in order to reach a comprehensive settlement. However, when in early 1992 most Yugoslav republics opted for independence, the EU lost the diplomatic initiative. It had to play second fiddle to the United Nations, which became the central institutional focus of peacekeeping operations in a conflict-torn region. The European Community's main involvement at that stage was in the administration of the Muslim-Croat town of Mostar in Bosnia–Hercegovina.

In the course of 1994 the EU was forced into the shadows by two member states – France and the UK – promoting the establishment of a Rapid Reaction Force, and by the United Nations, NATO and Russia. Main decisions were taken by the so-called Contact Group, of which Germany and the United States also were part. After the fall of Srebrenica and Zepa in 1995, the EU played second fiddle to the United States, which used coercive diplomacy via NATO in order to achieve an agreement in Dayton. The EU's post-1996 participation in the implementation of the Dayton Agreement has been only low key, and remained limited primarily to the continued administration of Mostar and to financial assistance. It seems, therefore, appropriate to concentrate on the period in which EC actions appear to have made a difference. As far as foreign policy is concerned, the EC was a key actor in 1991 and early 1992, although its refugee policies, including its support of the safe-area strategy, were central into 1995 and beyond.

One source of the fiasco must be the increasing restrictiveness of refugee and asylum policies in Europe, brought about in part by each state going for the least liberal stance possible in order not to be blamed by all other members for flooding the entire EU territory with refugees and asylum-seekers. The circumstances of the time, including the negotiations for the Treaty on European Union; the collapse of communism and fear of hundreds of thousands of new economic migrants; the policy of 'ethnic cleansing' and the fact that the majority of those displaced were Muslim at a time when xenophobia was apparently rising, all must all have played a role in bringing this fiasco about.

In sum, the EC's policies can be considered a disaster or a moderate success, depending on one's point of view. In the area of foreign policy, the EC successfully maintained its self-proclaimed goal of unity. This unity, however, had its price in terms of the achievement of the substantive policy goal of peace and stability in the region. In the area of displaced persons, not even an attempt at formulating a common policy was made. Individual states protected their perceived interest of keeping foreigners out. This, too, had an evident human cost. The EC formulated its policies on the basis of existing knowledge and available information, and in reaction to the unfolding of events in Yugoslavia itself. It is therefore appropriate to assess briefly the explanations of this crisis generally advanced at that time.

EC foreign and security policy towards the former Yugoslavia, 1991–92

The structure of the international system and the national interests of states offer an important first clue to understanding the initial lack of European involvement. Until the fall of the Berlin Wall in 1989, any grave development in Yugoslavia was bound to be defined in terms of the Cold War conflict between the two super-powers, the United States and the Soviet Union. This precluded independent European action. The dissolution of the Soviet empire in central and eastern Europe, however, brought about a gradual loss of interest in European security on the part of the United States, and an increasing eagerness of European actors to fill the power vacuum. The European Community took on several responsibilities in promoting and guiding stability in central and eastern Europe by administering many of the funds made available for that purpose (see Noelke and Stratman, forthcoming). When the Yugoslav crisis reached a first peak with the announce-ment of Slovenian and Croatian independence on 25 June 1991, the United States did not consider this a direct threat to vital American interests and was content to leave the Europeans to deal with the situation.

The phases of European involvement

European foreign and security policies towards Yugoslavia in 1991 can be succinctly divided into four stages (Glenny 1996; Wijnaendts 1993; Woodward 1995). Initially, there was *denial of the problem*. Until May 1991 there was no European policy towards Yugoslavia. In 1990 no one wanted to listen to the Austrian foreign minister, Alois Mock, who toured western Europe to warn against the dissolution of Yugoslavia after growing tensions in Slovenia (Woodward 1995: 148). Similarly, the Italian foreign minister, Gianni de Michelis, failed to interest the European Community in a common policy after Italy suffered from a huge influx of Albanian asylum-seekers (*ibid.*: 158). Instead, individual member states pursued individual policies, often signalling conflicting messages to the actors in Yugoslavia. Evidence from Dutch diplomats suggests that in 1991, under the presidencies of Luxembourg and the Netherlands, the Foreign Offices were displeased with reports from Belgrade warning against violence and dissolution. These same Foreign Offices wanted to press ahead with European integration and defined the Yugoslav problem away by arguing that, eventually, Yugoslavia would simply want to join the EC, just like all the other formerly communist European states (Huys 1994: 116–118).

Following denial, the EC switched to a stage of *acute awareness of the problem*. The May referendum on Croatian independence was the first event to stir the European Community. The declaration of independence by Slovenia and Croatia on 25 June, however, set the EC machinery in motion. Subsequently, the European Community would succeed in adopting a common foreign policy until 18 December 1991, when Germany unilaterally recognized the independence of both Slovenia and Croatia. In the six-month period between these two dates the European Community pursued a policy that was aimed at maintaining the unity of Yugoslavia in one way or another. It hoped to reach that objective by making use of two instruments: offering the carrot of autonomy for Yugoslavia's republics in a unified state and, to a lesser extent, economic carrots and sticks such as conditional loans and sanctions.

The president of the Council, Luxembourg's prime minister, Jacques Santer, and the president of the European Commission, Jacques Delors, travelled to Belgrade in May 1991 and made the issuance of a \$4.5 billion loan to Yugoslavia dependent on political reform and the introduction of a market economy (Woodward 1995: 160). After Slovenia's and Croatia's declarations of independence the EC *troika* employed shuttle diplomacy in the pursuit of ceasefires between the Yugoslav National Army (JNA), and Croatia and Slovenia, as well as eventual solutions that would be supported by all the Yugoslav republics. This comprehensive settlement seemed closer after the July 1991 EC-brokered ceasefire, the so-called Brioni Declaration. This declaration included a moratorium on moves towards independence for Slovenia and Croatia, and acceptance by the Yugoslav republics of an EC-sponsored conference in The Hague in early October, chaired by Lord Carrington and aimed at settling the future of the Yugoslav republics.

From mid-September 1991 Germany, and to a lesser degree Italy, indicated that solutions within the framework of a united Yugoslavia were no longer preferable to the immediate recognition of Slovenian and Croatian independence (Crawford 1996). At the meetings (formal as well as informal) of the twelve EC ministers of foreign affairs (14–15 September, 28 October, 8 November, 9 December and 15–16 December) Germany constantly indicated its willingness to go ahead with unilateral recognition if the other eleven would not agree to the soundness of immediately recognizing the independence of Slovenia and Croatia. Germany's argument was that Slovenia and Croatia were at that point barred from international assistance, while they risked losing the battle against the Yugoslav National Army. However, in this penultimate stage of 1991 EC policy towards Yugoslavia, *Germany followed the EC path*. Eventually, at the 15–16 December Summit, European unity was maintained: all Yugoslav republics were entitled to apply for recognition provided they filed their request within a week and the so-called Badinter Commission was convinced of their democratic status. The Badinter Commission's judgement was to be the basis of a final EC decision planned for 15 January 1992.

However, in the early morning of 16 December, after having reached this compromise with great difficulty, eleven worn-out foreign ministers were stopped in their tracks by their Greek colleague, Samaras. Samaras brought up the Macedonian question: Greece insisted that recognition would not be extended to Macedonia unless the republic's name was changed and the country made clear that it had no regional aspirations. Sheer fatigue prompted the eleven ministers to agree quickly (see Wijnaendts 1993: 162–163).

This scenario was only the beginning of the devastation of European unity. On 18 December Germany unilaterally recognized Slovenia and Croatia, without consulting its fellow member states and ignoring warnings from UN Secretary-General Perez de Cuellar and American President George Bush not to do so. This final stage, of *chain-gang diplomacy*, saw unity eventually restored, when the eleven other member states followed Germany and recognized Slovenia and Croatia, even before the Badinter Commission had pronounced its final judgement. Unfortunately for Macedonia, European unity was also maintained on the Greek front. Despite the Badinter Commission's approval of Macedonia's credentials, the European Community would not recognize its independence, on Greece's insistence. Meanwhile, the conference in the Hague had been co-sponsored by the United Nations, introducing Cyrus Vance as international mediator next to Lord Carrington and taking the main initiative in multilateral diplomacy away from the European Community.

The consequences of EC foreign and security policy

The EC's main aim was to avoid disunity among its member states, and to devise and stick to a common policy. Initially, this consensus was built on an attempt to design a comprehensive solution within the framework of some kind of Yugoslav unity, while its main policy instruments were the granting of international recognition and a mixture of economic sanctions. This emphasis on European unity helped bring about policies that had undesirable consequences.

Reinforcement of underlying causes

The EC's emphasis on maintaining a unified Yugoslavia aggravated several causes underlying the conflict in that country. A first instance is the financial assistance package the EC offered in the spring of 1991. The EC made its $4.5 billion loan of May 1991 conditional on Yugoslav 'good behaviour', for instance opening up their market, political reform and respect for human rights. By adopting this approach, the EC only added to the tensions already existing in Yugoslavia. The creation of a market economy was part of the struggle between the federation and the republics. Creating a Yugoslavia-wide market economy implied centralization of federal powers, which, of course, was at the heart of the Yugoslav problem. A second example is the way the EC defined the Yugoslav conflict once skirmishes occurred. The European Community defined the conflict in 1991 as a border conflict; this had several important consequences, all going back to the main failure of the European Community in never attempting thoroughly to analyse the problems of disintegration that had been bothering Yugoslavia since the mid-1970s. First of all, it implied that the European Community accepted without discussion the administrative borders drawn by the Yugoslav constitution, which were in fact at the heart of the problem. Actually, the European Community was trying to resolve a border dispute with the idea that all that was necessary was to create a ceasefire and put in place a monitoring mission. The EC did not attempt to set criteria to judge the various claims for self-determination; the Serbian minority in Croatia was thus denied the opportunity granted to the Croatians and Slovenians. Second, this approach to the problem strengthened the hand of extremists on both sides; recognition of Croatia's borders was bound to stir up Serbian extremism in eastern Croatia (Slavonia) and southern Croatia (Knin) at the expense of moderate parties in the region, such as the Serbian Democratic Party in Croatia (SDS). Finally, the focus on border disputes reinforced the tendency not to assess the long-term consequences of the EC's policies.

The eventual recognition by the EC of Slovenia and Croatia changed the game for many actors in the rest of Yugoslavia. Bosnia–Hercegovina and Macedonia saw no option but to declare independence as well, even though that implied that Croat and Serb minorities in Bosnia–Hercegovina would be deprived of their right to be part of a Croat or Serb nation, thus setting the stage for the violence that was to erupt in 1992. Time and again, President Izetbegovic of Bosnia–Hercegovina warned the EC against these consequences, but he did not succeed in restraining the member states from pursuing their recognition policy.

The choice of policy instruments legitimizes third parties

The EC's explicit definition of the Yugoslav conflict as a border issue between republics trying to become independent involved an explicit focus on maintaining ceasefires. The sending of monitoring missions constituted the principal policy instrument. The emphasis on the monitoring of ceasefire agreements forced the

EC to start dealing with, and focus its attention on, local warlords such as Buban (leader of the Bosnian Croats) and Hadjic (leader of the Serbs in Croatia's Knin region). This was deemed necessary in order to guarantee safety to EC monitors. At the same time, it implied the indirect recognition of such local war lords and the strengthening of their role vis-à-vis the moderate parties.

Spillover effects

The EC's explicit acceptance of existing borders between Yugoslav republics, coupled with the (eventually successful) German pressure to recognize Slovenia and Croatia, contributed to the spillover of the conflict, first into a war between Serbia and Croatia over Slavonia and the Knin, and next into Bosnia–Hercegovina. A further spillover, unforeseen or ignored by member states, was that these events would produce enormous waves of refugees, thus forcing the European Community suddenly to face another crisis, for another set of ministers in an intergovernmental setting: a refugee crisis.

The European Community's policies towards refugees

Some kind of EC institutional framework had at least been developed for external political relations in the 1980s. However, policies dealing with those consequences of individual mobility perceived as undesirable, such as immigration, terrorism, spreading drug addiction and crime, were developed in a setting completely outside the European Community. The Schengen Agreement, designed to cope with asylum-seekers, border-crossing criminals and trade in products such as drugs, arms and laundered money, was originally negotiated by five EC member states among themselves. European Community cooperation against terrorism and crime happened in many different, often secret, committees and working groups, such as Trevi (Bigo 1992; Hebenton and Thomas 1995) and the Intergovernmental Ad Hoc Group on Immigration and Asylum. Analysts have been quick to point out that this reluctance to discuss such matters in a strictly European Community framework comes as no surprise, because these policy areas touch the essence of national sovereignty, perhaps more than foreign policy does. They involve such pivotal matters as decisions as to who enters one's territory and the organization of legal and police systems, all elements that can be seen as primary constituents of statehood.

As has been discussed above, the conflicts erupted in former Yugoslavia in summer 1991 while the then twelve member states of the European Community were in the process of negotiating the Treaty on European Union. The Maastricht treaty, signed at the end of 1991, was to bring about institutional changes to cope with the expansion of areas of policy cooperation. As one of the two new pillars being added to the temple of European Union, intergovernmental cooperation on matters of justice and home affairs was being developed as part of a newly explicit political integration process. Justice and home affairs was set to cover three distinct but in some ways related branches of previously staunchly sovereign government activity: drugs policies; judicial cooperation, including law enforcement across frontiers and action against terrorism; and asylum and immigration. This latter area had already been the subject of much confusion through its linkage to these criminal activities in policy thinking. The sudden displacement of hundreds of thousands of former Yugoslavians, primarily from and within Bosnia–Hercegovina, was to prove an enormous challenge to the conceptualization of these issues and to the policy arrangements that had existed for the previous four decades.

Migration thought and policy action in Europe had been defined by the conjunction of two crises in the late 1940s. The 1951 Geneva Convention relating to the status of refugees was a nominally universal, but in fact Euro-centric document, defining a refugee as an individual with a well-founded fear of persecution on one or more of five discriminatory grounds, who was outside his or her country of origin and could not be returned there. This was intended to cover all those who had been displaced by Nazi activities and the outcome of the Second World War, and those who wanted to flee suppression in the communist east. The USSR and satellite states were not involved in the drafting of the convention, as they were more interested in a convention on statelessness to help them move unwanted peoples.

While in 1967 this document was universalized by the New York Protocol, it had served Europe's asylum purposes well until in the 1970s restrictions were imposed on legal immigration. All would-be immigrants thus became asylum-seekers, meaning that bona fide asylum cases had to demonstrate their credentials in a climate of increasing scepticism. Still the majority of the world's refugees did not make it to Europe, and the notion of political asylum in Europe remained largely a European concept, applied to east Europeans who managed to escape.

In 1989, as the Berlin Wall came down and leaving the east became an easy affair, the definition of a refugee ceased to apply to those for whom it had originally been meant. Under newly democratic systems persecution was no longer credible as a motive for westward migration. The crisis in former Yugoslavia broke out just as western governments were putting up higher barriers to all those fleeing former socialist states.

Asylum and immigration policies towards former Yugoslavs

European governments found themselves faced with a massive exodus, against a background of increasing restriction and continuing negotiations to develop harmonization of asylum and immigration policy. The very reason for trying to harmonize asylum and immigration policies was that a single market with free movement of people meant fewer checks for third-country nationals, even if the small print of free movement described it as only for EU citizens. Believing that an influx in one state meant horror for all, EU governments rushed to impose policies of limitation: visa restrictions, border controls and the safe third-country rule (whereby the first safe country transited en route is the one expected to deal with a claim and offer protection if appropriate).

185

Under pressure from non-governmental organizations (NGOs) and the United Nations High Commissioner for Refugees (UNHCR) European governments began to develop policies of temporary protection, whereby limited numbers of people would be granted a lesser humanitarian status for protection until the conflict was over. In the conclusions of the Edinburgh European Council in December 1992 the EU governments announced jointly that temporary protection would be applied only to vulnerable cases. The policy was essentially one of containment. The aim was to keep the displaced persons in former Yugoslavia – the Bosnians in Bosnia or, if necessary, in other former Yugoslav republics. This policy was facilitated or codetermined by at least two important factors other than the climate of limitations and initial harmonization and fear described above: the warring parties' policies of ethnic cleansing and the UN mandated 'safe areas'.

EU governments wanted to be seen not to be supporting the ethnic cleansing policies. If the policy on the ground was for each ethnic or religious group to try to remove the other groups, either through forced movement or extermination, then other states attempting to resolve the humanitarian dilemmas of the conflict felt the need to try to stop the extermination and stop the movement. In other words, to oppose the ethnic cleansing policy EU and other outside governments needed to try to keep people alive and in Bosnia, in the areas where they had lived for centuries. The EU member states supported the UN means of trying to effect this policy of opposition to ethnic cleansing through the creation of 'safe areas' – zones within which United Nations Protection Force (UNPROFOR) troops would operate within their severely limited mandate and in which humanitarian assistance (food, shelter, medicine) would be available.

The refugee policy fiasco to be described is a dual-faceted one. First, the policy decision taken was to go ahead with the creation of UN 'safe areas', thereby protecting the displaced persons close to their homes – or, put otherwise, protecting EU borders from the influx of enormous numbers of displaced persons and a new European Muslim diaspora. Second, the policy of offering temporary protection, while it meant that those who did escape received some form of protection, remains a fiasco in the making if return does not ensue as the Dayton Agreement stipulates. Having decided that civil war did not necessarily equate to persecution, the EC member states were not ready to grant refugee status according to the 1951 Convention to those fleeing Yugoslavia. Most of the EU member states took to ad hoc policy-making, developing structures of rights, residence, employment and education linked to the notion that the immigration of those temporarily protected would be short-lived. The foreign and security policies being employed would bring an end to the conflict, the thinking went, and then the 'refugees' could go home. Some states developed a legal basis to these new protection mechanisms; some looked to what neighbours were doing to add an element of coordination; but essentially it was policy-making at the state level, with rapid decisions and an assessment that the situation would not be long-lasting and return would be possible.

The 'safe area' policy was a UN approach supported by the EU. It lent an extra dimension to the actual refugee policies, in that it meant people would not so readily or easily arrive at EU borders. With the accession of Austria, these borders came much closer geographically to Bosnia–Hercegovina. While displaced people in Bosnia, the European and international media, and the general public may have understood the Security Council resolutions and fine words of the politicians to mean that areas of Bosnia were being actively protected and made safe, the actual situation was one of a symbolic guarantee of presence in besieged enclaves already filled with displaced people (Van Selm-Thorburn 1998). That the safe areas ultimately fell in 1995, and proved to be unsafe, is central to discussion of the success or failure of EU policy decisions with regard to asylum and protection of threatened people in former Yugoslavia. The repeat of humanitarian disaster for civilians who had been led to believe that they were secure through international protection demonstrated the humanitarian failings of the 'safe areas' concept.

Besides demonstrating the lack of protection in the enclaves, this episode showed gaps in the procedures and capacity developed by the international community, including the EU, to cope with a loss of the nominal protection provided. There were no aid agencies at the Tuzla camps to assist the displaced on their immediate arrival. There was confusion between the Bosnian 'Muslim' government and UNHCR over who was to take charge of relief (Radosavljevic 1995). An obliquely positive result of this initial confusion was that there was more preparation for those forced to flee Žepa a few weeks after the fall of Srebrenica.

Policies of temporary protection and burden-sharing

In response to UNHCR's call for at least temporary protection for those fleeing former Yugoslavia – a call which itself was prompted by the limitations imposed by west European governments on former Yugoslavs seeking asylum – EU member states began to develop policy positions. They were involved in intergovernmental discussion on immigration and asylum policies already. However, instead of developing a joint strategy on protection each government turned to its own statute books and policy orientations and developed something independent. Some member states, such as the Netherlands, drafted and passed new laws, others stuck with ad hoc policies (e.g. the UK). The Netherlands and Denmark developed sophisticated systems of progressive integration and a time limit after which 'temporary' could become longer term, with the accordance of full refugee status. The details of each individual policy or law are not the most essential point in discussing the success or failure of EU asylum policy. That ministers meeting regularly to discuss asylum matters could not develop a basic coordinated policy for those arriving on their territories shows how very far there is to go before any positive results emerge from this branch of intergovernmental cooperation.

The varied nature of the policies developed is reflected to some extent in the varying numbers of persons granted whatever form of protection was on offer in the different member states. In 1994 Germany tabled its burden-sharing proposal to the Immigration Working Group (not the Asylum Working Group). This was put on the agenda under its own presidency, three years after the massive influxes which prompted the proposal had begun. The essence of the notion was that if refugees are to be admitted only temporarily, with the aim of protecting as many as possible, then the financial and physical burden of their protection on EU territory should be shared by the member states on some sort of proportional basis rather than being the sole responsibility of the most generous. The resolution was not accepted, although a watered down version was passed in 1995.

The anticipated outcome of all the temporary protection schemes was and remains that those granted such a status would return home. The phraseology has (again as a result of the ethnic cleansing policies) always been of 'returning home', implying that people would go back to the very town, street and building which they left in fear. Those schemes which set deadlines used a three- to five-year plan. As the conflict formally ended with the Dayton Peace Agreements of November 1995 and temporary protection began in 1993, this deadline was not passed and, theoretically at least, those protected can be expected to return to Bosnia–Hercegovina. The possible next fiasco could be the result of too-hasty returns and, particularly, forced repatriations such as those the German government has recently embarked upon. Predicting a fiasco is risky business, but the possibility is there.

Explaining the disaster

Institutional constraints

Under the Maastricht treaty the two areas of foreign and immigration policy were given similar intergovernmental constructions. Yet the two institutional pillars operate slightly differently. This difference affected the way in which member states dealt with the Yugoslav situation from 1991 onwards. In foreign and security policy-making EC member states have been very reluctant to give up their sovereign prerogatives. Nevertheless, an institutional arrangement has developed, the European Political Cooperation (EPC), which gives an impulse to policy coordination and produces an incentive to certain member states to adopt and pursue a common perspective rather than a national one.

Until the ratification of the Maastricht treaty in 1993 the external political relations of the European Community were decided under strict intergovernmentalism via the EPC. This embodied a regime under which member states promised to inform each other of their foreign policy positions and to make an attempt at formulating a common policy before individual steps would be taken. To that purpose a small institutional framework was set up under the Single European Act of 1985. This included the formation of EPC working groups (comparable with the working groups of the Committee of Permanent Representatives to the EU–COREPER) headed by the so-called Political Committee and composed of senior civil servants from the foreign ministries, and the creation of an EPC Secretariat (comparable with the General Secretariat of the Council of Ministers) which dealt with daily matters. Some twenty foreign office diplomats ran the Secretariat at any one time.

They were sent to Brussels for a period of two years, coinciding with the period in which their home country participated in the EC *troika* (Nugent 1994: 391 ff.; Kirchner 1992: 78–79).

This system kept the European Commission at arm's length and ensured that foreign-policy making would not be overtaken by normal community decision-making procedure. As decisions had to be unanimous, each member state could be sure of the continued ability to pursue independent foreign policies when it deemed fit. The European Commission, keen to extend its competencies to the foreign policy realm, was not happy with this situation (Cini 1996: 83–84, Nuttall 1996). Most analysts have therefore retained a sceptical view of the EPC, claiming that national interests will ultimately prevail over a common European policy and that the EPC institutional framework was designed to ensure that.

In the search for a common policy, certain actors in the European Community usually adopt a 'common European perspective' in areas such as foreign policy. These include the member state holding the presidency of the Council, which usually has an interest in pursuing a common European foreign policy during its reign, because it is considered to add to the success of its presidential term. This consideration can also be extended to the other two members of the *troika*, and thus to the officials working at the General Secretariat of the EPC. Finally, those members and staff of the European Commission involved in these policies will push a unified line.

After Maastricht, decision-making in foreign policy continued to follow the unanimity rule and could generally be seen as decision-making characterized by lowest common denominator solutions (cf. Kirchner 1992: 13). We would not expect individual member states to forgo their national interests easily, but if they would it would be more likely in foreign policy, where one could argue that a European regime of cooperation had developed with EPC, than in immigration policy. However, that often means member states will obey only the rule to inform and consult other states, but will pursue individual foreign policies anyway.

In the area of immigration policies such an existing regime was not in place. Policy-making remained (and in 1998 still remains) outside the area of communitarian policy-making. In a strictly intergovernmentalist framework no actor saw an incentive to pursue a common European policy. The decisions to attempt a 'safe areas' approach via the UN and to use temporary protection statuses rather than granting asylum were clearly brought about by the whole combination of circumstances detailed above. 'Safe areas' had seemingly been effective from a potential host state's point of view when they had stopped thousands of Iraqi Kurds from leaving Northern Iraq and entering Turkey in 1991. With populations displaying a reluctance to accommodate newcomers and a fear of being overwhelmed by immigrants from eastern Europe, it is not surprising that EU governments would try to limit arrivals and the granting of refugee status. Media calls in western Europe centred far more on intervention to stop the displacements than on calls to offer protection within EU member states.

The implementation of ethnic cleansing policies by the warring parties cleared the way for the decision to try to keep people close to their homes. However, this understanding of the motives behind the 'safe areas' approach is two-edged. After all, the moral conflict over appearing to comply with ethnic cleansing, or encouraging or even forcing people (through the lack of available and practical options) to remain in the conflict area and face the possibility of death is not the least of the difficulties posed by the obvious failures of the 'safe areas' policy in Bosnia–Hercegovina. In addition, this failure highlighted the apparent European desire not to take in refugees, matched by a Bosnian and Croat desire to keep people in place to carry on the fight. In sum, policies towards displacements were not constrained by the existence of an evolved EC-wide practice, which would have been an incentive to attempt to construct a European policy. National interests prevailed.

Institutional games and the circumstances of the Maastricht negotiations

In strictly intergovernmental policy arenas which decide by unanimity decision rules, one would expect national interests to prevail. This is even more true in policy areas in which few incentives to achieve a common policy exist, as in the case of the EC's refugee policies. The best result that can be hoped for is the lowest common denominator. But even that was impossible in the case of refugee policies specifically aimed at former Yugoslavia. The more incentives towards pursuing a common line exist, the greater the likelihood that policy-making will be characterized by splitting the difference or upgrading the common interest (Kirchner 1992). Some of this can be observed in the EPC, where several actors have an institutionalized interest in developing a common policy. In the case of EC foreign policy towards Yugoslavia, once that crisis reached a first peak in the summer of 1991, the parallel negotiations on the Treaty on European Union affected the dynamics of EC policy-making. Many actors (Germany, France, Benelux) had defined the incorporation of the EPC into the EC legal framework as part of its success. This provided an extra incentive to try and develop a common policy towards the unfolding crisis in Yugoslavia. A failure in Yugoslavia might affect the future of EPC itself.

This increase in weight of the importance of unity, however, provides leverage to those actors that want to pursue a national interest anyway; because the others have a higher stake in cooperation per se, individual demands are likely to be accepted more easily (cf. Bueno et al. 1994). This is exactly what increased the leverage of Germany and Greece in pursuing their objectives of recognizing Slovenian and Croatian independence and isolating Macedonia, respectively.

Segmented policy-making

Finally, foreign and refugee policies were decided upon in different policy arenas, each with their own decision rules and composed of different ministers. No overlap between the two policy arenas existed. The major consequence of this was that during their formulation, the EC's foreign policies towards Yugoslavia were hardly judged for the consequences they might have on displacements in Yugoslavia. When the refugee problem reached crisis proportions, EC member states refused to adapt their foreign policies to this new crisis. Rather, EC member states preferred to leave the foreign policy part to other actors, such as the United Nations and the United States, and to leave refugee matters to the discretion of individual member states. They thus added to the suffering of many individual victims of the Yugoslav crisis.

Conclusion

The European Community's policies have had some dire consequences for the way the crisis in (former) Yugoslavia unfolded.[2] At important instances its preoccupation with European unity seems to have been more important than maintaining a substantive policy. This was especially the case with its recognition policies, which helped to speed up the disintegration of Yugoslavia, aggravated the ethnic conflict underlying it, and buried the international conference it had set up itself to bring about a comprehensive solution. Its previous policy line of maintaining Yugoslav unity was thwarted by specific choices on how to implement that policy. When faced with waves of displaced persons, the European Community member states were unable to design a common policy because national interests prevailed and because forty years of a universalized Cold War approach meant they had ready-made reasons to reject cases on legal grounds. The individual policies that prevailed added to the toils of individual Yugoslavs, whose country was torn apart, whose homes were destroyed, and whose family and friends suffered untold pain and death in yet another twentieth-century European disaster.

Notes

1 We employ the titular terminology of the European Community/Union as appropriate in the chronological framework.
2 The disintegration of former Yugoslavia has also been traced to deep roots in internal Yugoslav politics (Little and Silber 1997; Glenny 1996) and in cultural conflicts (Pfaff 1993), as well as to the tensions induced within a loosely federal system by economic crisis (Woodward 1995). Our analysis has focused instead on the contribution of the European Community to specific aspects of that crisis.

References

Bigo, D. (ed.) (1992) *L'Europe des Polices et de la Securité Intérieure*, Paris: Editions Complexe.
Bovens, M. and 't Hart, P. (1996) *Understanding Policy Fiascos*, New Brunswick: Transaction.
Bueno, D. Mesquita, B. and Stokman, F.N. (eds) (1994) *European Community Decision Making*, Yale, NJ: Yale University Press.

Cini, M. (1996) *The European Commission. Leadership. Organisation and Culture in the EU Administration*, Manchester: Manchester University Press.

Crawford, B. (1996) 'Explaining defection from international unilateral recognition of Croatia', *World Politics* 48(3): 482–521.

Glenny, M. (1996) *The Fall of Yugoslavia*, 3rd edition, Harmondsworth: Penguin.

Haas, E. B. (1983) 'Regime decay: conflict management and international organizations, 1945–1981', *International Organization* 37(2): 189–256.

Hebenton, B. and T. Thomas (eds) (1995) *Policing Europe. Co-operation, Conflict and Control*, Basingstoke: Macmillan.

Huys, T. (1994) *In opdracht van Hare Majesteit. Diplomaat in Crisistijd*, Weert: M & P.

Jones, R. (1996) *Politics and Economics of European Union*, London: Edward Elgar.

Kirchner, E. J. (1992) *Decision Making in the European Community. The Council Presidency and European Integration*, Manchester: Manchester University Press.

Lavdas, K. A. (1996) 'The European Union and the Yugoslav conflict: and re-institutionalization in Southeastern Europe', *Journal of Political and Military Sociology* 24: 209–232.

Little, A. and Silber, L. (1997) *Yugo-Slavia. Death of a Nation*, 2nd revised edition, Harmondsworth: Penguin.

Noelke, A. and Stratman, G. (forthcoming) 'The role of international financial institutions in central and eastern Europe', in B. Reinalda and B. Verbeek (eds) *Autononous Policy-making by International Organizations*, London: Routledge.

Nugent, N. (1994) *The Government and Politics of the European Union*, 3rd edition, Basingstoke: Macmillan.

Nuttall, S. (1996) 'The Commission: struggle for legitimacy', in C. Hill (ed.) *The Actors in Europe's Foreign Policy*, London: Routledge.

Pfaff, W. (1993) *The Wrath of Nations. Civilization and the Furies of Nationalism*, New York: Simon & Schuster.

Radosavljevic, Z. (1995) 'Muslims' flight brings no escape from despair', *The Independent*, 15 July: 8.

van Selm-Thorburn, J. (1998) *Refugee Protection in Europe: Lessons of the Yugoslav Crisis*, Dordrecht: Kluwer Law International.

Wijnaendts, H. (1993) *Joegoslavische Kroniek. Juli 1991–Augustus 1992*, Amsterdam: Thomas Rap; translated from the French, *L'Engrenage: chroniques yougoslaves. Juillet 1991–Août 1992*, Editions Denoël, 1993.

Woodward, S. (1995) *Balkan Tragedy. Chaos and Dissolution after the Cold War*, Washington, DC: Brookings Institution.

Part VI

CONCLUSIONS

11

EXPLAINING POLICY DISASTERS IN EUROPE

Comparisons and reflections

Mark Bovens, Paul 't Hart and B. Guy Peters

Policy disasters in Europe

Perhaps the most important aspect of policy failure and policy disasters is how mundane they really are. Policies fail regularly, and they continue to fail for many of the reasons that have contributed to the failure of policies for decades, if not centuries. Very few, if any, policy-makers set out believing that their prized plans and programmes are going to fail, but many do, and they often do so because they appear not to have learned from the experiences of other similar cases. Further policies often fail not so much because of their own inherent defects but because they are components of a larger universe of public policies that fail to mesh together properly. Again, the failure to coordinate has been endemic in government, but there has been very little improvement in the 'horizontal management' of governments despite the long recognition of the problem (Peters 1997).

In contemporary Europe there is an undiminished need to study the occurrence and antecedents of major governance failures. Major mishaps continue to emerge at all levels of governance, including the European Union, and span the entire range of governance domains. The present collection of recent cases suggests that even in the supposedly post-Keynesian, post-industrial, post-ideological and postmodern era, policy disasters appear to be an invariant feature of political life in European democracies. No doubt there may be important differences in the incidence of failure between (types of) countries, sectors and programmes; it remains for future research to ascertain whether this is the case, and what sort of comparative patterns and trends can be found. In the present study the authors have not sought to illuminate the relative frequency of failure, but have instead concentrated on qualitative descriptions and analyses of the genesis of failure in selected cases of national and EU policy-making. Combined, the case studies demonstrate that policy disasters take a variety of forms and have quite different origins. In this concluding chapter we reflect on this variety and try to put it into a broader analytical perspective. Let us begin to map out the terrain by comparing and contrasting different forms of failure that may be found in the case studies.

195

Identifying disasters: political versus programme failures

Multidimensional disasters

In the introductory chapter it was observed that the political identification of particular events and episodes as policy disasters is rooted in political time, political culture, and other sources of bias in evaluation methodology and discourse. The case studies show that a policy event can indeed come to be labelled as a disaster for different reasons, by different actors using different means. A most useful distinction is the one between political failures and programme failures (Mucciaroni 1990; Bovens and 't Hart 1996: 35–36). Roughly, a programme failure pertains to the technocratic, social-engineering dimension of policy-making. It occurs when a policy decision, plan or strategy that has been implemented fails to have the desired impact on target populations, or even produces major unintended and unwanted effects. The essence of political failure, in contrast, does not involve the social consequences of polices, but rather the way in which policies are perceived in the court of public opinion and the political arena. Specifically, a policy is a political failure when it lacks the political support and momentum necessary for its (long-term) survival as a prioritized area of government activity. In Figure 11.1 we have mapped the cases on these two dimensions, showing the different 'failure profiles' of the various policy episodes studied in this volume. Furthermore, the arrows for each case show the changing assessments of a particular case through time.

This figure highlights the intricacies and paradoxes of policy disasters. Not surprisingly in a volume on policy disasters, the 'complete success' box is nearly empty, with only the early years of the Common Fisheries Policy meeting the model of a more or less rational policy carrying broad political support (Chapter 9). Perhaps more surprisingly, given the efforts made by the country authors to select major disaster cases, it turns out that only a few of the case studies in this volume meet the 'complete disaster' profile (programme and political failure coinciding throughout). The purest example is EU policy during the early stages of the disintegration of Yugoslavia (Chapter 10). Put simply, despite its ambitions and rhetoric in this domain, there was no EU policy. The very lack of a united European stance contributed to the escalation of the conflict – and has widely been seen to have done so. Another major example is the Dutch case (Chapter 3). When consecutive inquiries revealed many embarrassing facts about the adventuristic, ineffectual and unaccountable methods used by the supposedly elite crime-fighters in the Netherlands, there was widespread political consensus that this deserved to be called a major disaster. Political agreement on the question of who should be blamed for it proved tenuous, resulting in the anomaly of a major policy disaster ending in a whimper, without the symbolic satisfaction of punishment and purification (Shklar 1990; Douglas 1992).

Certainly a paradox occurs when a policy performs according to the social-

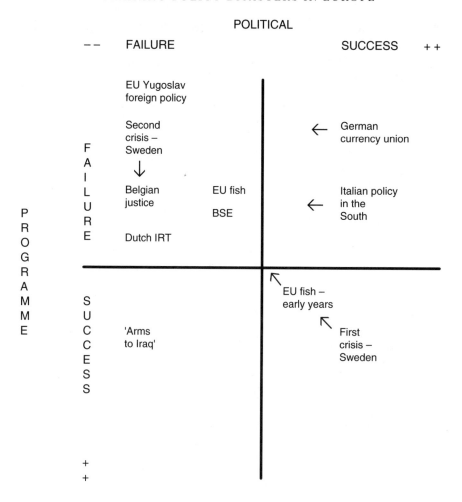

Figure 11.1 Mapping political and programme failures

engineering ambitions of its designers yet becomes branded as a major disaster in the court of public opinion or by society's 'legitimate value judges', such as parliament, courts of audit, the judiciary or an official inquiry (Dror 1986). In our sample, Conservative elites in the foreign and defence sector achieved their strategic aims in licensing exports to Iraq (Chapter 7), and were above all astounded when the issue first started to provoke huge political controversy. Underestimating the political sensitivity and the ability of media and opposition leaders to keep the issue alive, they mishandled the affair and exacerbated their political difficulties. Also, although the EU's handling of the refugee flows following the escalation of the Balkan crisis may be judged relatively mildly in comparison to the utter failure of its efforts to take a united diplomatic and security stance towards the disintegration of Yugoslavia, it still presents a bitter example of 'operation successful' (a coherent policy to minimize the influx of refugees into western Europe) yet 'patient deceased' (widespread moral and political criticism of the insensitivity to the plight of refugees).

The other paradox is presented by policies that entail major social costs or conspicuously fail to meet even modest performance standards and yet are not labelled a failure in the political arena. The paradigm case here is the Italian policy for the South (Chapter 5), where decades of financial injections and other government attempts to stimulate economic development produced little if any effect, but without any significant politicization of this failure taking place for many years. The explanation of the paradox in this case follows readily from Sykes's argument that the policy served the interests of powerful regional and national institutions. Similarly, the string of unsolved major crimes in Wallonia was for a very long time accepted by public opinion and the entire political caste as a seemingly inevitable part of 'the Belgian condition', as it were (Chapter 2). In case after case of apparent incompetence and alleged political cover-up, no political questions were asked and no blame was apportioned. Retrospectively, we can see that despite this lack of overt criticism a diffuse frustration was building up among the public. It took the psychodrama of large-scale child abuse to stem the tide and unleash a political firestorm at the grassroots level that swept far beyond the prime actors in the Dutroux investigation. Sometimes, potentially disastrous policies on the programme level are even championed as successes in the political realm. Around 1990 in Germany there was a clear discrepancy between the momentous risks associated with Chancellor Kohl's policy gamble on the monetary union with the former GDR, and the widespread political support that existed for this move at the time (Chapter 6). Clearly, the psycho-political momentum of the emerging reunification far outweighed the tenets of fiscal prudence and medium-term socio-economic feasibility. Several years later, and in the midst of a major budget crisis, more critical reassessments of the episode gain political respectability.

The variable scope of policy disasters

A final point concerns the seemingly difficult methodological issue of case demarcation. Policy disasters are like Russian dolls reversed: one policy disaster may well be viewed as being embedded in a larger set of problems in a policy sector, which in turn may be viewed as part of a yet wider institutional and even regime failure. The Belgian criminal justice system (Chapter 2) is a case in point. The failure of the police and the judiciary to put a timely end to the ring of child molesters was retrospectively linked in the public discourse to a series of other crime-fighting failures, which themselves came to be viewed as epitomizing the pathology of the criminal justice system, and indeed the Belgian polis as a whole. In the Dutch case (Chapter 3), likewise, what began as an incident – the forced dissolution of a police investigation team – gradually went through a political process of redefinition until it encapsulated the entire institutional make-up of the Dutch fight against organized crime. Finally, the depth and volatility of the 'Arms to Iraq' affair in the UK (Chapter 7) cannot be understood properly except when viewed against the back-drop of a string of controversial policies and political scandals that beset the latter half of the Conservative reign in the 1980s and 1990s. This process of perceptual widening and the linking of seemingly disparate policy disasters is not a self-evident matter, nor is it a merely analytical issue. The assessment of whether a policy disaster is a stand alone incident or a symptom of something bigger is the subject of political manoeuvring by stakeholders who seek to contain or expand the scope of controversy. It partly depends upon the mass media's ability to uncover pertinent evidence of linkage, its willingness to criticize incumbent elites and put forward daring conjectures about possible disasters looming behind current ones. Ultimately, however, the political boundaries of policy disasters may well rest upon the general public's inclination to lend credence to partisan argu-ments concerning their proper proportions. The public credibility of disaster arguments narrow and wide should be linked with the more general level of trust in political elites, the incumbent regime and the basic features of the political order (Easton 1965). When this is low (or going down), policy elites will have a hard time keeping their performance records untainted.

Explaining policy disasters: three key questions

Even though the question as such has not been studied systematically in this volume, one gets the distinct impression from reading the newspapers, watching the news and glancing over the titles of many scholarly works that the incidence of policy disasters has been on the rise. At the very least, the sheer abundance of recent cases for any of the countries included in this volume demands an explana-tion. In explaining this apparent ubiquity of policy disaster, it is crucial to keep in mind the distinction between the programme and the political dimensions of policy disasters. These are logically and often empirically distinct: a high incidence of political disasters in a particular country at a particular time does not neces-sarily mean that there is also a high incidence of programme disasters – it may simply reflect increasingly critical public opinion or a more successful opposition strategy. Observing these differences, the apparent ubiquity of policy disasters raises various major questions.

First of all, at the level of individual cases, such as the ones studied in this volume, we need to develop theoretical notions that can help us explain why particular policies are liable to become programme failures to begin with. Second, at the level of policy-making entities (governments, policy networks) we may wonder if there are any reasons why there might be more programme disasters, e.g. if policy-making itself has become more 'failure prone'. Finally, at the level of the political system as a whole, we may ask why there has been so much public attention recently to alleged cases of 'bad governance', e.g. a possible trend towards more political disasters. To these three consecutive questions we now turn.

Explaining cases of policy failure

The first question we must ask is why specific cases of policy disaster – both in programmatic and political terms – occur. While every case presented in this volume is to some extent sui generis, there are also a number of points of commonality that bind the cases together. These points provide some preliminary explanations for failures and therefore can serve as the starting point for a more refined theory of failure.

In the introductory chapter, four classes of explanatory approaches that may account for cases of policy failure were presented. The *problem-solving approach* views policy-making as a series of strategic choices and emphasizes the role of information and analysis as the crucial factors determining its success and failure. The *competing values approach* sees governance as a process in which multiple, partially conflicting values and interests have to be reconciled and traded off, with disaster occurring when the balance is lost and some parties systematically gain (or lose) more than others. The *institutional action approach* locates success and failure in the workings of the machinery of government, and highlights the complexity of organizations, procedures and routines. The *structural constraints approach* is deterministic in that it suggests that the success or failure of policies is determined in large part by the systemic context – e.g. the constraints of the international balance of power – in which they seek to have an impact. In highly complex, tightly coupled technical systems, for example, accidents are bound to happen, however carefully policy-makers manage to operate. Looking back at the case studies, it is interesting to see the differential importance of factors incorporated in these failure explanations for the course of the policy-making process. In Table 11.1 we provide our assessment of the disaster explanations given by the case authors recast in terms of the four models. Below, we discuss the various cases when we revisit the four explanatory approaches.

The limits of problem-solving explanations

The problem-solving account of policy disasters centres on the limits to analytical rationality that governments display when they try to make sense of their environment in order to steer it in purposeful ways. Karl Deutsch (1963) once conceptualized government as a cybernetic system, in close contact with signals from its environment and acting to adjust its behaviours to meet the demands of that environment. In the best version of this form of government the public sector would be sufficiently attuned to society to identify social trends before they became problems and 'lead' the moving target that society presents.

Deutsch was writing in an era with greater optimism about government and its capacity to solve social problems than our own, so that this conceptualization now appears somewhat quaint. Further, the numerous policy disasters already documented have tended to humble governments, so that they may have become more docile. Those things having been said, however, governments that are more

Table 11.1 Dominant explanations of failure: the cases revisited

	Problem-solving	Competing values	Institutional interaction	Structural constraints
Belgian criminal justice system		**	***	
Dutch IRT			***	
BSE	*	***	**	
Southern Italy		***	**	*
German union	**	***		*
Arms to Iraq	*	**	***	
Sweden's monetary crisis			**	***
EC/EU fisheries policy		***	**	
EC/EU foreign and refugee policy for Yugoslavia		***	**	

Notes:
*Denotes the category of factors most emphasized in the case study account.
An empty space denotes that the category in question is not emphasized in the case study.
In some cases a more or less clear hierarchy exists between different explanations.
Readers can judge for themselves whether they agree with our coding.

attuned to society and to information should be more capable of solving, or even avoiding, problems. Unfortunately, few governments have been able to develop such good systems for the collection and utilization of information. Most governments tend to behave in an almost contrary manner, and to close their systems of knowledge collection and utilization rather than opening them to more diverse sources of information (Dror 1986). Rather than being cybernetic, governments have tended to become autistic, and sometimes appear virtually unaware of their surrounding environment. In one terminology, government has become 'self-referential' and has lost contact with other points of reference in society (Teubner 1993). From a problem-solving perspective, a classical explanation of this phenomenon focuses on the personal idiosyncrasies and limitations, even personality defects, of top leaders and their most senior advisers, as well as on the interpersonal dynamics in policy-making groups (Janis 1972, 1989). The problem-solving approach acknowledges that policy-makers may choose not to reach out to new and different information on the basis of more or less rational calculations. Information is costly, and the search is even more costly when it is not clear exactly what information is needed to avert some as yet unidentified problem in the future. If a policy-maker and those surrounding him or her are sufficiently confident and sufficiently remote from social reality, they can convince themselves that they need not search for new information. Further, they can also believe that if a problem arises they will find the means then to solve it.

In the cases studied here, not much emphasis was placed on the role of individuals and groups in the policy-making process and possible information-processing pathologies stemming from their prominence as decision-making entities. The key questions asked by Wolfgang Seibel in his reconstruction of the German currency union fiasco (Chapter 6) are probably closest to a problem-solving approach. Each of his four questions suggests that German policy-makers behaved in exactly the opposite way to what a detached, rational analysis of the issues would suggest to be the best course of action. However, in his case analysis Seibel shows that it was not so much the inability, or even the unwillingness, of Chancellor Kohl and the members of his inner circle that produced the disaster, but rather the complex nexus between West German leaders struggling with what they experienced primarily as a political and not an economic threat, and an East German population in the grip of an acute revolution of rising expectations. In the case of the Swedish monetary disaster (Chapter 8), policy-makers were struggling with acute uncertainties about the likely responses of the international money markets to the various emergency measures considered by the government and the National Bank. However, the more significant uncertainty was political, and it stemmed from the institutional make-up of Swedish consensus democracy, which required opposition support for any government measures to gain credibility abroad. Tellingly, the 'learning' displayed by the Social Democratic opposition leadership had less to do with achieving more sophisticated macroeconomic insights than with deftly negotiating intra-party and domestic political pressures. Likewise, Baggott detects numerous instances of defective information-processing by British officials in the BSE case (Chapter 4), but sees these as symptoms of broader political and organizational dynamics rather than as autonomous causes of the government's inability to handle the crisis.

Competing values: power, conflict and motivated ignorance

In contrast, considerable evidence in the case study material seems to support the competing values interpretation of flawed policy-making. This approach contends that individual, group or organizational miscalculations are not the prime cause of the self-referentiality of governments and the policy disasters this may entail. From a competing values perspective, a classical weakness of the public sector is that its relative power and its conventional role in society have reinforced its isolation from the forces in society that might help it prevent policy disasters. The search for new information is resisted because of power and influence relationships between government and familiar sources of information, including a number of sources within government itself. Studies of the use of policy advice and expertise in government (Barker and Peters 1993; Peters and Barker 1993) indicate that, rather than the public sector being a marketplace for ideas, there are often cartels that serve to limit the sources of information. Government organizations establish linkages with information sources and tend to go back to them again and again. The narrowing of sources of information is a way of avoiding addressing and balancing the fundamental conflicts of values and interests that abound in most important policy areas. In part to seek a more comfortable life and in part because of real beliefs in their own definitions of social reality, organizations restrict the sources of information to which they attend. Furthermore, the segmentation of government and the autonomy which most government organizations enjoy permit them to segment policy and segment their sources of policy advice. In the Common Fisheries Policy (Chapter 9), different national policy communities made different choices in the economy–environment trade-off, depending on the relative power of the fishing industry lobby. In the BSE case (Chapter 4), some sources of expertise were definitely 'more equal' than others when it came to their access to and credibility with departmental officials and government leaders.

The segmentation of policy advice occurs horizontally as well vertically, so that governments tend to pay greater attention to more organized sources of advice and to elites rather than to mass-based sources. Governments in most societies have the power to exclude sources of information and advocacy, and in all have the capacity to winnow through the sources and give credence to some and not to others. The study of decisions such as the siting of hazardous facilities indicates that governments tend to ignore the less prestigious sources of information and to pay attention to organizations that conform to the norms of public organizations (Hunold 1997). Lode Van Outrive's study of Belgian policy (Chapter 2) is perhaps the best example of this pattern of policy failure. In some ways the simple arrogance of power was confounded by a pervasive pattern of corruption and suppression of information. Some political systems are more open than others, and the Belgian case documents well the consequences of closing down sources of information. The discourse on the Belgian case also exemplified the more general assertion that governments may not search for new sources or types of information because of close connections with vested interests, including vested interests within the public sector itself. The relationships of government departments with their clienteles is obvious and may operate as much through the sharing of information as through more overt forms of political influence. The relationships with information sources within government and the defining of the relevant types of knowledge are perhaps less obvious.

In fact, discursive practices are part and parcel of the influence process in and around government. Indicators of policy-relevant variables are socially and politically constructed, just as are almost all other parts of the policy process. They represent political as well as objective scientific choices (Majone 1989; Stone 1988). Take, for example, gross national product (GNP) as one of the most familiar of all variables used in making policy. Although familiar, the variable also has conceptual flaws that are becoming more evident in a globalized economy (Shaikh and Tonah 1994). Other more subjective measures, for example of poverty or even unemployment, represent even more difficult political bargains and compromises that any attempt to replace with new measures could well endanger. The BSE case (Chapter 4) shows the importance of discursive framing. BSE could be framed as a case of contaminated, and potentially deadly, daily food. The connection of BSE with hamburgers was a very powerful way of condensing the case. Moreover, similar food scares – about salmonella-infected eggs – had already attracted a large amount of public attention. BSE thus fitted within a frame that already existed. Furthermore, the symbolic pictures of the British minister of agriculture, John Gummer, feeding his own daughter hamburgers (quickly labelled

'Gummerburgers' in popular accounts) helped fuel the politicization of the BSE case. The 'bureaucracy' itself is now a sufficiently negative political symbol so that if the media, or other participants in the process, can frame the issue as one of bureaucracy persisting in its own inertial paths the political battle may be over. Likewise, the ability to personify a problem, as in the case Marc Dutroux and his teenage victims in Belgium (Chapter 2), may facilitate the creation of a political disaster when less clearly defined symbols could not. Other cases, such as the Common Fisheries Policy (Chapter 9) and the devaluation of the Swedish currency (Chapter 8), were not connected to such simple but powerful symbols, and were far more difficult to frame.

Condensatory symbols are often used to 'frame' a policy issue for mass political consumption (Edelman 1964). They may, however, also be turned against incumbent elites and institutions, and employed by third parties to create political disasters (Edelman 1971; 't Hart 1993). In the context of powerful organizations and political interests contending in a policy area, some amount of countervailing power may be needed to shift the definition of the issue. Therefore social movements and policy entrepreneurs become important for defining programmes as failures, or for defining the political dimensions of failure (Tarrow 1994; Kingdon 1995). Political disasters and their potential corollaries of crisis and instability may well be desired by various stakeholders. They offer important opportunities for political gain and institutional self-dramatization ('t Hart 1993). They can be played up and used as rhetorical devices, dramatic symbols of the need for structural change. This has, to some extent, occurred in Italy, with politicians such as Umberto Bossi developing a political movement around the issue of the failure of the policies for the South. Several British politicians attempted to use the EU fisheries policy as a way of creating or reviving political careers, and were able to get the issue defined as disastrous in the process.

Institutional action: incremental politics and bureaucracy as usual

In the institutional perspective, interest group politics and value conflicts make way for organizational complexity and fragmentation as the main explanatory device in the analysis of policy disasters. From this point of view, failed policies may represent the institutionalization of routines of 'policy-making as usual' when the circumstances are no longer usual. Politicians, as well as almost all other decision-makers in the private as well as the public sector, have a tendency to think about policies in a linear fashion. That is, if a programme has functioned well in the past there is a tendency to believe that it will continue to work well in the present and in the future (Neustadt and May 1986; cf. Rose 1993). Furthermore, if the policy has worked well in the past and if it fails to work, then simply doing more of the same thing will return the policy to an acceptable level of success. This linear and incremental thinking is likely to function well when policy problems are well defined and stable. As we have argued above, this is often not the case (cf. Dror 1983). If the fundamental nature of the policy problem has been transformed and if the incremental pattern of searching for a solution persists, then the best possible outcome for solutions picked in the usual manner would be simple failure, with large-scale negative synergies also being possible, and even likely. Even very familiar and well-known policies can be transformed in relatively short periods of time, and without any prior inklings that the change is coming. For example, Downs (1972) describes 'alarmed discovery' as the first stage of the agenda-setting process for a number of policies that had been around for some time but suddenly burst on to the agenda in a new, transformed format.

The persistence of this incremental pattern is easy to understand politically. Policies represent the outcome of long processes of bargaining among interests, especially in countries such as the Netherlands or Belgium, which have multiple social divisions and more consultative styles of decision-making. Thus, moving away from an agreed pattern for solving problems – especially one that has worked at one time or another – is very difficult politically and opens up the entire policy area to another round of bargaining. Further, there are often few objective signs that the policy area has changed, so that even arguing that there has been some sort of change involves opening up the policy area to more bargaining, and perhaps producing even less desirable outcomes.

Another variant of the same pattern of behaviour is concentration on a short-term 'fix' for a problem when the problem is actually more long term and persistent (Goodin 1982). This pattern has been observed in relation to poverty and social dislocation any number of times – governments have claimed to have *the* solution, only to find that they were merely addressing a symptom of the problem – urban policy in the United States and the United Kingdom being good examples of that pattern. Of course, hindsight is always perfect in these cases, but failure to think about the long-term causes and consequences of policy is endemic in the world of public policy. The cases contained in this book reflect how this incremental pattern of problem-solving can contribute to policy disasters. For example, Sykes's study of Italian policy toward the *Mezzogiorno* (Chapter 5) shows how a policy that really has not worked at all persists long after any possible utility has been exhausted. The clientilistic politics and the unique power position of the Mafia in that part of Italy virtually guaranteed this persistence, reinforced by a general pattern of incrementalism and a failure to correct errors. Also, the BSE case (Chapter 4) represents an attempt to cope with a long-term problem through a series of short-term policy responses, a pattern that appears to have compounded the problem.

From an institutional perspective, the dynamics of politics and those of bureaucracy are closely intertwined. Therefore the nature of public bureaucracy and the manner in which bureaucracies reflect established policy commitments also play a significant role in the genesis of policy disasters. First, the structure of government is a tangible reflection of an intellectual disaggregation of the policy problems of society. This division also defines a set of intellectual and policy blinkers worn by the occupants of those organizations. Thus, the division of government into ministries and agencies entails a certain degree of 'trained incapacity' of the members of organizations to perceive the world in other than the particular manners inculcated by the institutions to which they belong (March and Olsen 1994). As these organizations have developed, their collective viewpoints have tended to be reinforced by the educational and professional backgrounds of the members being recruited – departments of agriculture tend to hire agronomists and veterinarians, not engineers and artists.

As well as developing institutionalized professional perspectives about their tasks, public organizations also develop procedures for coping with policy questions. The problem with these 'standard operating procedures' is that they are indeed standard, but are applied to all circumstances unless there is a very good reason to do otherwise. Just as the incremental thinking described above tends to make organizations persist in established practices even after those practices have become sub-optimal or dysfunctional, so procedures tend to produce standard responses to non-standard problems. Graham Allison's (1971) analysis of the management of the naval blockade of Cuba and the continuation of air reconnaissance missions over the Soviet Union during the missile crisis of 1962 documented some of the more famous examples of this dysfunctional behaviour by public organizations. Likewise, Pat Gray's study of 'Arms to Iraq' (Chapter 7) points to the persistence of routines as one of the difficulties in identifying and addressing the issues in that scandal.

The problems produced by 'departmental views' and standard operating procedures are magnified when policy problems extend beyond the domain of a single government department to become problems that require the involvement and cooperation of multiple departments. In the first instance, departments (just as individuals) which lack a common conception or language for the policy will find it difficult to communicate effectively about those policies; they may be talking about the same thing but cannot recognize each other's interpretation of the issues. The case of the BSE debacle in the United Kingdom (Chapter 4) provides an example of these types of factors. The policy problem has been defined as one of agriculture rather than one of health, and this policy definition helps to explain why the problem has been treated as it has. Baggott points out that as the health departments became more involved in the problem the nature of the solutions shifted. Of course, the optimal solution might have been developed if greater coordination among those departments had been possible from the initial recognition of the issue. The salience of this problem has increased because governments now encounter fewer and fewer policy problems that fall conveniently into the dominion of a single organization (Peters 1997). Policies do not fall within the domain of a single area of policy expertise, despite the efforts of some disciplines (notably economics) to appropriate a wide range of issues as their own.

As well as having different professional and department perspectives on policy, public organizations may also have different values and different objective interests. These different interests are a basis of conflicts over 'turf', one of the all too familiar pathologies of bureaucracy (whether public or private). Even if organizations identify a problem in similar ways, they may still have different values and want it resolved differently, as agricultural and environmental organizations do over the EU fisheries policy. The recent case of the crash of TWA 800 in the United States illustrates these problems well. The investigation of the crash involved a number of federal organizations, most importantly the Federal Aviation Administration (FAA), the National Transportation Safety Board (NTSB) and the Federal Bureau of Investigation (FBI). Each of these organizations saw the crash differently (*New York Times*, 24 April 1997). The FAA, as a regulatory body, was looking for lessons it could apply to prevent other problems. The NTSB is an investigative body interested primarily in finding the answer – why did it happen? Finally, the FBI wanted to determine whether there was a federal criminal case, and, if there was, to preserve the legal 'trail of evidence' and prosecute the perpetrators. These organizations clashed over how to collect and assemble evidence, with the NTSB and FAA wanting to assemble it as quickly as possible to rebuild the plane and find a cause, and the FBI wanting to be sure that evidence was preserved in such a way that it could be used in court if needed. The same crash constituted a very different entity to the three organizations. Such a lack of interorganizational collaboration within government may even escalate into open rivalry, characterized by a reduction of communication and mutual secrecy about past or future decisions and actions in contested domains. Pat Gray's study of the 'Arms to Iraq' scandal in Britain (Chapter 7) and the Bovens *et al.* study of criminal justice policy in the Netherlands (Chapter 3) demonstrate the severe consequences of excessive secrecy in government in reducing the probabilities of effective policy coordination, and hence effective resolution of policy issues.

Structural constraints: systemic power or convenient excuse?

Some of the policy-makers whose actions were studied in this volume quite explicitly referred to various factors limiting their room to manoeuvre. Some argued that the issues facing them were highly intractable (the BSE case, Chapter 4); others referred to the overwhelming power of third actors and embedded practices (the Italian case, Chapter 5), the time-bound situational context (the German case, Chapter 6); yet others played up the constraints placed upon them by the institutional setting in which policy-making took place (both EU cases, Chapters 9 and 10). These arguments are no doubt in part to be understood as defensive rhetoric of policy-makers called to account for disastrous policy outcomes. However, in some instances the case study evidence bears them out. Perhaps the clearest example is provided by the Swedish monetary debacle (Chapter 8). What, after all, are the options left to policy-makers and financial institutions of a small state when faced with a concerted effort on the part of major operators in the international money market to speculate against the national currency? In many of the other cases presented in this volume, the evidence for the overwhelming influence of systematic factors is open to dispute. Of course, every new regime in the Italian South faces formidable odds in dealing with entrenched system of institutional corruption. But does this by itself make any reform effort impossible? Is it sufficient reason to throw in the towel at round one and join the system, as many lawmakers and bureaucrats in that region seem to have done over the years? The same applies to Belgium. The recent history of both countries shows that committed and courageous policy-makers are in fact able to make serious dents in the system, and that there is potential grassroots support for change agents. Likewise, in the EU cases, the complex, multi-level and seemingly erratic nature of European policy-making may always provide national authorities with a convenient scapegoat when they come home from Brussels and face national interest groups and party elites empty-handed.

More programme disasters?

The German currency union (Chapter 6), the malfunctioning of the Belgian justice system (Chapter 2), the enduring predicament of Southern Italy (Chapter 5), all testify to the reality of purely programmatic failures, regardless of their political fortunes. The case studies of these fiascos all show that the policy-makers in charge committed crucial failures that were both foreseeable and avoidable, even discounting the benefit of hindsight. Might it therefore be the case that the ubiquity of policy disasters reflects some very real problems of governance? There are at least some indications that suggest governance itself has become a more risky business.

Increasing social and technological complexity

Contemporary policy-makers in European liberal democracies find themselves confronted with increasing social complexity. Mass immigration from a variety of non-European countries has greatly enhanced the ethnic, cultural and religious diversity of society. Urbanization, increased levels of education and the rise of specific emancipatory social movements have increased the variety of lifestyle preferences enormously. This increasing socio-economic and cultural variety is a source of uncertainty for policy-makers. Policy-makers cannot rely fully on traditional socio-economic parameters and policy feedback. They find themselves confronted with an unstable, rapidly changing mix of social conditions, cultural trends, fashions and hypes, a growing number of increasingly refined, yet uncoordinated classification mechanisms used in different policy sectors. Sometimes it takes acute disruptions and crises to convince policy-makers that there are new social groups 'out there', some of which never even appear in the official statistics (Rosenthal *et al.* 1994). This, one can argue, leads to a heightened chance of unforeseen consequences and negative side-effects.

Moreover, social and cultural pluralism is a source of value-driven uncertainty and conflict. Policy-makers find themselves confronted with competing frames when they try to define and to delineate the policy problem which appears to be at stake. Examples of these 'intractable policy issues' in Europe are abortion, euthanasia, drugs, environmental conservation, immigration, and minority rights, such as the right of Islamic female students to wear headscarves (Hoppe and Peterse 1993; Rein and Schon 1994). Different stakeholders have different interpretations of the nature of the issue and they evaluate potential solutions differently. In these polarized policy arenas governance is a formidable task and often bound to fail, as one party's success is automatically perceived as failure by the other side (Bryson and Crosby 1992).

This increasing social complexity is mirrored by technological complexity. Biotechnology, informatization, and the rapid expansion of the Internet and new telecommunications technologies are examples of emerging technological spheres with a high impact on society as a whole, yet which are very difficult to govern. Technical expertise is hard to come by and often only available within the community of the regulated. It is often unclear, even for specialists, which new technologies will prove feasible, what their impact on society will be and which areas will be effected. This unforeseeability often comes with a high degree of uncontrollability, as many of these contemporary technological innovations are driven by large, transnational corporations that operate in a global market. Nevertheless, governments are expected to respond in an adequate and timely fashion.

Tighter coupling

We live in an era of accelerating time–space compression (Harvey 1989). Physical barriers to the diffusion of people, ideas, information, technology, weapons, bacteria, tastes, in fact any conceivable natural and man-made phenomenon, become smaller. This change is facilitated by major advances in transport and communications technologies. People move more, and do so faster. Markets are becoming global, and businesses and governments are reorganizing accordingly. Events occurring in one social sphere or country spill over rapidly into others. As a result, previously segmented policy arenas and policy problems tend to become more tightly coupled: small and seemingly straightforward policy interventions may turn out to have big consequences, often defying attempts by policy-makers to control the process and its outcomes. Tighter coupling is, however, also produced by semi-autonomous processes within government itself. Policies originating in different time periods accumulate. New policy initiatives compete and interact with existing policy programmes in unexpected and not always beneficial ways.

Spillover effects between previously segmented policy sectors increase the need for policy coordination. In an age of mass transport and increasingly open borders within the European Union, some policy problems can travel very fast. A failure of European diplomacy and peacekeeping in the Balkans can give rise to massive refugee flows into Germany, Austria, Italy, Denmark, Sweden and the Low Countries, which in turn may suddenly pose major challenges for local immigration authorities, housing agencies, and education, health and welfare programmes. Economic globalization has reduced the leeway for monetary and fiscal policy-making and strongly enhanced the volatility of national economies. Monetary authorities in most countries often stand empty-handed when faced with a sudden increase in the American interest rate or a concerted attack on the national currency. At a time when meat is exported globally, outbreaks of BSE and other veterinarian diseases can have a devastating economic impact upon national cattle industries far beyond the original problem area virtually overnight.

More political disasters?

The final question of this chapter deals with the trend towards more political disasters. In day-to-day political discourse, the analytical subtleties of political versus programme failures are often lost. Media attention and public scandal substitute for programme evaluation, and political failures are portrayed as indications that the policy-making process is not functioning properly. In this vein, many critical observers of government use a tip-of-the-iceberg argument, which claims that the failures of governance that become political disasters through media attention and public scandal are only a small sample of the total number of instances where government policies go seriously wrong. Only some programme failures make it to the political agenda, but many more are hidden below the surface, waiting to be discovered and politicized. Political scandals, therefore, are not isolated incidents, but symptoms of endemic problems in governance. If this argument were true, governance in many western societies would be in serious trouble. However, the current ubiquity of political disasters may well be a bad predictor of the quality of policy-making. There are various alternative explanations for this phenomenon.

Mass media vigilance

In most western societies the role of the media in framing policy disasters is pivotal. Negative coverage in the media is the *sine qua non* for political failure. However, as indicated by Bovens *et al.* in this volume (Chapter 3), the role of the media in many western societies has gradually changed from one of deferential lapdog to one of vigilant watchdog or, in some cases, even to that of a roaming 'junkyard dog'. Many news media no longer limit their role to the passive reporting of political events, but actively seek evidence of cases of waste, fraud, abuse and other forms of government failure. In fact, some political failures are not just reported by the media, but rather are media-made. This seems at least partly the case in the 'Arms to Iraq' (Chapter 7) and the BSE affairs (Chapter 4). The main reason for this may be the proliferation and commercialization of the media, and the fierce competition between the various news media. Claims about policy failures, political corruption and bureaucratic pathology make for attractive copy and network time ('bad news is good news'). Ironically, the institutional and personal drama of government scandals has a high amusement value and can boost newspaper sales or the ratings for TV news. Second, in many countries the ties that existed between the media and the political establishment have been loosened. This is, for example, the case in the Netherlands and Belgium, consociational democracies in which, until recently, the major political parties used to have strong financial and social bonds with specific newspapers or networks. A new generation of highly educated, independent journalists, working for new, commercially operated media, feels much freer to report on corruption and government incompetence than its predecessors (Bovens 1996). In short, more publicity for malpractice and underperformance does not necessarily mean an increase in malpractice itself. There have always been cases of bureaucratic infighting among the Dutch police, and the Belgium justice system has been malfunctioning for many years, but only recently have journalists taken an interest in publicizing these things. These explanations amount to a friendly form of blaming the messenger: governance itself has not changed, but the media are less and less willing to give policy-makers the benefit of the doubt.

Decreasing deference to public authority

The irony of contemporary mass democracies is that, although governments may have reason to claim that they are doing better, many citizens are more likely to feel that they are doing worse (cf. Wildavsky 1987). Not only the media, but also the public at large have become less deferential towards public authorities in many western countries. The silent majority has become vocal and demands value for the taxes it pays. Maladministration is no longer taken for granted, as it has been for decades in Belgium and Italy. The reasons for this are manifold. First of all, there are some long-term social trends in most western societies. There has been a large increase in the level of education of the general public, in the level of urbanization and in the proliferation of information throughout society. Partly as a result of this, social structures which traditionally supported authority claims, such as organized religion, science or intermediate associations, have been severely weakened. There is an increasing awareness of the political nature of expert knowledge and a rising distrust in the authority of scientific experts (Beck 1992, 1995). Political parties and other intermediary organizations have been confronted with a loss of status and supporters. New social movements and other critical protest groups have emerged and are able to mobilize large parts of the public against traditional political establishments (Tarrow 1994). In some countries, confrontation, contestation and crisis management have replaced traditional patterns of cooperation, consultation and co-optation. This also explains the more aggressive media approach towards political and bureaucratic elites: a well-educated, critical public wants to stay informed about government performance, particularly in times of cutbacks and economic reforms.

Institutionalization of watchdogs

Trends towards more political disasters may also be the paradoxical byproduct of the ongoing administrative and constitutional modernization in many countries. Many liberal democracies have institutionalized the watchdog function within the political and administrative system itself, through the establishment of a number of watchdog agencies, such as courts of audit, ombudsmen and inspection boards. Their very task is to uncover and remedy malpractice and underperformance by public institutions, and they have been doing this with increasing success and authority (Hertogh and Oosting, forthcoming). In addition, some of the traditional watchdog institutions, such as courts and parliamentary committees, have become increasingly vigilant and active. In Belgium and Italy, a new generation of magistrates has played an important role in uncovering the systemic failure of large parts of the executive. Similarly, in the Netherlands parliamentary activism has risen sharply in response to the increasing criticism of parliamentary impotence. For example, between 1985 and 1997, the Dutch parliament used its ultimate investigative powers (the official *Enquête*, inquiry) eight times, compared to only once in the first four postwar decades. This parliamentary activism has played an important role in uncovering the crises in the system of criminal justice. Within the executive branch, administrative modernization manifests itself, for example, in increasingly hefty forms of bureaucratic politics and in the subsequent rise of a less deferential and much more politicized administrative ethos (Bovens 1998). Competition between bureaux in a context of fiscal austerity, endemic coordination problems, administrative 'entrepreneurship', and social networking between senior bureaucrats and journalists makes for increasingly sophisticated politics of leaking (Bovens *et al.* 1995). The crises in the criminal justice systems of both the Netherlands (Chapter 3) and Belgium (Chapter 2), for example, have been characterized by a series of leaks from within the police and the prosecutor's offices. As in the BSE crisis in Britain (Chapter 4), the politics of expertise can add to the political agitation and upheaval in the media, and can create a generalized impression of discontent and discontinuity (Fischer 1990).

Conclusions

The distinction between programme and political failures is clearly important in beginning the process of classifying, and hence understanding, the events which have been described in this volume. Our analysis has shown that such events may vary greatly in their characteristics, yet generate certain common patterns of explanation. Our case authors have explained failure predominantly by underlying inequalities and imbalances in the handling of competing values, and by the institutional complexity and fragmentation of government. These are by no means the only explanations for such failures. As we have argued above, broader trends towards increasing social and technological complexity, and the 'tighter coupling' of social, technological and political systems may render programme failures more likely. The changing role of the mass media, less deferential public opinion and the institutionalization of new channels for criticism of government may well explain why political failure may accompany such programme failures, whether they are real or not. Under such circumstances, the study of failures in governance has a bright future.

References

Allison, G. T. (1971) *Essence of Decision*, Boston, MA: Little Brown.

Barker, A. and Peters, B. G. (1993) *Advising West European Governments: Inquiries, Expertise and Public Policy*, Edinburgh: Edinburgh University Press.

Beck, U. (1992) *Risk Society: Towards a New Modernity*, London: Sage.

—— (1995) *Ecological Politics in an Age of Risk*, Cambridge: Polity Press.

Bovens, M. A. P. (1996) 'The integrity of the managerial state', *Journal of Crises and Contingencies Management* 4: 125–132.

—— (1998) *The Quest for Responsibility: Accountability and Citizenship in Complex Organisations*, Cambridge: Cambridge University Press.

Bovens, M. A. P. and 't Hart, P. (1996) *Understanding Policy Fiascoes*, New Brunswick: Transaction.

Bovens, M. A. P., Geveke, H. G. and de Vries, J. (1995) 'Open administration in the Netherlands: the politics of leaking', *International Review of Administrative Sciences* 61: 17–40.

Bryson, J. and Crosby, B. (1992) *Leadership for the Common Good: Tackling Public Problems in a Shared Power World*, San Francisco, CA: Jossey Bass.

Deutsch, K. (1963) *The Nerves of Government*, New York: Free Press.

Douglas, M. (1992) *Risk and Blame: Essays in Cultural Theory*, London: Routledge.

Downs A. (1972) 'Up and down with ecology: the issue–attention cycle', *The Public Interest* 28: 38–50.

Dror, Y. (1983) 'Policy gambling: a preliminary exploration', *Policy Studies Journal* 12: 9–13.

—— (1986) *Policymaking Under Adversity* New Brunswick: Transaction.

Easton, D. (1965) *A Systems Analysis of Political Life*, New York: Wiley.

Edelman, M. (1964) *The Symbolic Uses of Politics*, Urbana, IL: University of Illinois Press.

—— (1971) *Politics as Symbolic Action: Mass Arousal and Acquiescence* New York: Academic Press.

Fischer, F. (1990) *Technocracy and the Politics of Expertise*, London: Sage.

Goodin, R. E. (1982) *Political Theory and Public Policy* Chicago, IL: University of Chicago Press.

't Hart, P. (1993) 'Symbols, rituals and power: the lost dimension of crisis management', *Journal of Contingencies and Crisis Management* 1: 36–51.

Harvey, D. (1989) *The Condition of Postmodernity*, Oxford: Oxford University Press.

Hertogh, M. and Oosting, M. (forthcoming) 'Introduction: the ombudsman and the quality of government', in J. J. Hesse and T. A. J. Toonen (eds) *European Yearbook of Comparative Government and Public Administration*, vol. 3, Boulder, CO: Westview Press.

Hoppe, R. and Peterse, A. (1993) *Handling Frozen Fire*, Boulder, CO: Westview Press.

Hunold, C. (1997) 'The politics of nuclear waste siting in Canada, Germany and the United States', unpublished PhD dissertation, University of Pittsburgh, Department of Political Science.

Janis, I. L. (1972) *Victims of Groupthink*, Boston, MA: Houghton Mifflin.

—— (1989) *Crucial Decisions*, New York: Free Press.

Kingdon, J. W. (1995) *Agendas, Alternatives and Public Policies*, Boston, MA: Little Brown.

Majone, G. (1989) *Evidence, Argument and Persuasion in the Policy Process*, New Haven, CT: Yale University Press.

March, J. G. and Olsen, J. P. (1994) *Democratic Governance*, New York: Free Press.

Mucciaroni, G. (1990) *The Political Failure of Employment Policy, 1945–1982* Pittsburgh: Pittsburgh University Press.

Neustadt, R. E. and May, E. R. (1986) *Thinking in Time: The Uses of History for Policymakers*, New York: Free Press.

Olsen, J. P. and Peters, B. G. (1996) *Lessons from Experience*, Oslo: Scandinavian University Press.

Peters, B. G. (1997) *Managing Horizontal Government: The Politics of Policy Coordination*, Ottawa: Canadian Centre for Management Development.

Peters, B. G. and Barker, A. (1993) *The Politics of Expert Advice*, Edinburgh: Edinburgh University Press.

Rein, M. and Schon, D. A. (1994) *Frame Reflection: Towards the Solution of Intractable Policy Controversies*, New York: Basic Books.

Rose, R. (1993) *Lesson-drawing in Public Policy*, Chatham: Chatham House.

Rosenthal, U., 't Hart, P., van Duin, M. J., Boin, R. A., Kroon, M. B. R., Otten, M. H. P. and Overdijk, W. (1994) *Complexity in Urban Crisis Management*, London: James & James.

Shaikh, A. M. and Tonah, E. A. (1994) *Measuring the Wealth of Nations: The Political Economy of National Accounts*, Cambridge: Cambridge University Press.

Shklar, J. (1990) *The Faces of Injustice*, New Haven, CT: Yale University Press.

Stone, D. A. (1988) *Policy Paradox and Political Reason*, Glenview: Scott, Foresman.

Tarrow, S. (1994) *Power in Movement*, Cambridge: Cambridge Univeristy Press.

Teubner, G. (1993) *Law as an Autopoietic System*, Oxford: Blackwell.

Wildavsky, A. (1987) *Speaking Truth to Power: The Art and Craft of Policy Analysis*, New Brunswick: Transaction.

INDEX